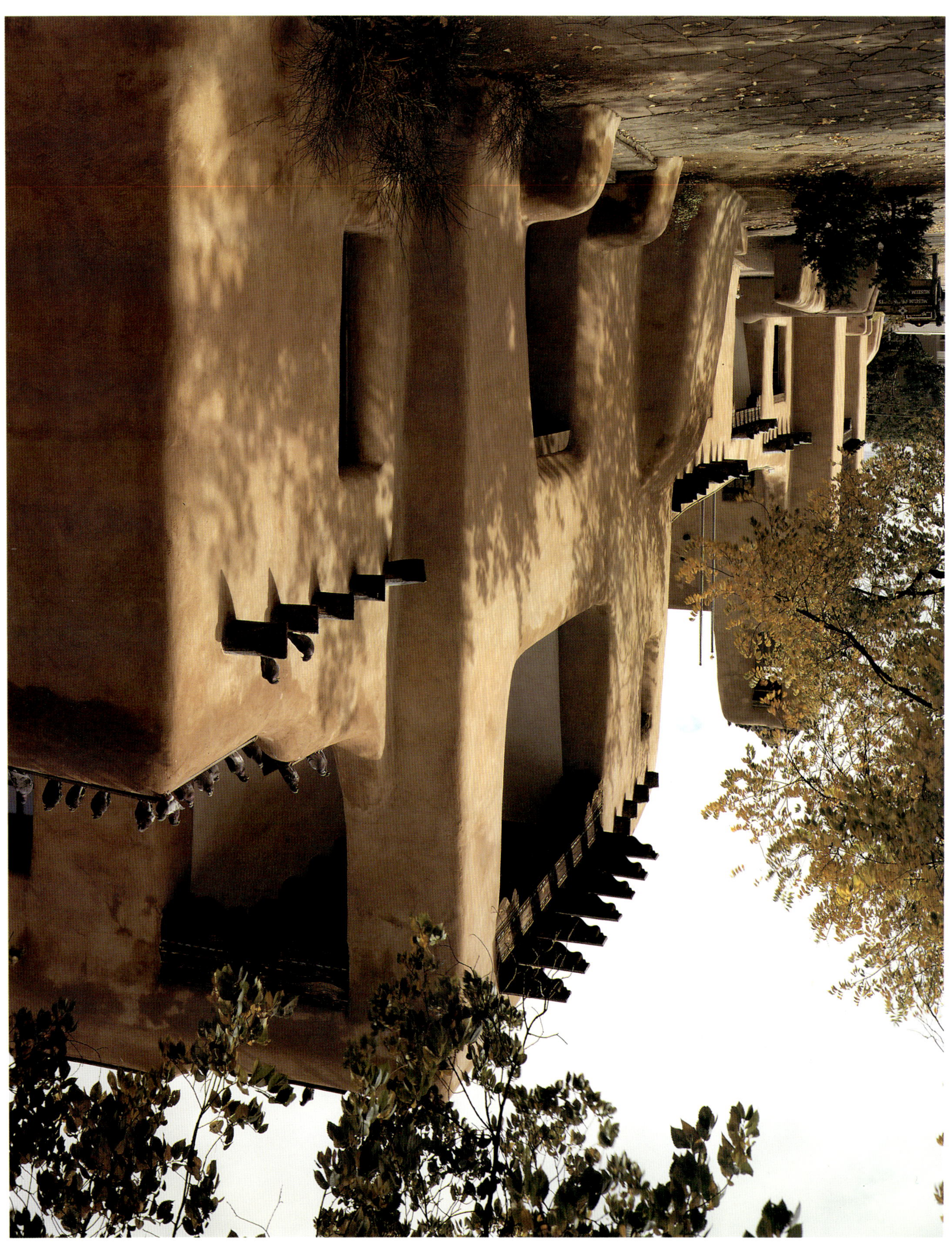

ARTISTS OF 20TH-CENTURY NEW MEXICO

THE MUSEUM OF FINE ARTS COLLECTION

MUSEUM OF FINE ARTS, SANTA FE

MUSEUM OF NEW MEXICO PRESS

MUSEUM OF NEW MEXICO PRESS
Post Office Box 2087
Santa Fe, New Mexico 87504

The Museum of Fine Arts and the Museum of New Mexico Press are units of the Museum of New Mexico, a division of the State Office of Cultural Affairs.

This publication is made possible through the generous support of funding from the National Endowment for the Arts, the Museum of New Mexico Foundation, and the L. J. Skaggs and Mary C. Skaggs Foundation.

Printed in Japan
Composition by Wilsted & Taylor
in Aldus and Palatino
Photography: Blair Clark
Design: Eleanor Caponigro
Project editor: Mary Wachs

LIBRARY OF CONGRESS
CATALOGING-IN-PUBLICATION DATA

Museum of Fine Arts (Museum of New Mexico)
Artists of twentieth-century New Mexico : the Museum of Fine Arts Collection.
p. cm.
Includes index.
ISBN 0–89013–230–5. ISBN 0–89013–231–3 (pbk.)
1. Art, American–New Mexico–Catalogs. 2. Art, Modern–20th century–New Mexico–Catalogs. 3. New Mexico in art–Catalogs. 4. Art–New Mexico–Santa Fe–Catalogs. 5. Museum of Fine Arts (Museum of New Mexico)–Catalogs. I. Title.
N6530.N6M87 1992
709'.789'07478956–dc20 91–26150
CIP

Frontispiece: The Museum of Fine Arts, south-east corner, 1988. Photograph by Terry Husebye.

10 9 8 7 6 5 4 3 2 1

CONTENTS

PREFACE

IN 1992, a year when many will observe the quincentennial of Columbus's voyage to the New World, the Museum of Fine Arts in Santa Fe will celebrate its own anniversary, marking the seventy-five years since its founding in 1917. Three-quarters of a century is a long history for a public museum in New Mexico, a territory that joined the Union as the forty-seventh state only in 1912.

In essence, this book is about both the artists whose works have had an impact on New Mexico art history and this museum's involvement with them. Throughout its seventy-five-year history, the Museum of Fine Arts has collected and exhibited significant artworks created by artists who have traveled to and lived in this beautiful land. In retrospect, it is evident that the museum itself, because of its involvement with the New Mexico art community, has played an important supportive role in the history of art in New Mexico. By looking at the development of the museum's collection and exhibition history, we simultaneously glimpse art-making in New Mexico in this century, as well as some of the developments in art elsewhere in the world.

The focus and scope of this book were determined through a process of elimination. The museum staff first decided that this publication should not be a handbook of the collection, although the museum's only handbook, produced in 1974, seriously needs updating since almost three thousand objects have been added to the collection during the intervening years. A new computerized collections management system that now allows staff and researchers to easily access and update acquisition information has filled this void to a large extent since it is a more efficient means of documenting the breadth of the ten-thousand-piece collection.

The museum's staff also agreed that this book should not attempt to present a definitive history of art in New Mexico. Such a history, still to be written, is long overdue. Although good surveys about the early art history of New Mexico and the arts and crafts of the area's Native Americans and Hispanics already exist, very little has been written about contemporary art in New Mexico.

After rejecting these various approaches, staff members concluded that this book should focus on the development of the Museum of Fine Arts' collection. While the museum's collection is extensive, its strengths are in the areas of representational painting of the early twentieth century, photography, and works on paper—the styles and media for which New Mexico is best known. Because of its policy of relinquishing to its sister museums within the Museum of New Mexico specialty collections such as Native American pottery, weaving, jewelry, and traditional painting, as well as Hispanic religious art and decorative crafts, the Museum of Fine Arts' collection naturally is weak in these areas. At the same time, the museum is beginning to strengthen its collection of contemporary art by both emerging and nationally recognized artists working in New Mexico.

Though a regional museum, the fine art collection goes well beyond its provincial boundaries. Over the years, serious efforts have been made to broaden the scope of the collection in order to show that New Mexico art was not produced in a vacuum. Beginning with Joseph Henry Sharp's visit to Taos in 1893, artists have traveled to New Mexico, inevitably influencing local artists and trends. Many artists who had gained recognition for their work while residing elsewhere moved to New Mexico, bringing with them a broader, more sophisticated context for approaching art. They include Georgia O'Keeffe, John Sloan, Agnes Martin, Bruce Nauman, and Paul Caponigro. Still other artists represented in the collection, such as Paul Cézanne, Alfred Stieglitz, Diego Rivera, and Harry Callahan, have never set foot in New

Mexico, and yet their work has strongly influenced art produced in this area.

Volume 1 of this two-volume edition presents a historical overview of the Museum of Fine Arts and its vital role in the region. One hundred and thirty-nine works were selected to represent both the diverse artistic activity of artists working in New Mexico and the major national movements that found their influential way to New Mexico.

Volume 2 comprises an illustrated anthology of essays presenting in-depth examination into areas important in the study of art in New Mexico. These include topics such as federal patronage and mural painting in New Deal New Mexico, the influence of Cézanne on Southwest modernists, printmaking in New Mexico, photography's response to the cultural landscape, and aspects of modern and contemporary art.

We intend by this two-volume publication to gratefully acknowledge the generous donors whose gifts have enabled the museum to build its collection. Although an active museum must continually be involved with procuring works in connection with the current art market, such involvement on the part of the Museum of Fine Arts is severely limited due to inadequate acquisition funds. However, sympathetic collectors have often helped the museum acquire important pieces of art because they shared our goal to match a significant artwork with an appropriate museum collection. In many cases, artists themselves have come forward to help the museum acquire a superb piece of their own art, a tradition that began with Robert Henri's gift, *Portrait of Dieguito Roybal of San Ildefonso*, and that continues to the present time.

It is the museum's role to document the high level of artistic activity here by carefully building a collection that represents the best work available. The Museum of Fine Arts aims to collect in both breadth and depth. It wants an extensive collection that represents many of the movements influential to the area. However, it also acknowledges the importance of having a wide range of the work of selected artists, particularly those who have created art for many years and whose work has gone through a number of stylistic changes.

The publication of a book like this is an opportunity to take stock of our collection. Although much more work is needed to make the collection even more extensive than it is and there are still many artists who need to be recognized, the Museum of Fine Arts can feel proud of the progress that has been made over seventy-five years, for we have a unique collection that has proved invaluable to the artists and public of New Mexico, as well as to the state's many visitors.

DAVID G. TURNER
Director, Museum of Fine Arts

ACKNOWLEDGMENTS

WHEN A MUSEUM embarks on a complex project concerning the history of its collection, collaboration among numerous artists, curators, and writers, each with a distinctive point of view, inevitably produces stronger results. In addition to the individuals and institutions listed here who contributed directly to this project, there are many people not named here who have contributed indirectly through the considerable time they have devoted to the study of the history of art in New Mexico and the Southwest, including those who have been intensely involved in the operation and development of the Museum of Fine Arts. In their own ways, they have contributed to the production of this book through considerable research, lecturing, publishing, and curating, and their work has created valuable files in public and private research libraries that are used as the basis for further research.

The museum is indebted to these authors for their contributions to this body of research and writing: Clinton Adams, Professor Emeritus, Department of Art, University of New Mexico; Van Deren Coke, Professor Emeritus, Arizona State University and former Director of the University of New Mexico Art Museum; Earl Stroh, artist, Taos; Sharyn Udall, art historian, Santa Fe; Malin Wilson, former curator, Jonson Gallery, University of New Mexico; and David Witt, Curator, Harwood Foundation, Taos.

The staff members of the Museum of Fine Arts accepted this publication project into their already busy schedules with a commitment that reflected their understanding of the importance of such a publication. While working together to select the images for this book and to determine their sequencing, the curators and myself learned a great deal from each other about our respective disciplines and approaches to the arts. I sincerely thank Sandra D'Emilio, Curator of Paintings and Sculpture, 1900–1945; Steve Yates, Curator of Photography; Susan Benforado, former Curator of Contemporary Art; and Sandy Ballatore, Curator of Contemporary Art. May this fruitful relationship continue on future projects.

Much of the material in this book was based on research of the art and artists in the collection, and thus Phyllis Cohen, the librarian at the Museum of Fine Arts, was invaluable in guiding the writers and researchers to the proper sources. In addition to her support of our research, Ms. Cohen, with the tireless assistance of Leanne Walther, also assembled two highly significant lists for this publication (more complete listings exist in her library files): a complete exhibition history of the Museum of Fine Arts and a biographical index of artists who have worked in New Mexico. The compilation of both these lists reflects exemplary research. She was assisted in this task by volunteers Melody Schneider, Peggy Hemmendinger, Katherine Korbell Brown, Jr., George and Rose Kaplan, Melinda Elliot, Rusty Andrews, and Bri Knorr. Researchers helping to gather information for the curators included Susan Levy, Barbara Kramer, Anna Hansen, Jay Rabinowich, Joseph Fleck, Jr., John Miegs, the late Don B. Shuster, the late Helmuth Naumer, Virginia Hunger Ewing, Dorothy Morang Emmett, Donald Van Soelen, Tom Lea, Eliseo Rodriguez, Gene and Phillips Kloss, Charles ("Chuck") Barrows, William Lumpkins, Leo Bushman, James Ridgely Whiteman, Stephen Dietz, Pamela Rogers, and Peter Birmingham, University of Arizona Art Museum; Peggy Giltrow, New Mexico State Library; David Farmer, DeGolyer Library, Southern Methodist University, Dallas; Octavia Fellin, Gallup Public Library; Jeffery Ball, Museum of Art and Archaeology, University of Missouri at Columbia; Betty Lloyd, Arthur Johnson Memorial Library, Raton; Mary Jo Walker, Golden Library, and Winston Cox, Eastern New Mexico

University, Portales; Bob Reed, Donnelly Library, and Janice Odom, Highlands University, Las Vegas; Susan Berry, Silver City Museum; Terry Gugliotta, University Archives, University of New Mexico; and Karen Mobley, University Art Gallery, New Mexico State University, Las Cruces.

Assisting in the research of the objects in the collection, including their provenance and acquisition records, were Diane Block, former Curator of Collections, and Stephanie Turnham, Registrar at the Museum of Fine Arts. They were in turn assisted by a group of interns from the University of California at Davis, Princeton University, and Dartmouth University.

Other staff members at the museum have also been invaluable in assembling materials for this book, including Lorraine Cook, administrative secretary, who handled all of the financial transactions and much of the typing; Theresa Arellano, secretary, who transcribed the manuscripts and kept information updated in our computers; and Charles Sloan, preparator, who moved much of the art to be photographed.
All of the photographs were taken by the museum's photographer, Blair Clark, who did an exceptional job in a short period of time. His attention to detail is evident in the excellent reproductions.

After this project progressed to the Museum of New Mexico Press, it took its final form with expert vision. Mary Wachs, editorial director, contributed experienced advice and project direction, as well as the final edited manuscript. Ron Latimer, director, kept a sharp eye on the financial aspects of the project. Susan Benforado, a former curator at the Museum of Fine Arts, edited much of the first-draft material. Thanks also to Denice Anderson for proofreading the final text, Ann Mason for intermediary editing, and Joan Chernock for a professional typescript.

The museum's commitment to quality publications suggested Eleanor Caponigro to design this book. Her familiarity with and sensitivity to the material are unequaled. The beauty of the book is totally to her credit.

Funding for this project has been made available by a major grant from the National Endowment for the Arts, with matching funds from the L. J. Skaggs and Mary C. Skaggs Foundation and the Museum of New Mexico Foundation.

A PLACE FOR THE MUSEUM OF FINE ARTS

HISTORICALLY, the combination of several factors has made the New Mexico art community especially vigorous. Foremost, perhaps, are the qualities of the region itself, its unique light, physical beauty, and colorful history, all of which have attracted numerous artists to the area. Another factor has been the presence of many local artists who reinforce the importance of traditional skills and customs. Moreover, in recent history, strong individual leaders such as Edgar Lee Hewett and Mabel Dodge Luhan have emerged to infuse the community with the energy of their pioneering visions. One additional component of a thriving art community is a vital museum, a place where the language of art can speak to the artist, to the researcher, and to the general public.

The fact that New Mexico is a state whose regional art is easily identifiable poses a serious question for institutions such as the Museum of Fine Arts. Should the state's publicly funded art museum be a regional museum of New Mexico art or should it be a museum that presents regional, national, and international art to the people of New Mexico? What may seem a simple matter of policy has yet to be definitively stated in the seventy-five-year history of the museum. Perhaps it is the consequences of this unresolved issue that make the Museum of Fine Arts the dynamic and popular regional museum that it is during a time when our regional museums are too often dismissed.

All art museums strive to develop individuality that will distinguish them from the growing number of other institutions competing for the public's attention. Museums develop strategies to do this by concentrating their resources on a specialty for the museum, a strategy often necessary for museums founded in this century without large bequests of money or masterpieces. These newer museums tended to develop collections and exhibition programs of regional or media focus, thus allowing them to specialize in given fields of interest.

Outside the metropolitan art centers, where the blockbuster exhibitions are mounted and the "art stars" of the moment are made, smaller museums are playing an important role in studying and presenting the art made in their own regions. These museums can feature the work of artists whose milieus, often to the enhancement of their art, are removed from the recognized art centers. At the same time, regional museums can help these artists approach eventual national recognition.

The allure of the American Southwest has drawn artists for nearly a century. The attraction has been complex, but certainly key elements have been the landscape, the persistent indigenous cultures, and the region's identification with a true American vernacular. By 1910, the population of New Mexico was a mere 327,300, yet already the area was an important artistic center. By 1915, the Taos Society of Artists had formally convened. Two years later, the Museum of Fine Arts opened in Santa Fe, thus christening that town's art colony. The enduring influence of Hispanic and Native American arts, steady in the region for centuries, contributed immeasurably to the sensibilities of arriving artists.

This concurrence of new artists to New Mexico with the increased recognition of indigenous artists had demanded the establishment of an art museum. In 1908, only a few years before New Mexico earned statehood in 1912, the territorial legislature of New Mexico established the Museum of New Mexico as a cooperative venture between the School of American Archaeology and the Historical Society of New Mexico. The immediate goal of the new institution was the preservation of the historic Palace of the Governors, the oldest public building in the United States, and the objects housed there. Early exhibitions at the Palace focused mainly on the history of the region, but occasionally the museum hosted exhibits of local art as well as annual shows of the works of Taos and Santa Fe colony painters.

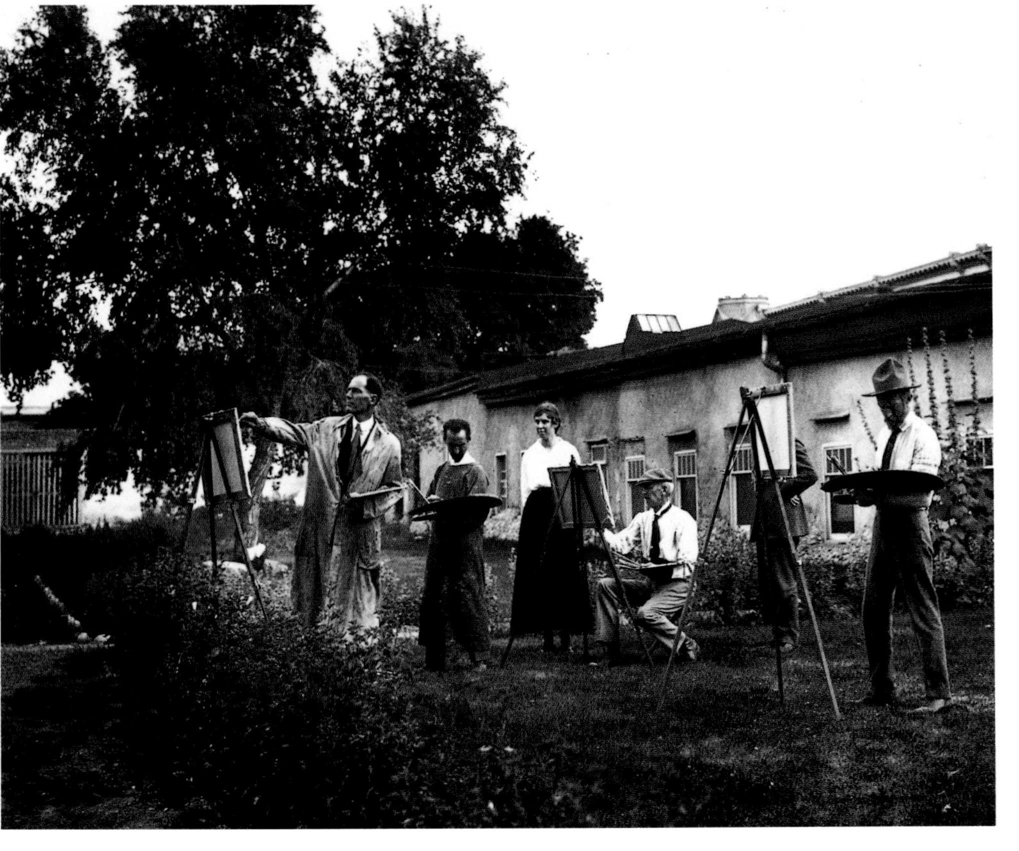

Artists in the patio at the Palace of the Governors, 1917. From left, Kenneth Chapman and Carlos Vierra. Sheldon Parsons is at far right. Photograph by Wesley Bradfield. Museum of New Mexico Photo Archives.

The year 1915 saw eighteen exhibits, and by 1917, the Palace was providing studio space to such artists as Robert Henri, Paul Burlin, Warren E. Rollins, Gerald Cassidy, William Penhallow Henderson, Marsden Hartley, and Sheldon Parsons and later to Pueblo artists Ma-Pe-Wi, Cresencio Martinez, and Awa Tsireh.[1]

For all its good intentions, however, the Museum of New Mexico could not keep up with the demand for exhibition space. To alleviate the problem, the farsighted director of the museum and the School of American Archaeology, Dr. Edgar Lee Hewett, a scholarly entrepreneur and accomplished archaeologist, enlisted the support of prominent artists from the East. Among those who responded was the esteemed American artist and teacher Robert Henri, who came to Santa Fe in 1916 to help Hewett promote the idea for a new art museum. The following year, Henri returned with two of his colleagues, the painters George Bellows and Leon Kroll, to assist in the effort.

At the same time, Hewett organized a lobbying team to persuade the 1915 legislature to construct a building "to be devoted to the purpose of an art gallery."[2] By early 1916, influential citizens of New Mexico, including eastern New Mexico rancher and territorial senator Frank Springer and Judge John R. McFie, met with Hewett to unveil plans for the new building. It was agreed that the total building costs would not exceed $60,000, half of which would be appropriated by the state and the balance to be solicited from private donors, Springer in particular.

The site chosen for the new art museum was the centrally located corner of Palace and Lincoln avenues, directly adjacent to the Palace of the Governors. This land had once been the site of the Fort Marcy barracks but at the time was owned by the Santa Fe Board of Education. Some additional lobbying by Hewett and his friends successfully convinced the school board and the county that the land should be deeded to the museum in exchange for $15,000 raised by a tax levy for the schools.

The architectural style of an art museum can make an important statement about the art to be collected and exhibited. The Museum of Fine

1. Hester Jones, "The Museum of New Mexico," *El Palacio* 42, nos. 1, 2, 3, 6, 13, 20 (January 1937): 4.

2. J. K. Shishkin, "An Early History of the Museum of New Mexico Fine Arts Building," *Museum of New Mexico Fine Arts Building* (Santa Fe, N.Mex.: Museum of New Mexico Press, 1968), unpaginated.

Arts was a larger replica of the official New Mexico building, called the "Cathedral in the Desert," at the 1915 Panama-California Exposition in San Diego, designed by architects I. H. Rapp and William M. Rapp.

In creating the building for the Panama-California Exposition, the Rapp brothers combined components from several regional styles, including elements from the facades of the mission churches at the pueblos of Acoma (southeastern end of the museum facade), Laguna (east door), and San Felipe (facade of St. Francis Auditorium). The fine arts building emerged as one of the largest structures in the city. Its Pueblo Revival style inaugurated what the city's Historic Preservation Ordinance, passed in 1957, codified as "Santa Fe Style."

Construction of the new art museum took a little more than one year and involved many skilled local craftsmen, who carved the large vigas and made the interior furniture. Santa Fe painter Donald Beauregard was commissioned to paint a set of murals dedicated to the life of St. Francis, the patron saint of Santa Fe, for the large St. Francis Auditorium. The six murals were finished by Carlos Vierra and Kenneth M. Chapman after Beauregard's untimely death in 1914. They depict both known and imagined scenes from the life of St. Francis, with some focus on a regional interpretation of his imagined influence on events connected with the discovery of America. Of similar regional focus were the Spanish Colonial Revival designs used for the interior furnishings of the building. The beautifully patterned chairs, tables, chests, and sideboards were designed by Jesse Nusbaum, Chapman, and Sam Huddleson to complement the exterior design. Interior detailing, such as the concrete floors painted to resemble traditional pounded earth and ox-blood sealed floors, further proclaimed the historical spirit of the place. The imposing stuccoed walls of the exterior, whose facade stretches a full city block, dominated the architecture of downtown Santa Fe. A renovation and addition, designed by Edward Larrabee Barnes and Antoine Predock and completed in 1982, increased exhibition space dramatically while adding to the impressive nature of the building.

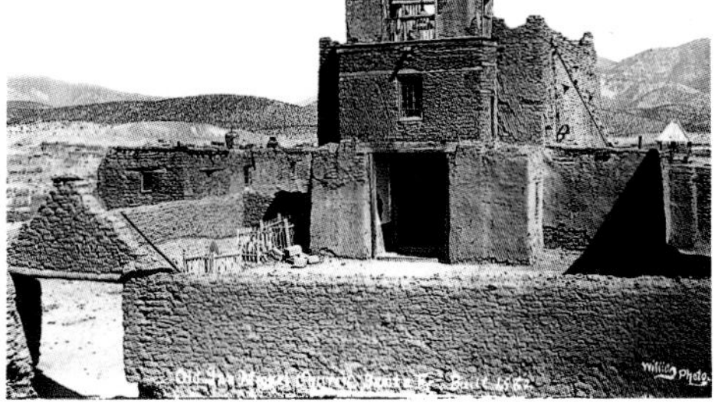

Ben Wittick, Old San Miguel Church, Santa Fe, built 1587, *1880. Museum of New Mexico Photo Archives.*

New Mexico Building at Panama-Pacific Exposition, San Diego, California, 1915. Museum of New Mexico Photo Archives.

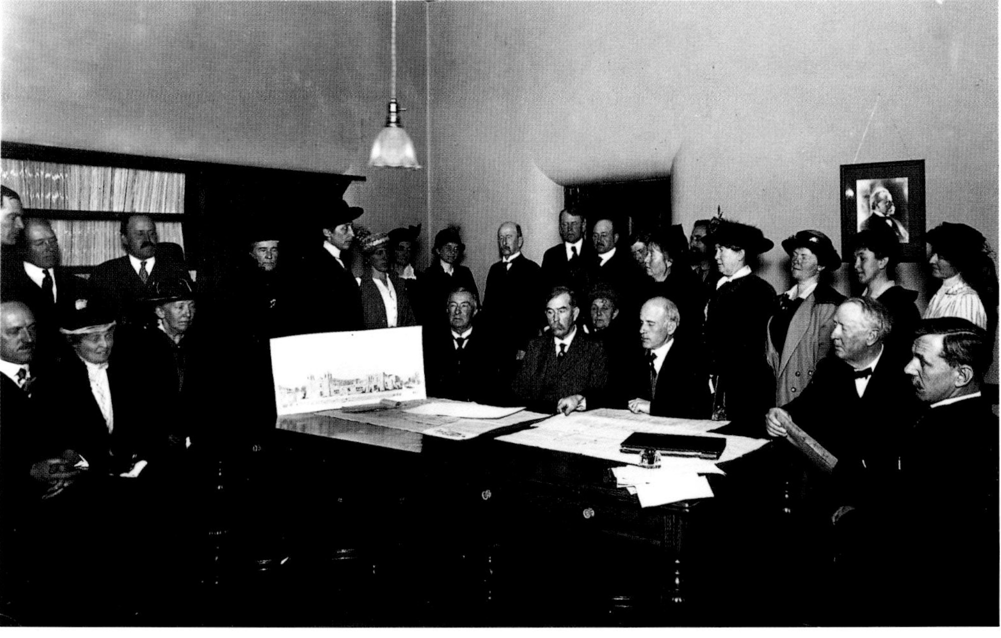

Committee considering proposed Fine Arts Museum, meeting in the Palace of the Governors in 1916. Included are Paul A. F. Walter, Frank Springer, Carlos Vierra, Mrs. R. E. Twitchell, Edgar L. Hewett, William C. McDonald, and John R. McFee. Museum of New Mexico Photo Archives.

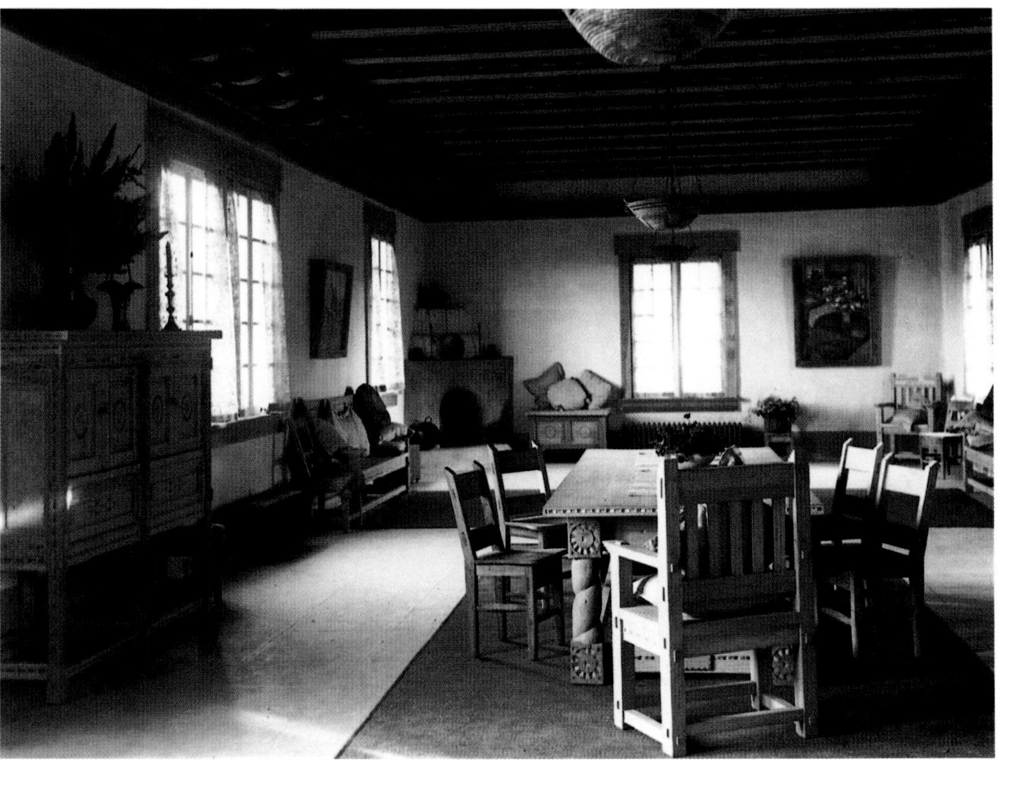

The museum's second-floor Women's Board Room, 1917. Photograph by Wesley Bradfield. Museum of New Mexico Photo Archives.

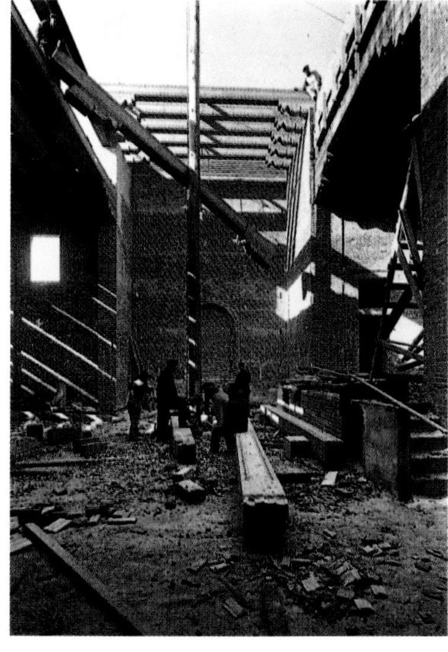

The museum's St. Francis Auditorium under construction, ca. 1917. Museum of New Mexico Photo Archives.

On November 24, 1917, the museum was dedicated and opened to the public. More than a thousand people overflowed from St. Francis Auditorium to hear congratulatory speeches by Springer, Hewett, and New Mexico's Secretary of State Antonio Lucero. Following the speeches, which were printed in full on the front page of the Santa Fe *New Mexican* the next day, the Women's Board of the Museum hosted the first of many receptions in the art galleries.

The inaugural art exhibition included paintings by several of the celebrated artists of the day: Robert Henri, Oscar Berninghaus, William Penhallow Henderson, Carlos Vierra, and Julius Rolshoven.[3] An article two days later in the *New Mexican* boasted that "the New Mexico Art Museum was comparable to the Carnegie Museum in Pittsburgh, the Chicago Art Institute, and the Corcoran Art Gallery in Washington."

From the beginning, two things were special about this museum: its architecture, which was a summation of the region's historic styles, and its commitment to exhibiting the contemporary art of the period.

Hewett's policy statement of 1920 was incontrovertible:

> *The Museum extends its privileges to all who are working with a serious purpose in art. . . . The Museum seeks to reflect what is passing in the minds of the artists who are working in this environment. It wants to put before the public in the most favorable light possible a view of the art that is being produced in the Southwest, to promote education in art by affording an opportunity to see all phases of modern work. The Museum thus becomes a forum for free artistic and intellectual expression, and must accurately reflect the cultural progress of our time.*[4]

Also contained in Hewett's policy was an acknowledgment of the educational role the museum must play in the community, principally through its diverse exhibition program.

The exhibition history of the museum confirms that it has remained faithful to Hewett's intentions. Virtually every artist of distinction working in New Mexico in the first decades of this century has been the subject of a one-person show, and many of these exhibitions were accompanied by a gallery brochure or

3. The *New Mexican* (25 November 1917): 4.

4. Author anonymous, "The Santa Fe Art Exhibit," in the catalog *Eighth Annual Exhibition by the Santa Fe Artists at the Museum of New Mexico* (September 1921), unpaginated.

catalog.[5] The majority of these one-person shows have come under the "Alcove Show Series," an innovative exhibition program that continues to this day.

As Hewett remarked at the museum's twentieth-anniversary celebration, "[The museum's] alcoves have been open to the most eminent painter or sculptor, to the unknown beginner, and to the humblest Indian, all on equal terms. There has been no jury, no favoritism for any theory or 'school' of art. The director's idea was to provide all the facilities possible within our means, then keep out of the way and give art a fair field."[6]

This liberal open-door policy gave artists of the time access to the museum's gallery spaces.[7] It also made the museum vulnerable to the risk of showing mediocre art as more and more artists of varied caliber moved to New Mexico.

Moreover, Hewett's liberal idea of exhibiting modern art met with a certain amount of skepticism from the conservatives in the local art community. Following an exhibit of the works of Marsden Hartley and B. J. O. Nordfeldt, the *New Mexican* ran an article (29 September 1920) titled "Real Bolshevists," in which it criticized the state museum for showing work by artists who claimed themselves to be modernists but whom the newspaper saw as Bolshevists. Hewett published in *El Palacio* a lengthy rebuttal to this attack on modern art[8] and was supported by community cultural leaders such as anthropologist Natalie Curtis Burlin and Alice Corbin Henderson, whose unpublished polemic stated that the "Art Museum should have little concern of a painter's political view or his religion, his bank account, or domestic affairs. The sole function of a museum is to foster art."[9]

5. The museum's exhibition history can be researched using records in the Fine Arts Library, including an exhibition file and past issues of *El Palacio*.

6. Edgar L. Hewett, foreword for the catalog of the "Twentieth Anniversary Exhibition," 1937.

7. The first show under this new policy was in April 1927 and featured paintings by Willard Nash, B.J.O. Nordfeldt, Raymond Jonson, Jozef Bakos, and Olive Rush. See "Modernist Alcove," *El Palacio* 22, no. 15 (9 April 1927): 311–313.

8. Edgar L. Hewett, "Art Policy of Museum and School," *El Palacio* 10, no. 5 (5 February 1921): 2–3.

9. This was written in a lengthy reply drafted by Alice Corbin Henderson and hand-delivered to the newspaper by Natalie Curtis Burlin on 11 November 1920. The publisher of the *New Mexican* had no interest in printing the rebuttal.

Though its principal commitment has been to New Mexico artists, the museum has throughout its years periodically shown the work of non–New Mexicans. Initially, this direction was challenged by those who felt that the Museum of New Mexico should show only art by New Mexicans,[10] but soon they realized that artists benefited not only when their work was exhibited but also by seeing the work of other artists.

Museum of Fine Arts, 1929. Photograph by T. Harmon Parkhurst. Museum of New Mexico Photo Archives. Gift of Ruth Louise Parkhurst, Caroline Grace Parkhurst, and Don Talcott Parkhurst.

Among the more significant art historical exhibitions organized by the museum have been "The Prewar French School of Painting" (1939); "Jean Charlot: Oil Paintings" (1947); "Graphic Works by Pieter Brueghel, the Elder" (1963); "Japanese Prints" (1934 and 1987); "Cubist Paintings and Sculpture from the Menil Collection" (1972); and "Goya: The Disasters of War" (1988).

Throughout its history, there also has been an attempt by the museum to present shows that collectively feature work by a number of artists,

10. Dr. K. Ross Toole and James Taylor Forest, "The Fine Arts Museum: A Policy Statement," no. 1 (January 1962): 9.

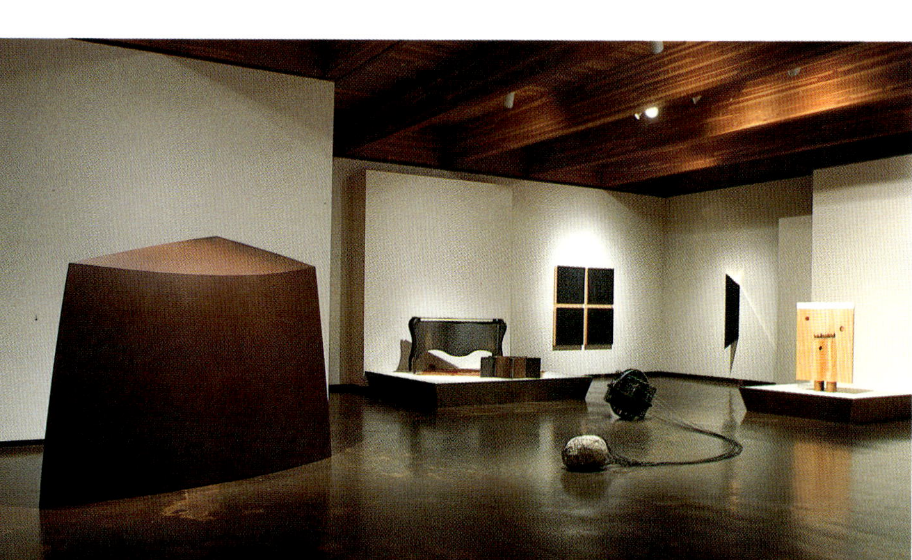

Installation view of the 1991 exhibit "Singular Visions: Contemporary Sculpture in New Mexico." New Wing galleries, completed in 1982, were designed by Edward Larrabee Barnes and Antoine Predock. Photograph by Blair Clark.

either organized around a distinct curatorial theme, such as "The Poetics of Space," a contemporary photography show presented in 1984,[11] or grouped by subject, as in "Images of Ranchos de Taos Church," an exhibition of paintings, prints, and photographs of that New Mexico landmark.[12]

By far the most popular group shows have been the museum's annuals of paintings by New Mexico and Southwest artists, begun as early as 1914 and still continuing today. Originally, these group shows featured the latest work by both acclaimed and emerging artists working in the area. In the museum's first three decades, the open-door policy allowed virtually every local artist to exhibit. By the early 1950s, however, the museum was forced to reevaluate its policy to determine how it could best serve both the artists and the public. The 1951 Annual Exhibit of New Mexico Artists was the first juried show, resulting in the inevitable, and desirable, exclusion of some artists. When longtime summer Santa Fean John Sloan learned of the shift in policy, he fired off a now legendary telegraphic response to Will Shuster in Santa Fe:

Dear Shus,
I have just heard that S.F. Art Museum is having its first Juried Ex. STOP! This means there will be no more distinction about the Annual Ex. STOP. The famous Open Door Annual of Santa Fe will be no more. STOP. Robert Henri and Edgar Hewett will "turn in their graves" muttering. . . .[13]

In a review of the next year's "Thirty-ninth Annual Exhibition for New Mexico Artists," then commonly referred to as the "Fiesta Show" because it coincided with the fall Santa Fe Fiesta events, Dorothy Morang explained the process of selecting works for the show and noted that "those [works of art] not used in the Fiesta Show are being held, on the option of the artists, for the new annual 'Autumn Exhibition.'"[14] To some, this may have seemed like a local version of the *Salon des Refuses*, where artists rejected by the salon jury in Paris in 1863 were shown together.

The annual exhibitions of the 1950s and 1960s represented artists from all over the state. Of two hundred artists in the 1952 annual, there were seventy-two from Santa Fe (including Randall Davey and Jozef Bakos); thirty-nine from Taos (including Louis Ribak and Howard Cook); thirty-eight from Albuquerque (including Kenneth Adams and Howard Schleeter); nine from Las Cruces (including Dorothea Weiss and Ken Barrick); six from Las Vegas (including Elmer Schooley); and one or two artists from each of twenty-six smaller cities across the state.[15] This broad distribution has continued in group shows through to the present.[16] As greater numbers of artists have relocated to New Mexico, the fierce competition for wall space, on occasion accompanied by heated controversy, has also been a steady feature of Museum of Fine Arts programming.

While its exhibition program was the museum's principal focus in its first three decades, the museum never lost sight of its commitment to building a permanent collection. Fortunately, some of the artists who had helped to establish the museum were from New York and other art centers and were aware of the importance of a collection to a museum.

Unlike some of the notable art institutions in the East, the Museum of Fine Arts did not begin building a collection around a core private collection donated by a single patron, although some major donations were made, such as Frank Springer's large gift of more than two hundred paintings and drawings by Donald Beauregard, Carlos Vierra, and Sheldon Parsons and Edgar Hewett's gift of many paintings by American Indian artists. To these were added the gifts of individuals and artists to the museum, and along

11. "The Poetics of Space," curated by Steve Yates, at the Museum of Fine Arts, 19 December 1986 to 22 March 1987. See *El Palacio* 92, no. 3 (Spring 1987), for additional information.

12. "Images of Ranchos de Taos Church," curated by Sandra D'Emilio, at the Museum of Fine Arts, 17 December 1982 to 24 April 1983. Also see the book *Spirit and Vision: Images of Ranchos de Taos*, with essays by Sandra D'Emilio, Suzan Campbell, and John L. Kessell (Santa Fe, N.Mex.: Museum of New Mexico Press, 1984).

13. Reprinted in full in Edna Robertson and Sarah Nestor, *Artists of the Canyons and Caminos: Santa Fe, The Early Years* (Layton, Ut.: Peregrine Smith, 1976), 154.

14. Dorothy Morang, "Thirty-Ninth Annual Exhibition for New Mexico Artists – A Review and Historical Comparison," *El Palacio* 59, no. 9 (September 1959): 271.

15. Ibid., 272.

16. One example is "New Mexico '87: A Fine Arts Competition," at the Museum of Fine Arts from 7 November 1987 to 21 February 1988, with accompanying catalog that lists the places of residence of the eighty artists in the exhibition.

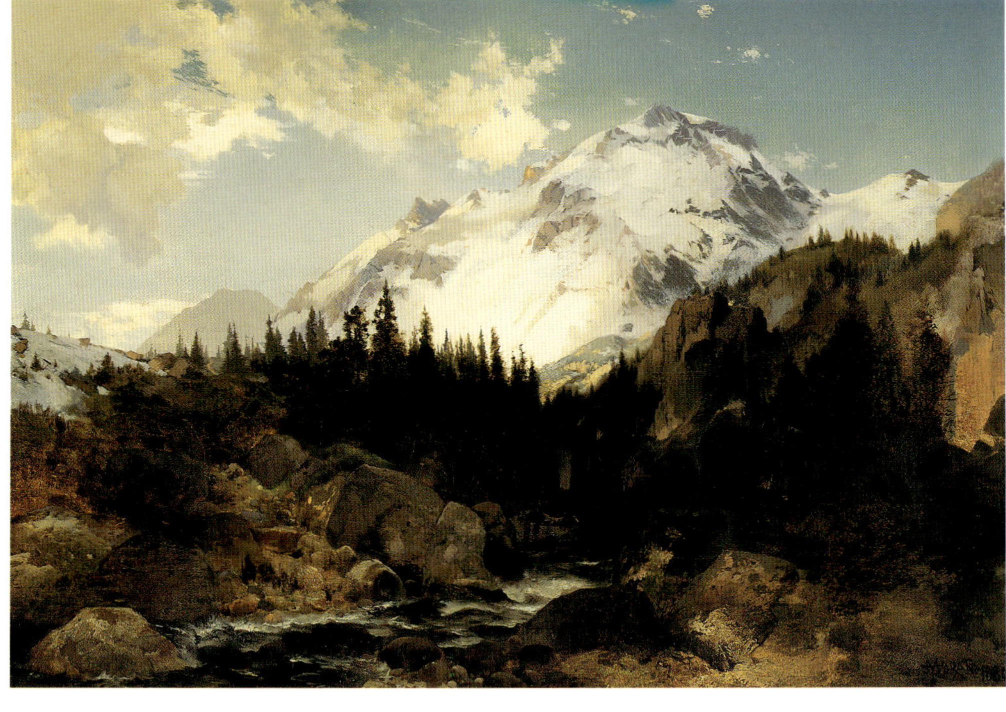

Thomas Moran, The Arkansas Divide, Colorado, *ca. 1873. Oil on canvas, 20 × 30 in. Gift of Mrs. Grace Brownell Daniels.*

with works purchased, a respectable collection slowly has emerged.

By far the largest portion of works in the museum's collection are ones that were produced here in New Mexico, which is not surprising, given the large number of artists who have worked in the area over the years. However, the collection also contains important paintings and photographs that have little or no reference to the state but have a connection with artistic traditions and styles that have influenced work produced in New Mexico and thus are appropriate to the collection. For instance, the great American romantic landscape painters of the late nineteenth century, such as Albert Bierstadt and Thomas Moran, never visited New Mexico. Yet their tradition of producing works that focused on the majestic, untamed West had a direct impact on the romanticized scenes painted by the members of the Taos Society of Artists.

If museums are to develop worthwhile collections, they must cultivate personable relationships with important donors and community supporters, and in cooperation with these donors and supporters, the museum must take a leadership role in guiding the growth of its collection. Moreover, in order for this leadership to be effective, there must be a clear understanding among the staff and board members about the goals of the museum as well as effective communications with people who can help the museum accomplish these goals. In 1962, the Museum of Fine Arts published a document that stated its collecting policy, including a specific list of priorities for the enhancement of the collection. For the most part, this list concentrated on contemporary and historical work from New Mexico but also included such wide-ranging fields as Japanese and Chinese art.[17] An even more specific acquisitions policy was approved in 1985 (revised in 1991), one that focused on twentieth-century

17. Toole and Forest, 14–18.

Albert Bierstadt, The Rocky Mountains, *ca. 1860. Engraving (J. Smillie, engraver), 19 × 29½ in. Museum of Fine Arts, Museum of New Mexico.*

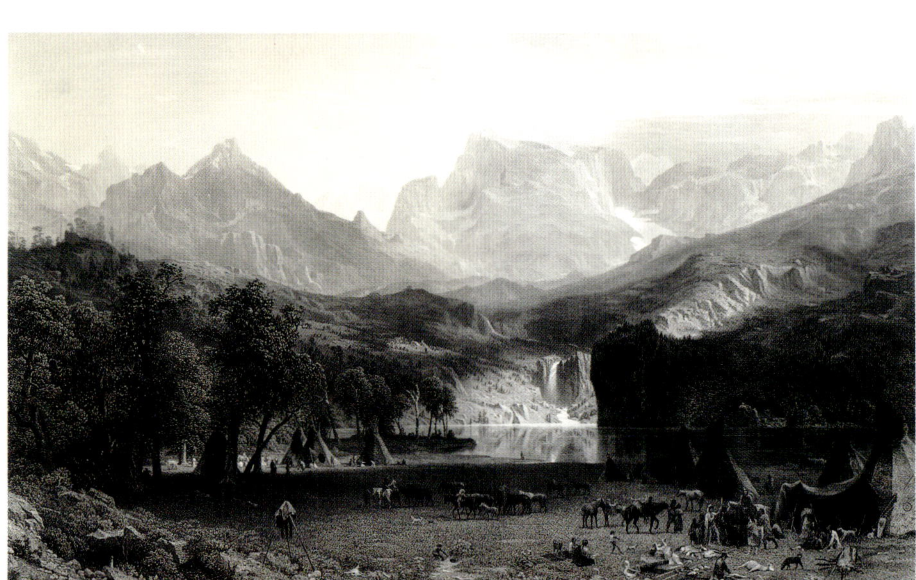

art of the U.S. and Mexico, with a particular emphasis on work produced in or related to New Mexico and the region.[18]

Once policy statements and goals for the future are made, money needs to be raised for acquisitions. Because the state has never made any substantial appropriation of public money for the purchase of works of art, the Museum of New Mexico Foundation was founded in 1962 as a private, nonprofit organization whose sole purpose is to support the various departments within the museum. In the first decade of the foundation's existence, this support went primarily to the purchase of works for the collection.

However, this foundation support alone has not been sufficient to build a collection of quality and depth. The Museum of Fine Arts, like all other museums, must look to individual donors for major support. Since this personal patronage is most effective when the museum is friendly, but aggressive, in letting people know of its needs, museum staff members have worked diligently to keep potential donors informed of the types of objects desired for the collection and in asking for help in securing them. Many times, an expressed wish of the museum is turned into a generous gift.

A museum's success in expanding its holdings is greatly assured when private collectors share with curators and directors a similar sensibility and philosophy about collecting. The museum has enjoyed two such relationships with collectors in New Mexico, Rebecca Salsbury Strand James and Joann and Gifford Phillips. Both have proven to be perfect examples of the crucial role that individuals have played in committing the Museum of Fine Arts to important art of the twentieth century.

Rebecca Salsbury Strand James was a distinguished member of the American art community. She was once married to the modern photographer Paul Strand and was a close friend of Georgia O'Keeffe, whom she accompanied on O'Keeffe's first trip to New Mexico in 1929. Through Strand and O'Keeffe, James met Alfred Stieglitz, who exhibited her Colcha embroidery and glass painting at least twice in his An American Place gallery in New York. There she began to collect the work of O'Keeffe, Stieglitz, John Marin, Marsden Hartley, Gaston Lachaise, and Paul Cézanne, among others. Her longtime residency in Taos, from 1932 until her death in 1968, and the many friendships that she cultivated in her adopted state led James to bequeath her private collection to the Museum of Fine Arts. This gift greatly bolstered the museum's collection of twentieth-century art.

Similarly, Joann and Gifford Phillips helped the Museum of Fine Arts broaden its collection at a time when it was interested in expanding its focus beyond New Mexico. The Phillipses have been serious collectors of contemporary art in both New York and California for many years and have been strong in buying the work of emerging artists. In 1983, they offered sixteen paintings by important California artists to the museum, a gift that was gratefully accepted and showcased in a special exhibition, "A California Connection."[19] The Phillipses continue to support the Museum of Fine Arts through additional gifts and involvement with museum projects.

The list of private collectors who support the museum is constantly growing. Gil Hitchcock and Jane Reese Williams have guided the museum's photography collection through a major expansion with significant gifts of works by American and international masters of the medium, with special focus on women photographers in the case of Williams's gift. Mel and Dicky Pfaelzer and Mr. and Mrs. Ford Good have contributed to the growth of the print collection through their support of printmakers in New Mexico. Frank Ribelin, Rosalind Constable, Ray Graham, and Dr. Thomas Jackson have built and donated significant collections of contemporary New Mexico art.

Through long-term relationships between donors, the museum, and the Museum of New Mexico Foundation, many outstanding artworks from estates have been added to the collection, including works that would otherwise have been impossible for the museum to acquire due to financial constraints. Most notable was the gift of two important paintings by Georgia O'Keeffe, bequeathed to the museum by Helen Miller

18. In the minutes of the Fine Arts Committee on the Museum of New Mexico Foundation, 17 June 1985 and September 10, 1991.

19. See exhibition catalog, "A California Connection: 16 Paintings from the Works Donated by Gifford and Joann Phillips Collection," with essay by Anne Carnegie Edgerton (Santa Fe, N.Mex.: Museum of New Mexico Press, 1983); exhibition dates, 21 October 1983 to 19 February 1984.

Jones, a longtime resident of San Antonio and frequent visitor to Santa Fe. Jones, who collected fine twentieth-century American art, felt that her collection of New Mexico paintings, which also included works by Marsden Hartley, Robert Henri, and John Marin, should remain in New Mexico to be enjoyed by the people of the state.[20] Other significant estates that have come to the Museum of Fine Arts through the Museum of New Mexico Foundation include a large selection of paintings, drawings, photographs, and letters by Victor Higgins from the estate of Joan Higgins Reed, daughter of Victor and Sara Parsons; the estate of Eugenie Shonnard, a prolific sculptor in New Mexico from the 1930s to the 1950s; a collection of New Mexico art gathered by Vivian Sloan Fiske, an active artist and socialite in Santa Fe during the 1950s; the complete set of wood-block prints by Gustave Baumann, left to the museum by his wife, Jane; an extensive collection of drawings and paintings by E. Martin Hennings, donated by Mrs. Hennings, through the encouragement of his daughter, Helen Hennings Winston, and art historian Robert White; and more than two hundred drawings by Ernest Blumenschein, placed with the museum by his daughter, Helen.

The museum's collection of O'Keeffe paintings was enhanced dramatically with the settlement of that estate. Four paintings were acquired by the Museum of Fine Arts in 1987, bringing the total of O'Keeffe paintings in the collection to eight. Fortunately, the museum was given the freedom to select these four from material in the estate, thus broadening the collection to include representative examples of O'Keeffe's work from the different periods of her long career.

New Mexico law allows the donation of artwork to the Museum of New Mexico for credit of estate taxes owed to the state.[21] A fortunate result of this law and of the expediency of estate planning was the generous donation of more than one hundred and sixty color photographs by Eliot Porter, donated by the artist. The Museum of Fine Arts today has one of the country's most extensive collections of Porter's work.[22]

A museum's collection not only consists of major works of art but also includes supporting material that illuminates artists' careers. To accommodate such materials, the Fine Arts Library has begun a limited archival program that currently focuses on documents of a manageable number of artists. Thus, researchers now have access to original material that includes working drawings and photographs, correspondence, and business receipts. Thus far, the museum has acquired archival material related to Victor Higgins, Will Shuster, and Ernest Blumenschein.

Across the street, at the Museum of New Mexico's Photo Archives, more than 360,000 photographs and negatives are kept, many of them illustrating the history of art-making in New Mexico.

At any one time, a visitor to the Museum of Fine Arts may find less than 4 percent (sixty to one hundred works) of the collection on view. As with all museums, space limitations in the galleries restrict the number of works that can be effectively displayed at a given time. The Museum of Fine Arts therefore maintains an active loan policy. Recently, the museum made a major loan of twenty-one works to a traveling exhibition organized by the National Museum of American Art, "Art in New Mexico, 1900–1945: Paths to Taos and Santa Fe."[23] At the same time, the museum organizes exhibitions utilizing the collections of other institutions, as in the 1986 show "The Extended Line," which combined nineteen works from the museum's collection with special loans from area artists and collectors.[24] Moreover, some exhibitions organized by the Museum of Fine Arts are traveled to other museums nationally, as with "Art of New Mexico: The Early Years,"[25] "Inspirations: Churches of New Mexico in Art,"[26] and "Light and Color: Images of New

20. David Turner, "Refining the Fine Arts Collection," *El Palacio* 92, no. 2 (Winter 1986): 4–9.

21. See Article 7–7–15 to 7–7–20, NMSA 1978, being Laws 1983, Chapter 209, Section 2, as amended, and Chapter 164, Section 1, as amended in 1987, commonly referred to as the Art Acceptance Law.

22. For a partial listing of works donated, see checklist of exhibitions, "Eliot Porter: A Special Gift to New Mexico," at the Museum of Fine Arts, 16 December 1988 to 16 April 1989.

23. The touring exhibition was organized by the National Museum of American Art, Washington, D.C., and traveled to Cincinnati, Houston, and Denver in 1986 and 1987. See catalog of the same name.

24. Curated by Sandra D'Emilio and Susan Zwinger and shown in the galleries, 6 April 1986 to 15 June 1986.

25. Organized by David Turner and Sandra D'Emilio and exhibited at eleven locations in the United States during 1988 and 1989.

26. Organized by Christine Mather for the museum and circulated to five museums in 1986 and 1987.

Mexico."[27] The traveling exhibits program is complemented by smaller shows that continually are circulated throughout the state.

As the Museum of Fine Arts looks to the future, it will doubtless continue to evaluate itself and its role in the community it was established to serve. When the museum opened its doors in 1917, it served a small but growing art colony whose stance with respect to the rest of the world was largely escapist. In 1992, the museum finds itself serving an increasingly sophisticated and pluralistic community, yet one in which traditional cultures continue to exert strong influence. The Museum of Fine Arts has grown from an art gallery representing local artists and a smattering of acclaimed outsiders to a professional museum whose survival depends upon its ability to position its collection within a more national and international context. With the continued support of its community, the museum will retain its intimate, regional character while showing art of major significance.

DAVID G. TURNER
Director, Museum of Fine Arts

27. "Light and Color: Images of New Mexico," organized by Norman Geske and Ellen Bradbury and circulated throughout the United States from 1981 to 1982. See catalog of same name.

SELECTIONS FROM THE MUSEUM OF FINE ARTS

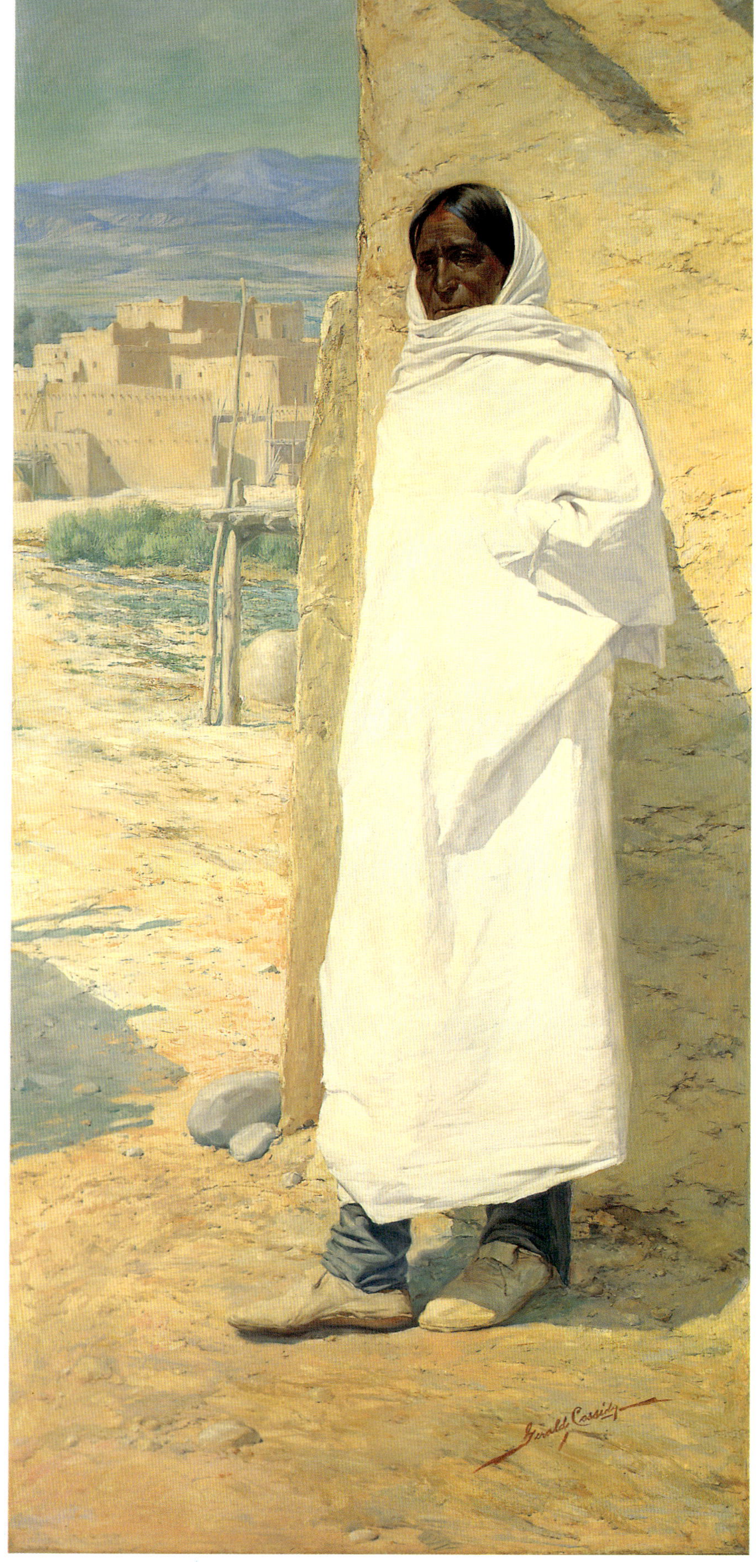

GERALD CASSIDY
Cui Bono?, ca. 1911
Oil on canvas
$93\frac{1}{2} \times 48$ in.
Gift of the artist, 1915

CASSIDY'S DRAWINGS of Indians, reproduced on postcards in the early 1900s, stood apart from similar work of other artists by their vitality and skill in craftsmanship. Cassidy was among many artists to receive commissions from the Santa Fe Railway, whose popular calendars promoted travel in the Southwest. Cassidy's *End of the Santa Fe Trail*, also in the museum's collection, was used as the reproduction in the 1940 calendar.

Cui Bono? is one of the most popular paintings in the museum's collection, a life-size portrait of a Pueblo Indian wearing traditional dress and posed against the adobe architecture of Taos Pueblo. With a steadfast gaze, he appears to look out from the disappearing world he protects for himself and his people to curious visitors representative of an encroaching modern culture. He asks "Cui Bono?" or Who benefits from this? A prime example of Cassidy's work, this painting reflects not only his interest in the light and color of the arid landscape but also the mystery and fascination his subjects held for him.

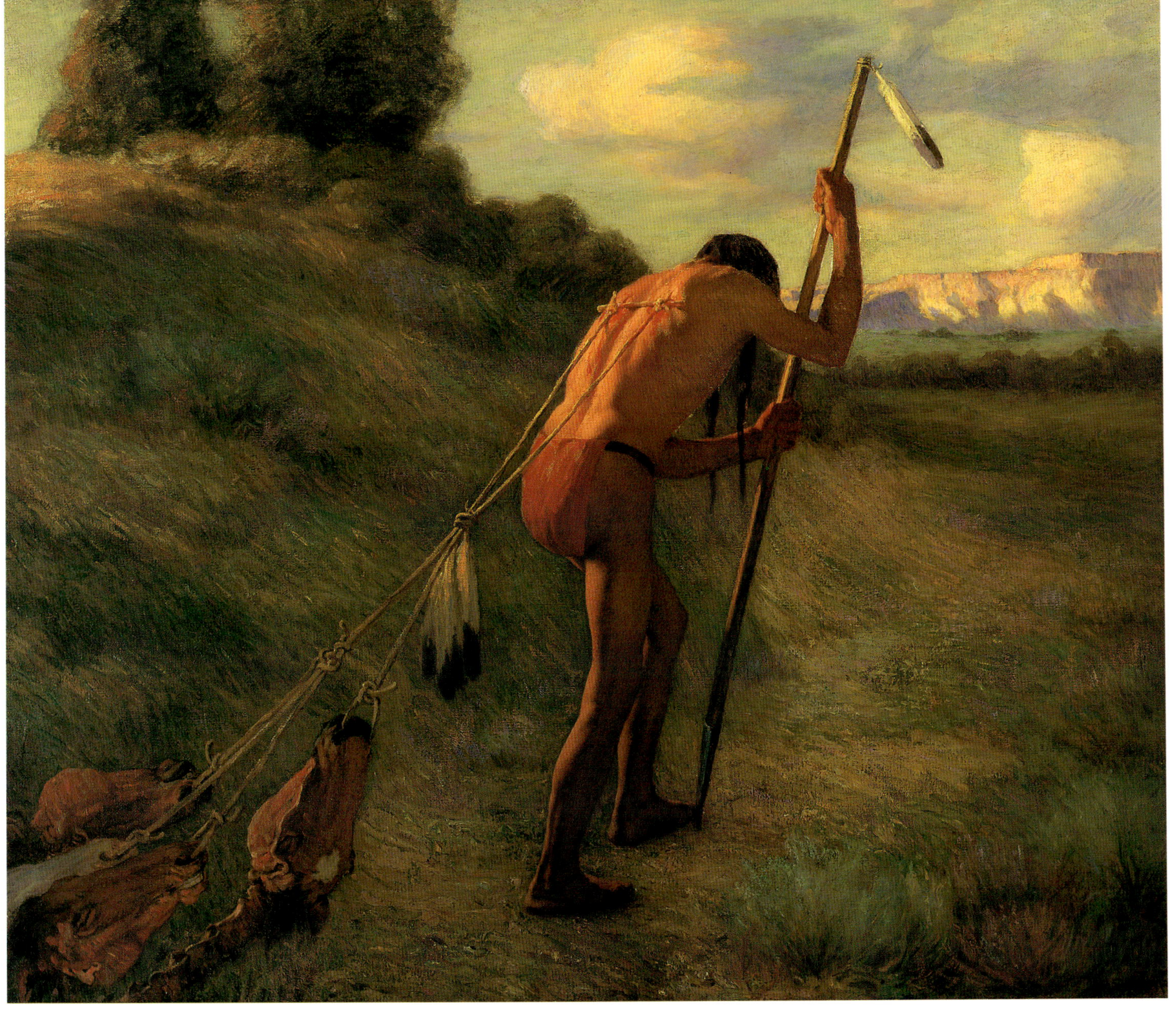

JOSEPH HENRY SHARP
The Stoic, 1914
Oil on canvas
$52\frac{1}{2} \times 61\frac{1}{2}$ in.
Gift of the artist, 1917

INDIAN LIFE fascinated Sharp from the time he read the works of James Fenimore Cooper in his youth up until the time of his death. He was keenly aware that Native American cultures were vanishing, and he worked with a special urgency among both the Plains and the Pueblo tribes to portray their traditional customs that could not survive the onslaught of modern civilization.

Sharp, who first came to Taos in 1893 and is considered the "father of the Taos art colony," personally identified with the spirit and fortitude of the Indian. *The Stoic* depicts a Plains Indian ritual in which an individual sought purification and enlightenment by testing his physical and spiritual strength. In this ritual, the skin was pierced to insert bone spatulas onto which long ropes were attached to horse heads. The warrior would then drag these horse heads for days without food or water, chanting and hallucinating. This ritual was practiced in times of great turmoil in the hope that the ensuing visions would provide a solution to the problem.
As Sharp was himself a quiet, stoical, self-made man, the painting could be seen as a spiritual self-portrait.

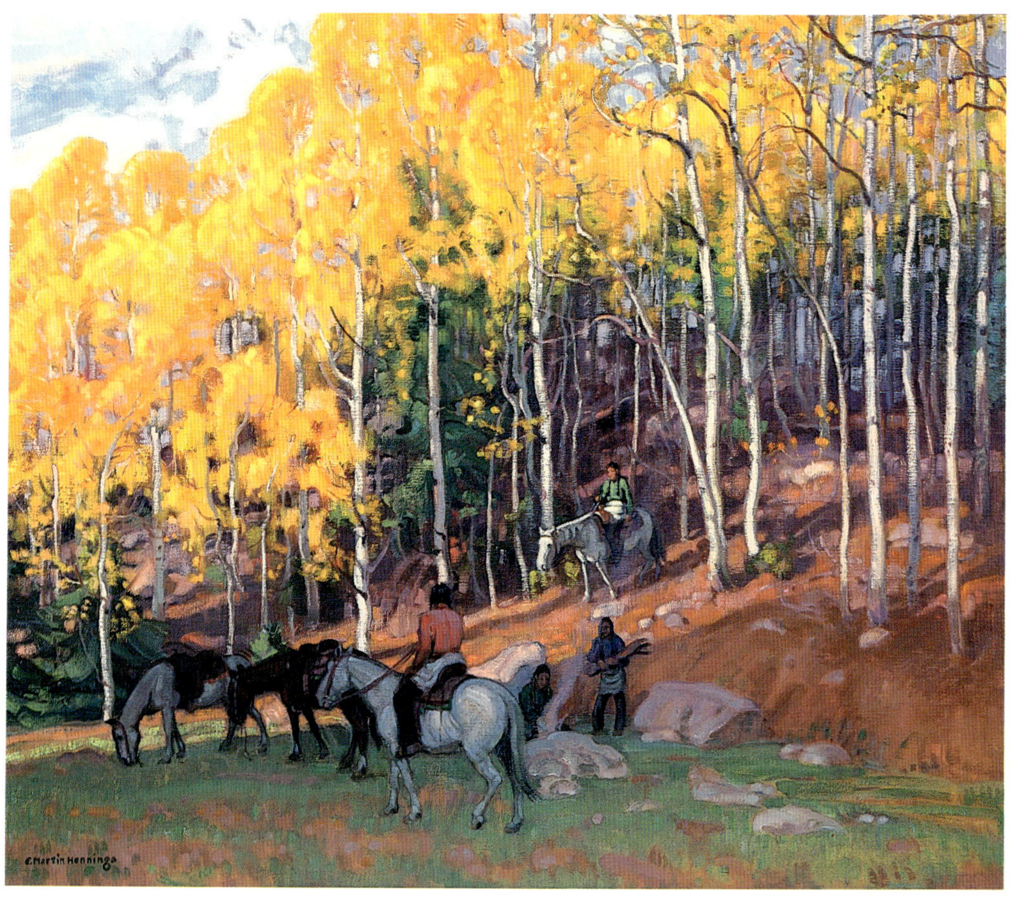

HENNINGS'S childhood ties with Chicago continued through his attendance at the Art Institute of Chicago (1901–4) and the start of his career as a commercial artist. Eventually, he became disillusioned with pure illustration, deciding to study in Munich from 1912 to 1914 under Franz von Stuck, the developer of *Jugendstil*, the German equivalent of art nouveau. The outbreak of World War I forced Hennings to return to Chicago, at a time when Oscar Mayer and Chicago's mayor, Carter H. Harrison, Jr., had begun to sponsor artists' trips to New Mexico via the Santa Fe Railway. He visited Taos in 1917 and in 1924 became a member of the Taos Society of Artists.

Hennings's admiration for the Taos Indians and his love of southwestern landscape are evident in his work. He often painted his figures on horseback amid a strong composition of trees or foliage, a personal style governed by his temperament rather than by a style modeled through the intellect.

E. MARTIN HENNINGS
The Rendezvous, ca. 1950s
Oil on canvas
25¼ × 30 in.
Purchase, Museum of New Mexico Foundation, 1977

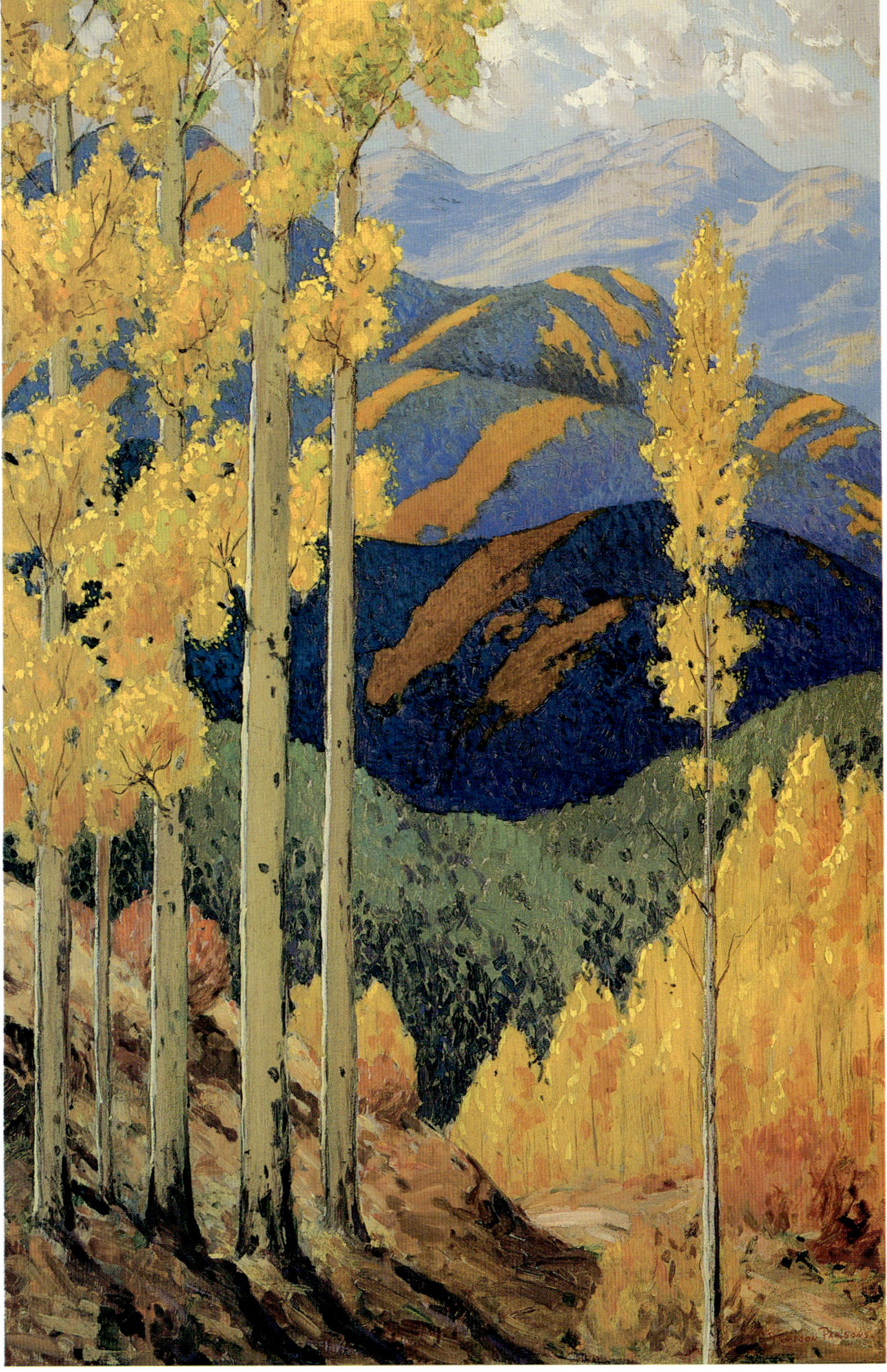

SHELDON PARSONS
Santa Fe Mountains in October,
ca. 1919–22
Oil on plywood
36 × 24 in.
Acquired by the museum, ca. 1922

PARSONS'S serendipitous discovery of Santa Fe in 1913 resulted from a flare-up of his tuberculosis while en route from New York to San Francisco to paint murals for an exposition. After his recovery at Sunmount Sanatorium, Parsons, who had been a prominent portrait painter in the East, settled permanently in Santa Fe and turned to the surrounding landscape for subject matter.

Santa Fe Mountains in October is representative of the paintings Parsons did in and around Santa Fe. The painting reveals the influence upon the artist of the Barbizon and impressionist schools in the saturation of light and the use of a high-key, bright palette. He often turned for subject to golden aspens, flowering chamisa, bright blue skies, red chile *ristras* hanging from adobe homes, and the nearby desert. Although most of Parsons's own works are representational in style, as the Museum of Fine Arts' first curator, he often exhibited works of modernists such as Paul Burlin, Marsden Hartley, and Andrew Dasburg.

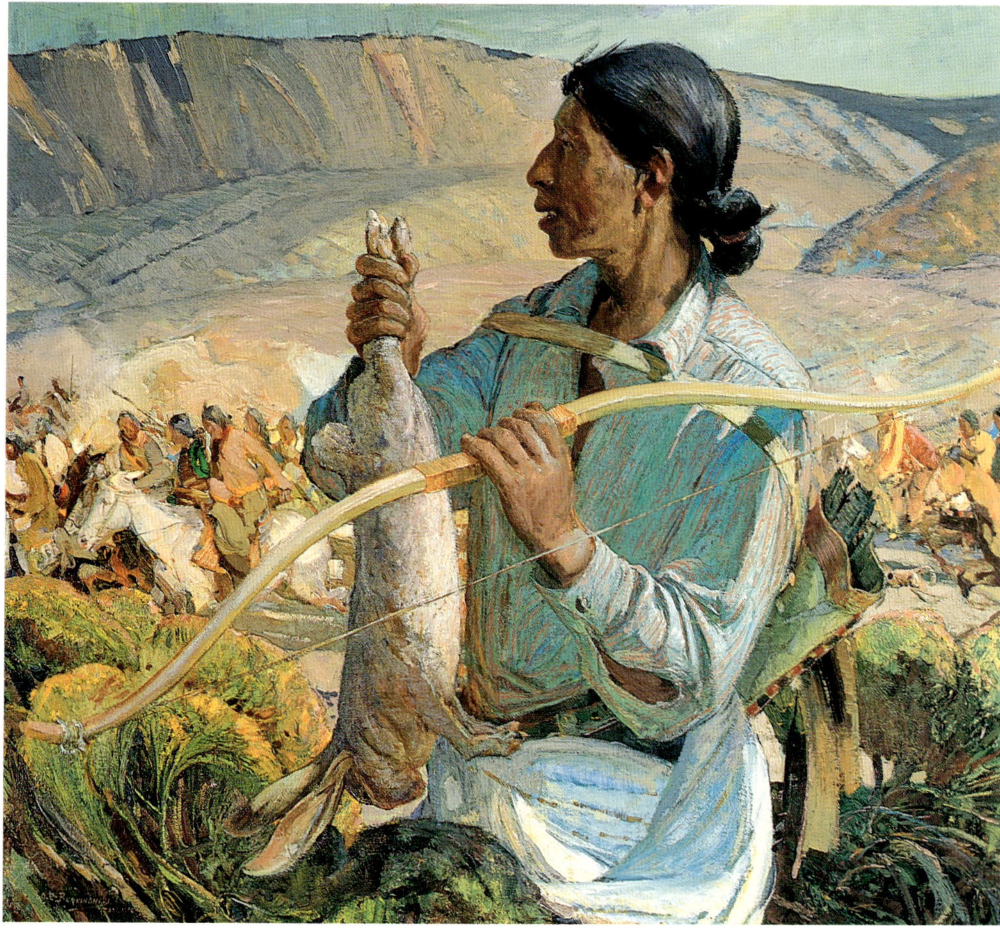

BERNINGHAUS, who had never studied in Europe, felt that the time was auspicious for a true American art to appear and that such an art would emerge from the cultural climate of Taos.

Embracing the divergent views of both a romantic and a realist, Berninghaus meticulously researched his subjects in order to accurately depict rituals and places while simultaneously being inventive with colors and compositions. He repeatedly painted his favorite Indian ceremonies, among them the rabbit hunts that usually took place on the day preceding major ceremonials.

OSCAR E. BERNINGHAUS
The Rabbit Hunter, ca. 1945
Oil on canvas
$34\frac{1}{2} \times 39\frac{1}{2}$ in.
Given in memory of Maurice N. Mikesell by John A. and Margaret Hill, 1975

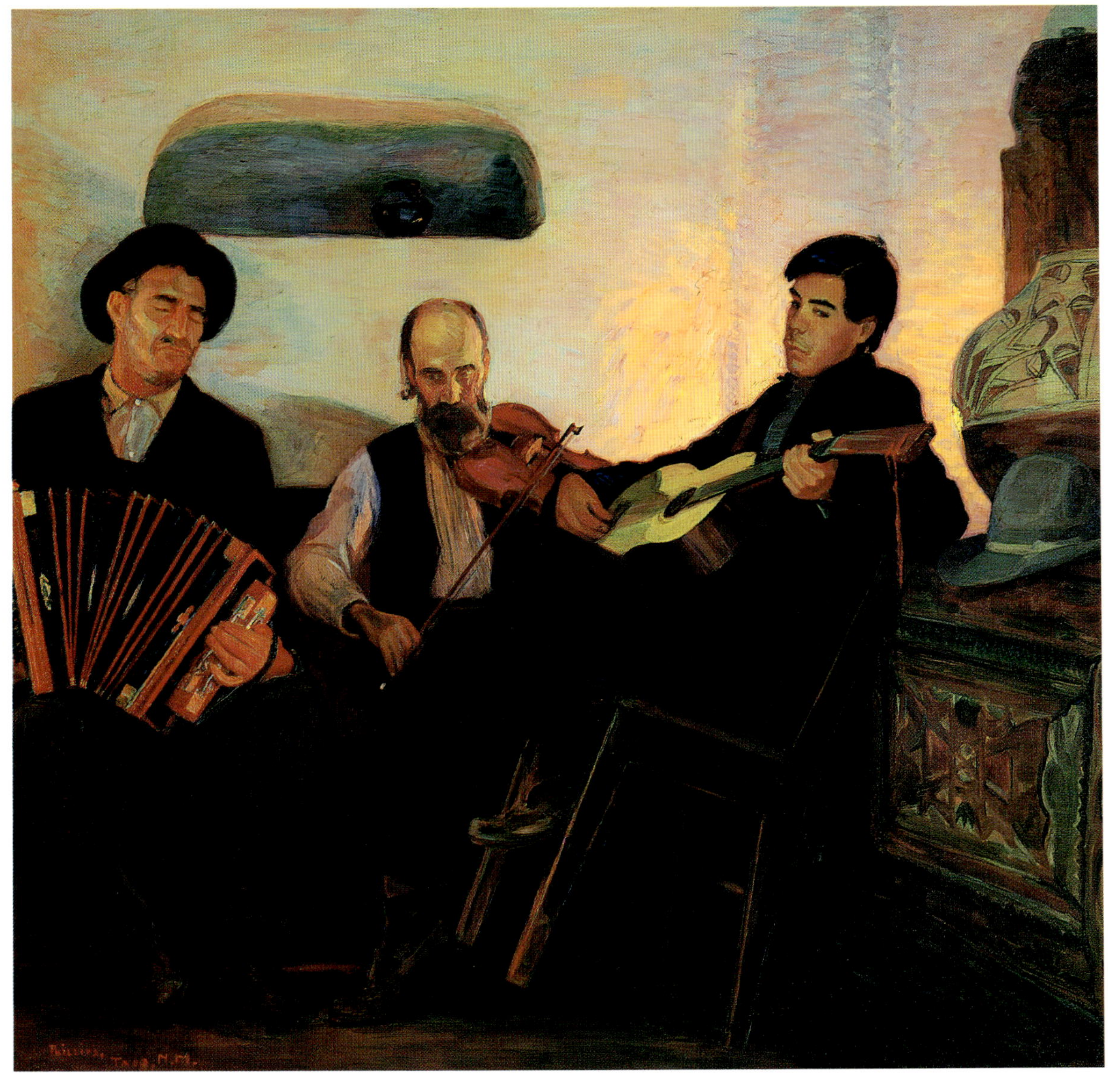

BERT G. PHILLIPS
Three Musicians of the Baile, ca. 1920
Oil on canvas
40 × 43 in.
Gift of Gov. and Mrs. Arthur Seligman, 1929

PHILLIPS was among the first academically trained artists to establish residency in Taos and was a central figure in that young art colony. Bringing an outsider's inquisitiveness to the local culture, he produced many regional portraits with a perceptive and sensitive objectivity.

While most Taos artists of the era produced idealized and often stereotypical views of Native Americans, Phillips turned instead to the Hispanic culture for inspiration. *Three Musicians of the Baile* is a casually arranged, pragmatic view of musicians preparing for a dance. The chest in the right foreground at one time held the vestments at Ranchos de Taos Church and is now in the collections of the Museum of New Mexico.

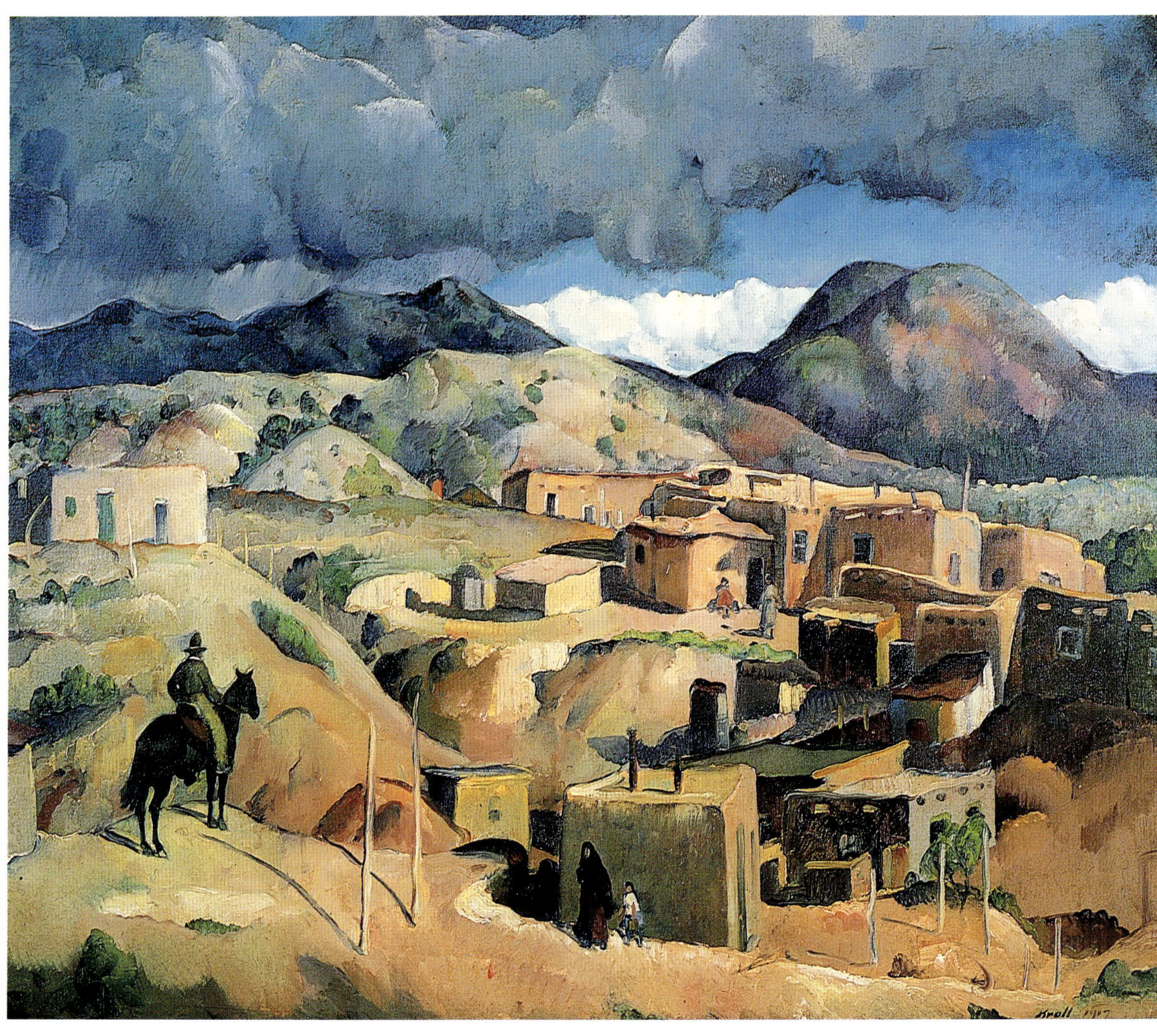

KROLL, an established New York genre and portrait painter, visited Santa Fe the summer of 1917 in the company of fellow painters Robert Henri and George Bellows. The trip produced one work of real significance—*Santa Fe Hills*—and caused the artist to reflect on Santa Fe as "a beautiful city" and the time as "a grand period."

Kroll viewed the painting as unique among his works. The palette and brushwork are reminiscent of Cézanne, but there is here a more realistic sense of perspective and detail. A man on horseback is about to embark on a ride into the nearby hills, or perhaps we have caught him in a moment of hesitation before an approaching storm.

LEON KROLL
Santa Fe Hills, 1917
Oil on canvas
34 × 40¼ in.
Purchase, Museum of New Mexico Foundation, 1972

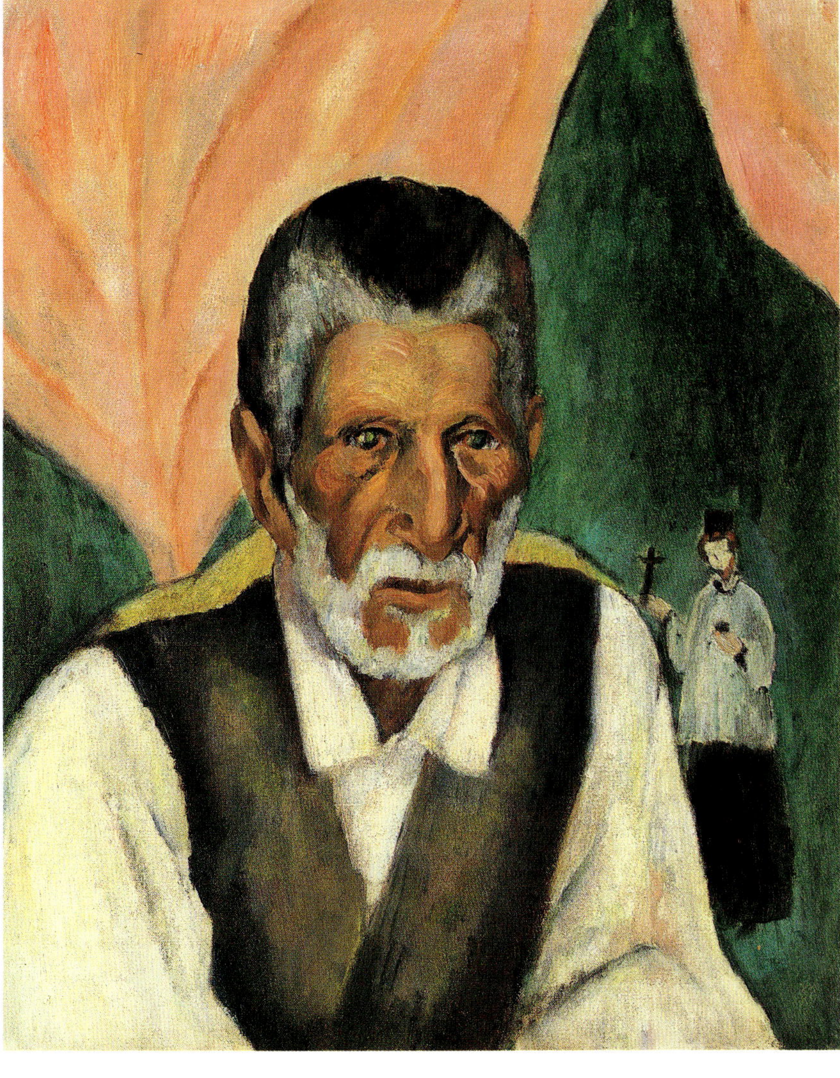

PAUL BURLIN
The Sacristan of Trampas, ca. 1918
Oil on canvas
24 × 20 in.
Acquired by the museum, 1922

ONE OF THE youngest artists to exhibit at the New York Armory Show in 1913, Burlin was deeply affected by his exposure to primitive, especially African, art and decided to seek out the primitive in his own country. This search brought him to the Southwest, where he married ethnomusicologist Natalie Curtis; through her, he became fascinated with Indian art. Burlin played a pivotal role in introducing fauve and expressionistic modes to the art of New Mexico, for in his art, he replaced realism with strident colors and sentimentality with expressive invention.

The sacristan in this painting was the keeper of the vestments at Las Trampas. Burlin obliquely alludes to the Brotherhood of the Penitentes, in whose homes a *bulto* of San Juan Nepomuceno, the patron saint of silence and secrecy, is often found.

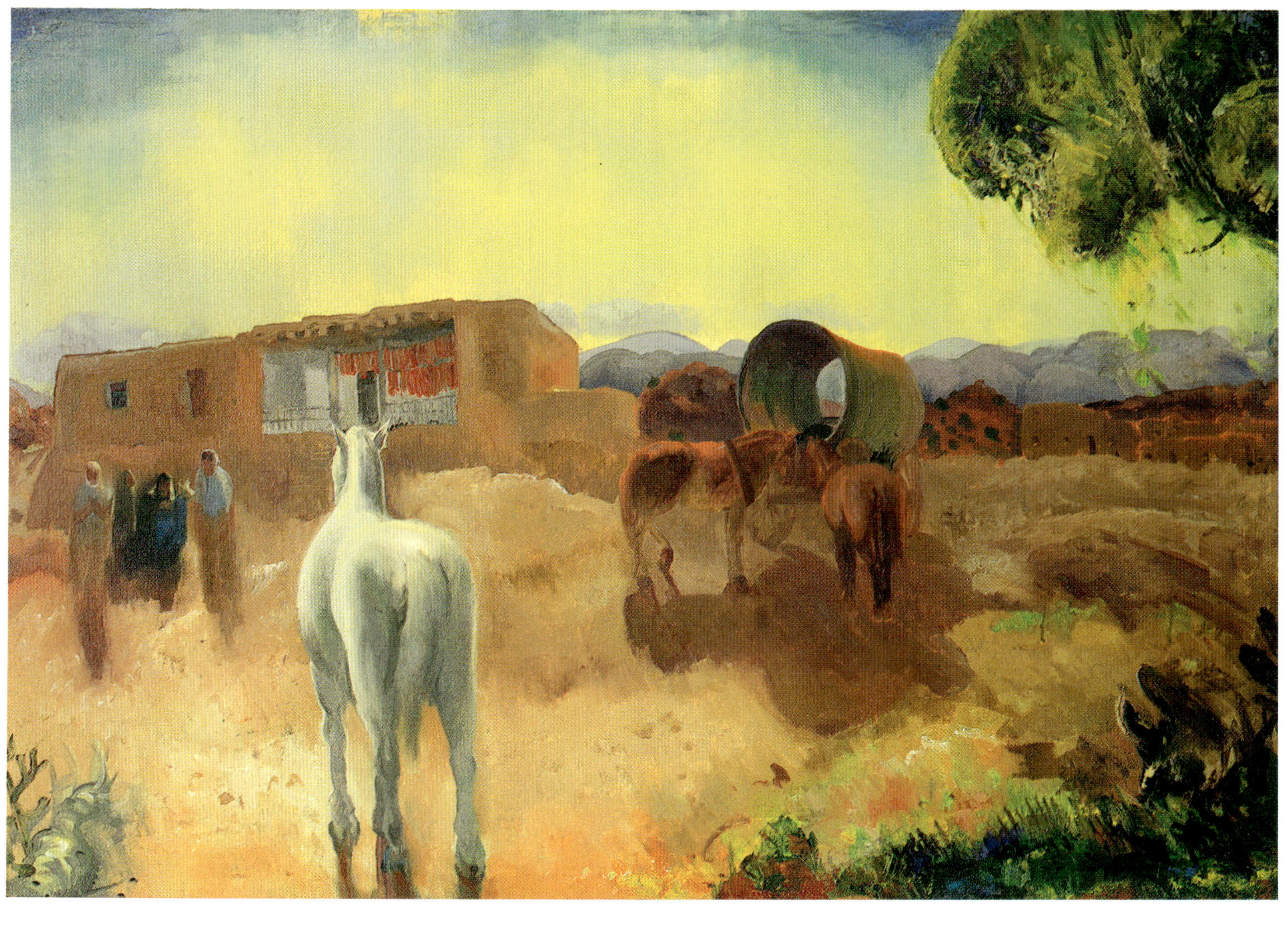

IN 1904, after attending Ohio State University, Bellows enrolled in the William Merritt Chase School of Art in New York City, where he became the student of Robert Henri. Later as a member of Henri's group The Eight, and throughout his artistic career, Bellows followed Henri's advice to draw subject matter and realize beauty in the commonplace.

At Henri's request, Bellows came to Santa Fe in 1917. Here, stimulated by New Mexico's landscape, its people, and its architecture, he painted numerous genre scenes. In *Chimayo*, Bellows translates the natural beauty and village life of a rural northern New Mexico community.

GEORGE BELLOWS
Chimayo, 1917
Oil on canvas
$30\frac{1}{2} \times 44\frac{1}{4}$ in.
Anonymous gift, 1974

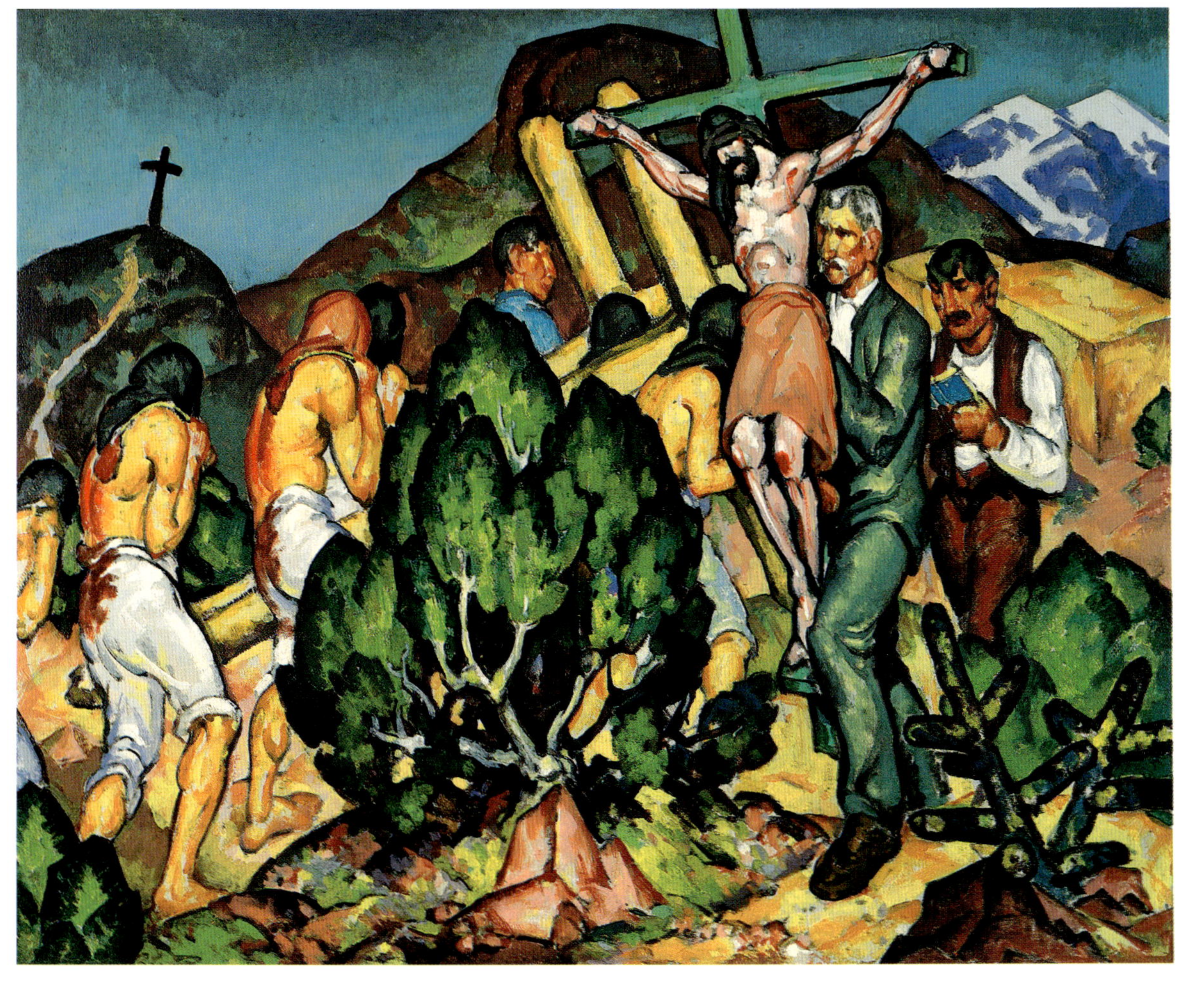

WILLIAM PENHALLOW HENDERSON
Holy Week in New Mexico, 1919
Oil on panel
32 × 40 in.
Gift of Mrs. Edgar L. Rossin, daughter of the artist, 1952

HENDERSON'S relocation to the Southwest from Chicago, necessitated by his wife's ill health, revitalized his artistic spirit and inspired his finest painting. Henderson and Alice Corbin became central figures in the Santa Fe art colony, championing the popular issues of Native American and Hispanic cultural preservation.

In *Holy Week in New Mexico*, the artist interprets the ritualistic reenactment of the Passion by members of the lay religious society known as the "Penitente Brotherhood." The Penitentes' order arose as a response to the shortage of priests in eighteenth-century colonial New Mexico. By Henderson's time, the Penitente tradition was deeply entrenched in the Hispanic Rio Grande. Unlike other artists who painted this ritual, he has deemphasized the bloody backs of the flagellants by depicting them in profile, focusing instead on the procession moving through the mountainous terrain to the cadence of chants.

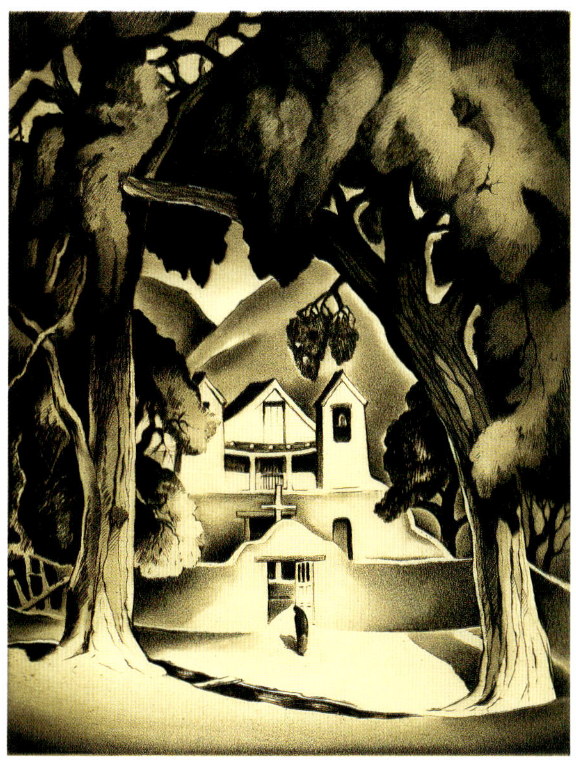

KLOSS WAS already a highly respected California printmaker by 1925 when she and her husband, the poet and musician Phillips Kloss, began summering in Taos. Her artistic response to the landscape and the people of New Mexico was immediate. Although a virtuoso printmaker, Kloss's superb technique never overshadows her obvious sensitivity toward her subject.

The Santuario de Chimayo, built in 1816 and restored in 1929, is a beloved subject of New Mexico artists. Located near a spring whose dirt is known for its healing properties, the Santuario draws thousands of pilgrims during Holy Week and throughout the liturgical calendar.

GENE KLOSS
The Sanctuary, Chimayo, 1934
Aquatint and drypoint on paper
13¾ × 10¼ in.
Public Works of Art Project

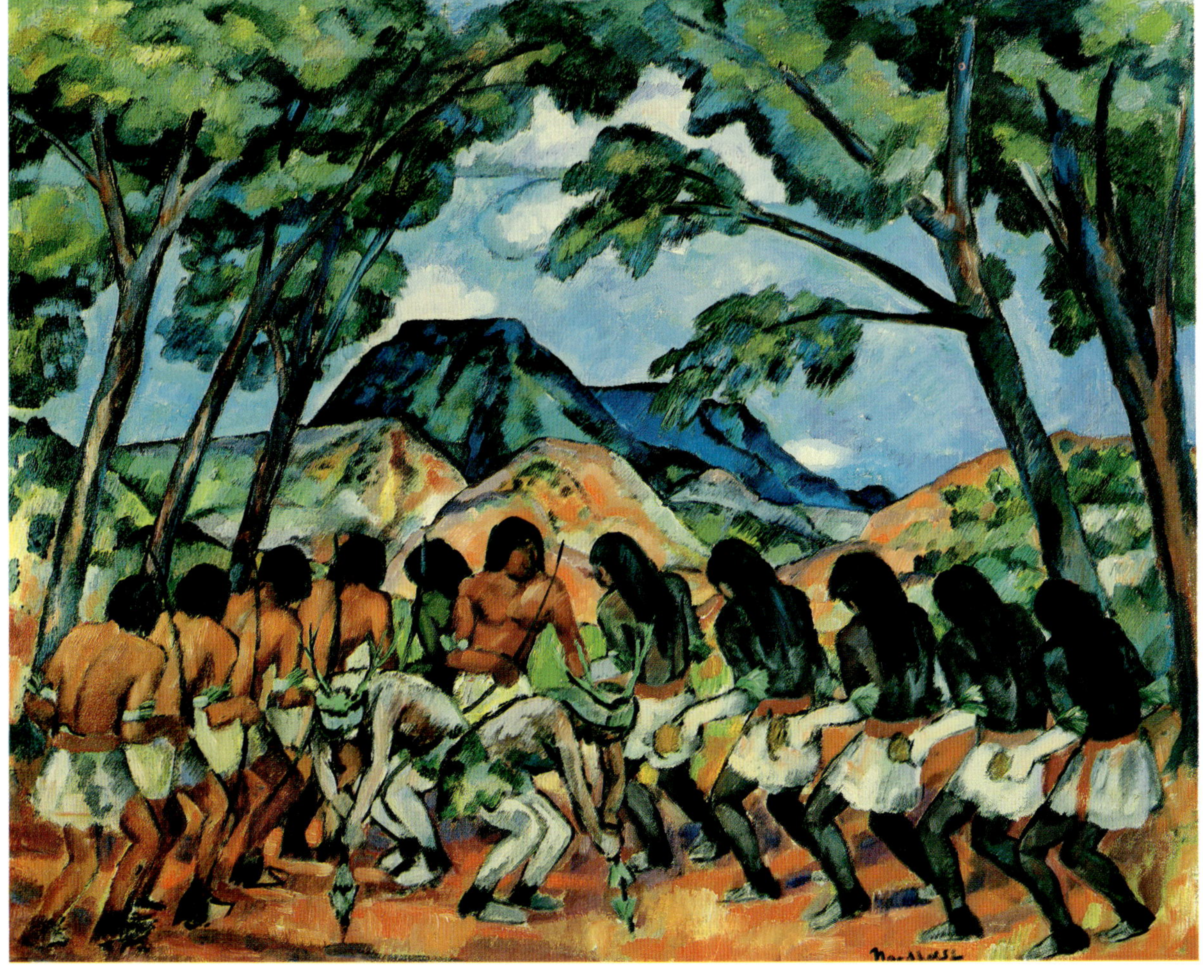

B. J. O. NORDFELDT
The Antelope Dance, 1919
Oil on canvas
33⅝ × 43 in.
Purchased by the Museum of Fine Arts, the Archaeological Society, and Friends of Southwestern Art, 1920

AFTER STUDYING at the Art Institute of Chicago, Nordfeldt extensively traveled and studied in Europe at a time when a momentous change was occurring in French art. French modernism, especially the works of Cézanne, had a significant impact on the growing simplicity and monumentality of Nordfeldt's own work, and he, in turn, influenced many artists in his adopted New Mexico.

Among the local customs of New Mexico that found their way into the artist's work, none were more compelling than ceremonial dances. *The Antelope Dance* is a vibrant response to the colors, rhythms, and geometric structure of that sacred animal ritual. It is a tangible expression of the mysterious and intangible dance, emphasizing the powerful spiritual resonances of this Native American ceremony through the rhythmic repetition of shapes. The canopy of trees over the figures and the distant mountain are Nordfeldt's homage to Cézanne.

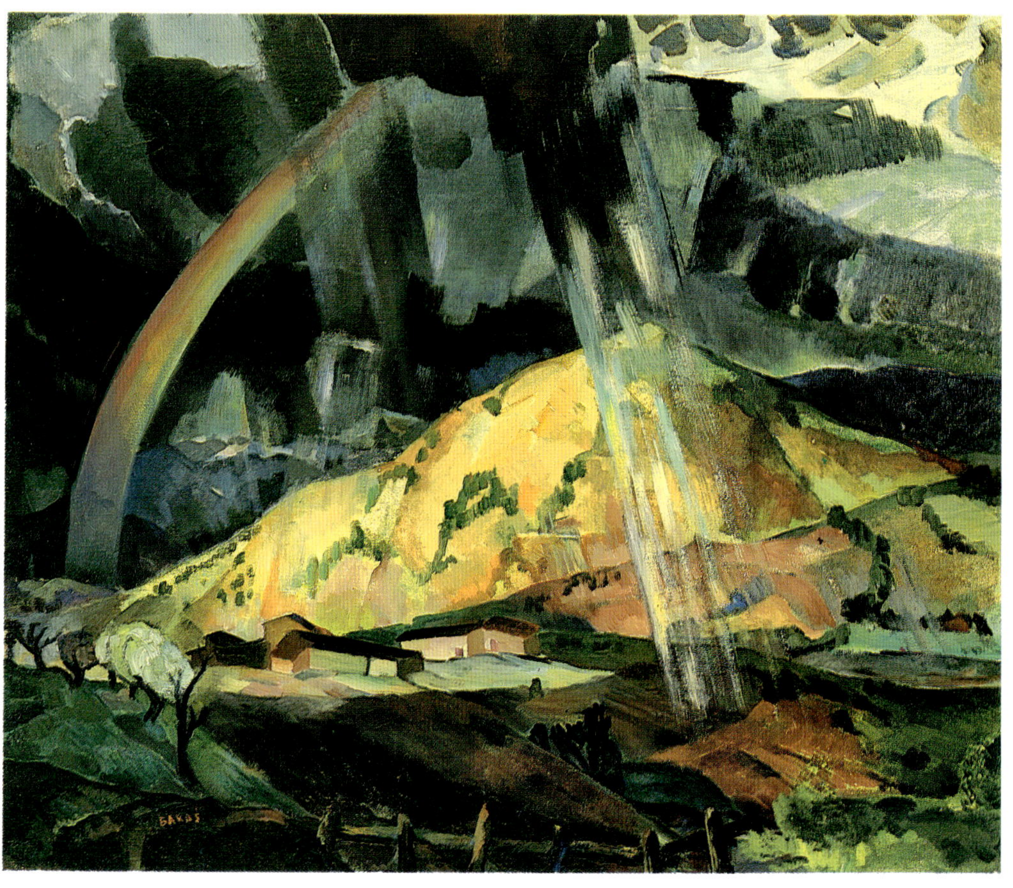

BECAUSE OF Bakos's modernist tendencies, he was refused admission to the Taos Society of Artists and became instead one of the founding members in 1921 of Los Cinco Pintores. While the five members of the Santa Fe group represented divergent artistic styles and temperaments, they shared the goal of wanting to bypass the museum system in presenting art to the people. As much as anything, they were struggling to find a vehicle for making their living by their art.

Encouraged by B.J.O. Nordfeldt to pursue his expressionist tendencies, Bakos painted various moods of the New Mexico landscape, almost always on location. Many consider *The Springtime Rainbow* to be his tour de force. While the planar structure is reminiscent of Cézanne, both the vigor and the lyrical quality of the painting are characteristic of Bakos's personal style.

JOZEF BAKOS
The Springtime Rainbow, 1923
Oil on canvas
$29\frac{1}{2} \times 35\frac{1}{2}$ in.
Gift of the artist in honor of Teresa Bakos, 1974

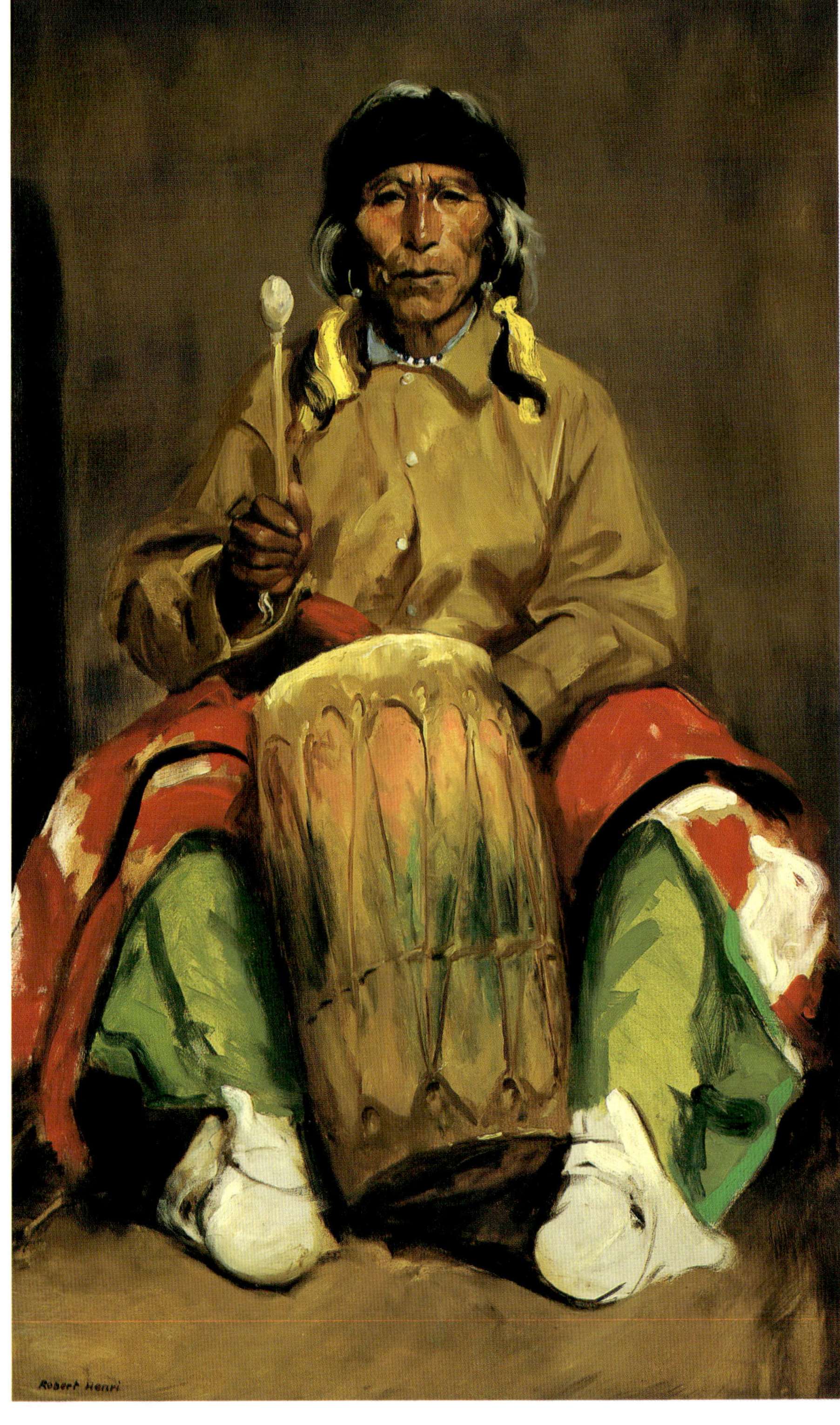

ROBERT HENRI
Portrait of Dieguito Roybal of San Ildefonso (Po-Tse-Nu-Tsa), 1916
Oil on canvas
$65\frac{3}{8} \times 40\frac{7}{8}$ in.
Gift of the artist, 1916

HENRI WAS already a well-known and influential artist and teacher of painting by 1916 when Dr. Edgar Lee Hewett, Director of the Museum of New Mexico, urged him to come to New Mexico and consult on the new museum. Using Santa Fe as his base, Henri visited Taos and other pueblos, completing thirty portraits, among them *Portrait of Dieguito Roybal of San Ildefonso*.

Dieguito, Rain Priest of San Ildefonso and ceremonial drummer, was one of more than three hundred Navajo Indian captives adopted into Pueblo communities in New Mexico after the military campaigns of the 1860s. Here he is seen in his Eagle Dance costume. Dieguito commented after seeing his portrait: "Now I will live forever."

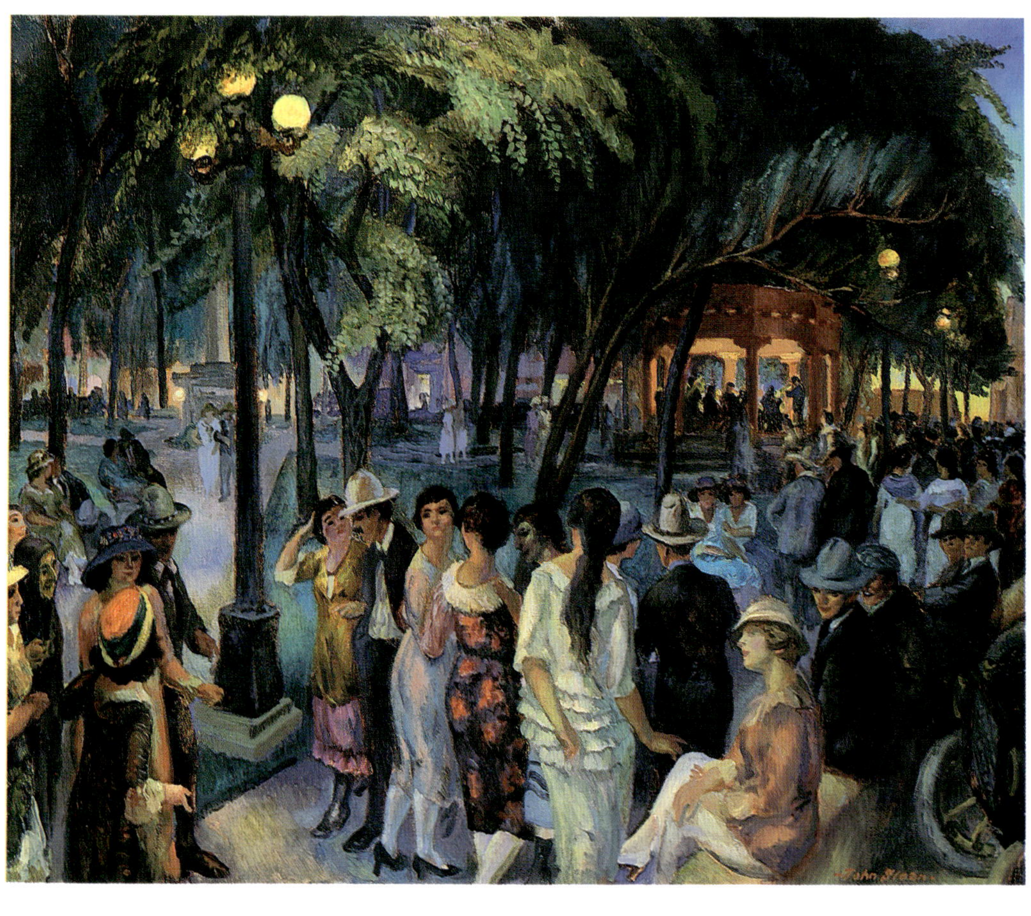

IN 1919, Sloan first visited Santa Fe, encouraged by fellow easterner Robert Henri, with whom he shared an association in The Eight. At the time, Sloan was a prolific, though not fully established, painter who eschewed the idealization of art and instead advocated painting the unglamorized subjects of real life. In New Mexico, over the course of some thirty years, his canvases depicted local genre scenes, Indian ceremonies, and the landscape.

In *Music in the Plaza*, the artist portrays the leisurely activity of groups of people mingling on the town plaza, though the painting is not without its formal concerns. The strong verticals of the plaza's obelisk and the lampposts counteract the rhythmic oscillation of the trees. Nor does the painting lack of autobiographical note: Sloan's family is present in the lower left corner, and it appears that Sloan painted himself as the bespectacled observer in the lower right.

JOHN SLOAN
Music in the Plaza, 1920
Oil on canvas
26 × 32 in.
Gift of Mrs. Cyrus McCormick, 1952

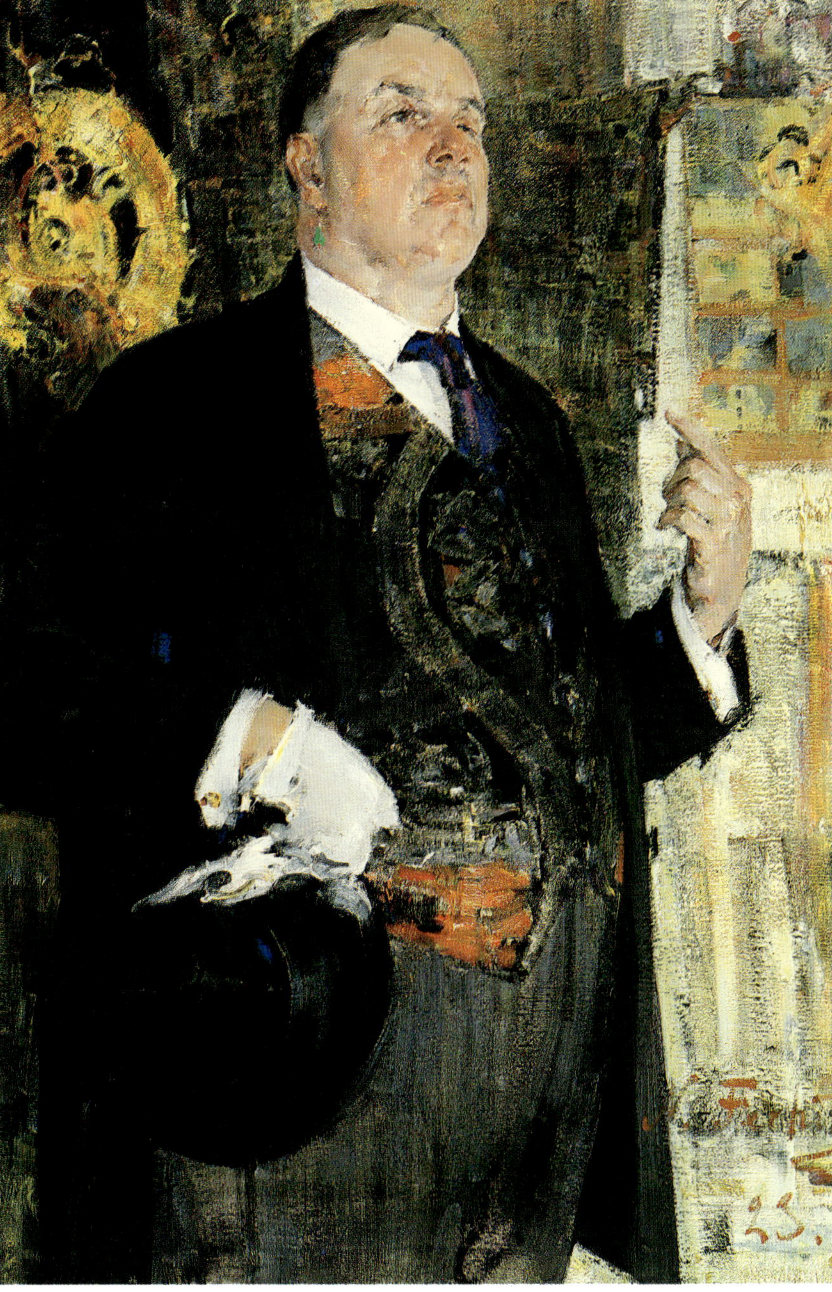

NICOLAI FECHIN
The Artist Burliuk, 1923
Oil on canvas
$49\frac{1}{4} \times 33\frac{3}{8}$ in.
Gift of Edwin C. Lineberry in memory of Duane Van Vechten Lineberry, 1980

BEST KNOWN for his portraits, Fechin studied at the Imperial Academy in St. Petersburg and was influenced by pre-Communist Russian impressionism and its trademark vibrant palette. Fechin emigrated from Russia to the United States in 1923 and in 1927 moved to Taos, where he rented a studio from Mabel Dodge Luhan and spent the next six years painting the many portraits for which he is remembered.

The Artist Burliuk, painted shortly after he arrived in America, is a portrait of Russian classmate and fellow émigré David Burliuk, founder of the Russian futurist movement. The painting is typical of Fechin's portraits in that the figure merges with a background that is an abstraction of freely applied paint strokes.

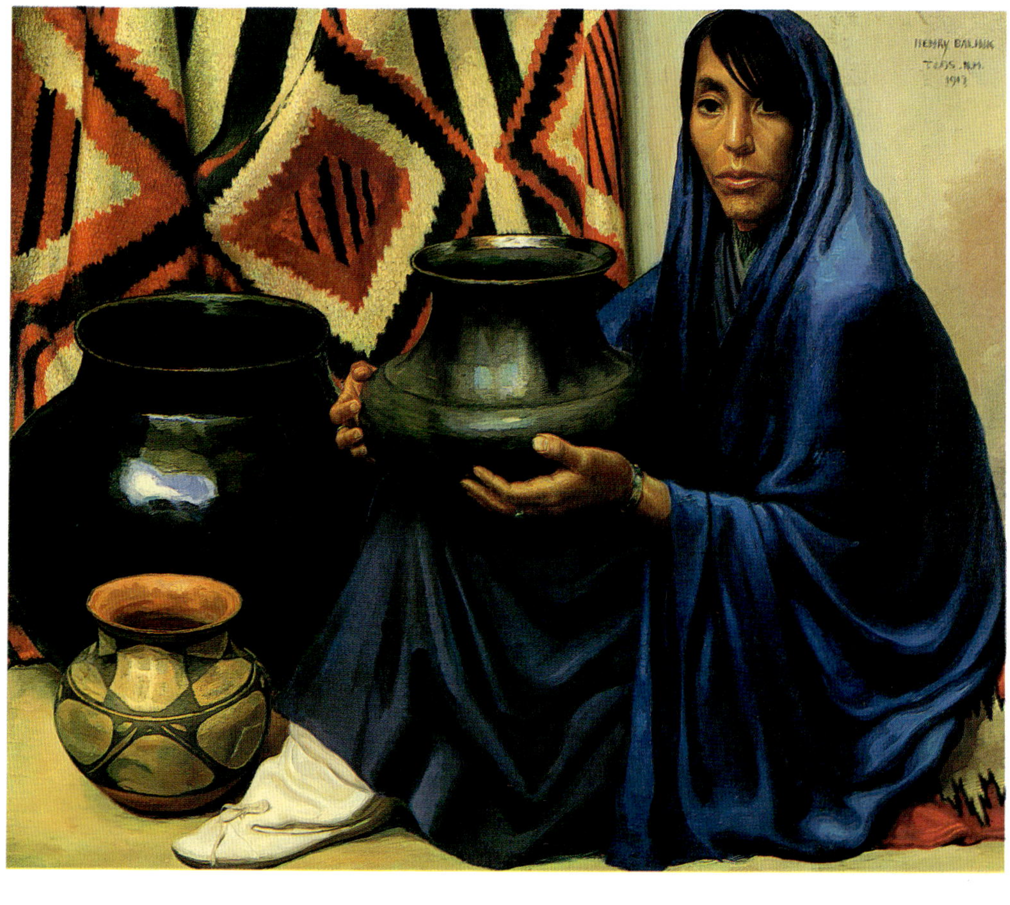

THE SON of a Dutch baker, Balink studied at Amsterdam's Royal Academy before being sent in 1914 to the Metropolitan Museum in New York to copy Greek vase paintings for the Berlin Archaeological Institute and the Louvre. He stayed in America, traveling to Chicago, Denver, and finally in 1917 to Taos, where his work was remarkably well-received. (He painted and sold eight works in his first six weeks there.) Three of Balink's Taos paintings, including *Pueblo Pottery*, were included in the inaugural exhibition at the Museum of Fine Arts that year.

In all, Balink's portraits of Native Americans represented some sixty-three tribes. As in *Pueblo Pottery*, his subjects were most frequently of Taos Pueblo. Given the work that the artist was commissioned to do in America, it is not surprising to note the objective detail in his work. The *olla* with black-on-cream geometric design is from Santo Domingo Pueblo; the woman holds an *olla* from Santa Clara Pueblo; and behind her is a Navajo Chief Blanket, Phase III.

HENRY C. BALINK
Pueblo Pottery, 1917
Oil on canvas
27 × 33 in.
Gift of Herman C. and Bina L. Ilfeld, 1977

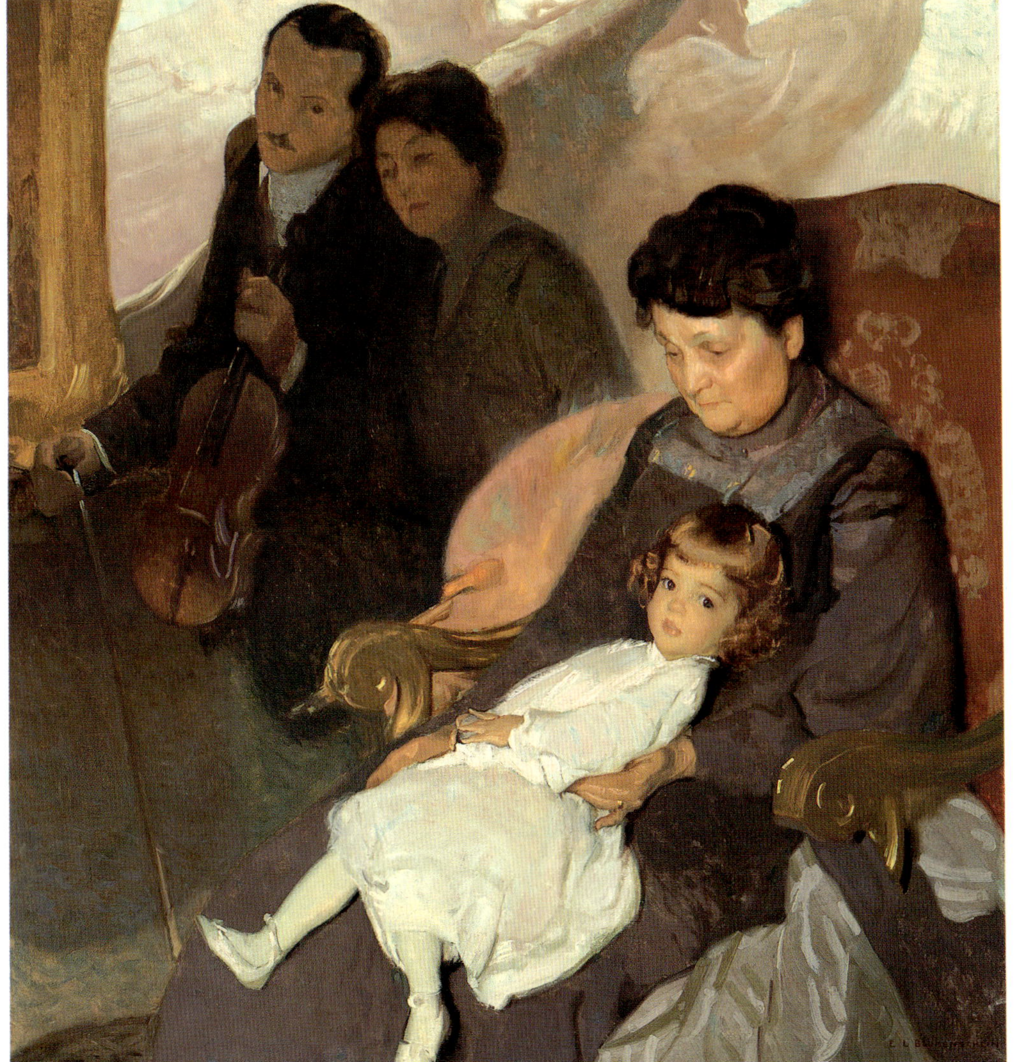

ERNEST L. BLUMENSCHEIN
Portrait of the Artist and Family, 1913
Oil on canvas
46×45 in.
Gift of Helen Greene Blumenschein, 1982

THE BEST-KNOWN and arguably the most versatile painter among the first generation of Taos artists, Blumenschein was a highly successful illustrator whose commercial work in New York supported his higher artistic pursuits in New Mexico between 1910 and 1919, when he relocated permanently. He was a founding member of the Taos Society of Artists in 1915, and his work in the society epitomizes this school of western realism.

Portrait of the Artist and Family, a significant autobiographical painting, was completed in New York while Blumenschein was teaching at the Art Students League. The influence upon the artist of his many years studying in Paris and the postimpressionism he encountered there is evident in this work. Shown in the painting are the artist; his wife, the artist Mary Greene Blumenschein; and daughter Helen, who followed in her parents' profession.

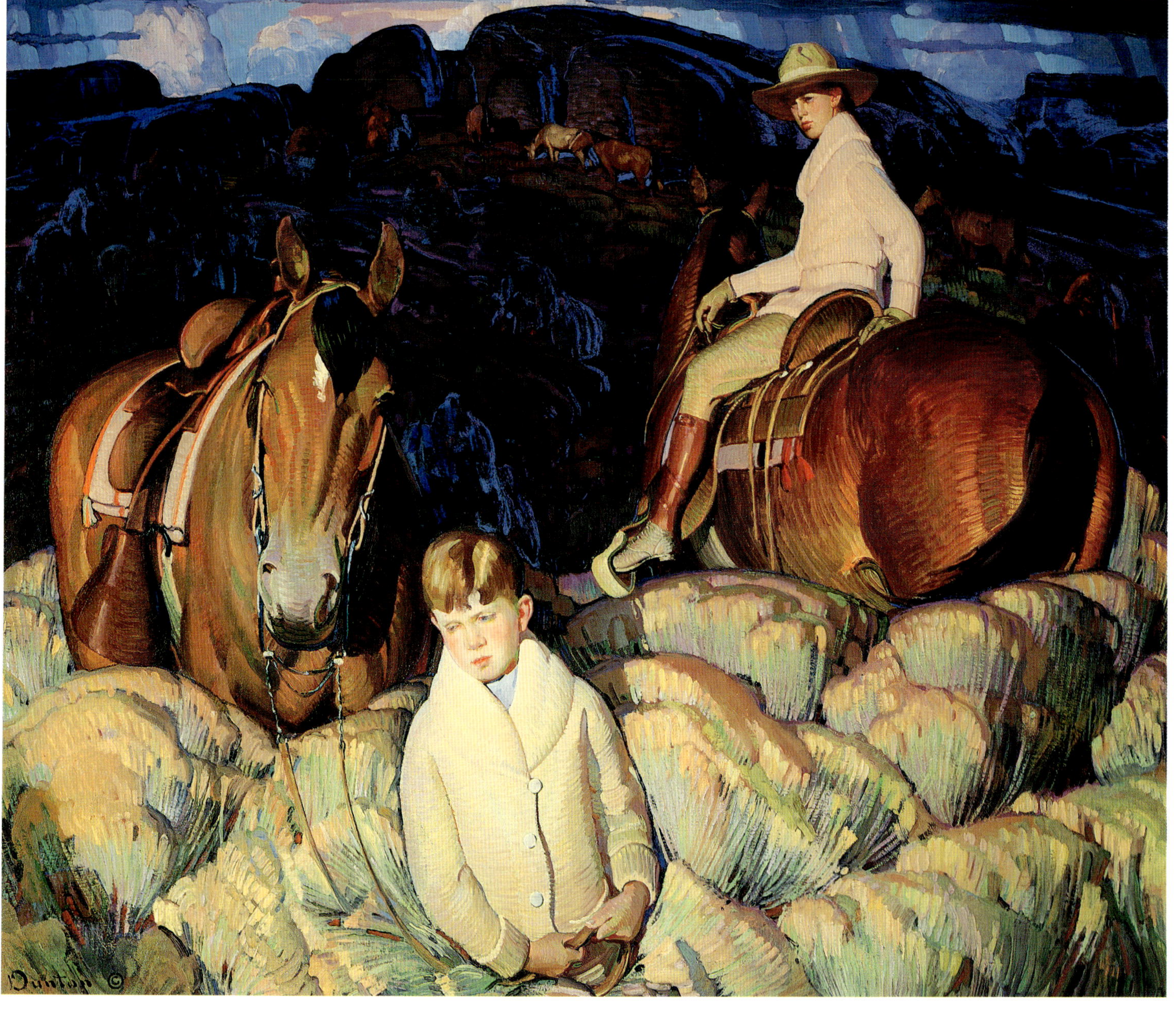

ONCE A PROMINENT American illustrator, Dunton largely abandoned this career upon moving to Taos in 1914. Unlike many of his peers, he had little artistic interest in the culture and ceremonies of Native Americans, preferring instead to paint the life of the cowboy.

My Children is atypical of Dunton's work in its focus upon the private world of his children during the time of the artist's marital separation. Set in a dramatic landscape usually reserved for his cowboy images, the painting is filled with chilling colors evocative of Dunton's dark mood and executed with a strong weave of side-by-side strokes, a style that is more characteristic of his later work.

W. HERBERT DUNTON
My Children, 1920
Oil on canvas
50 × 60 in.
Anonymous gift, 1927

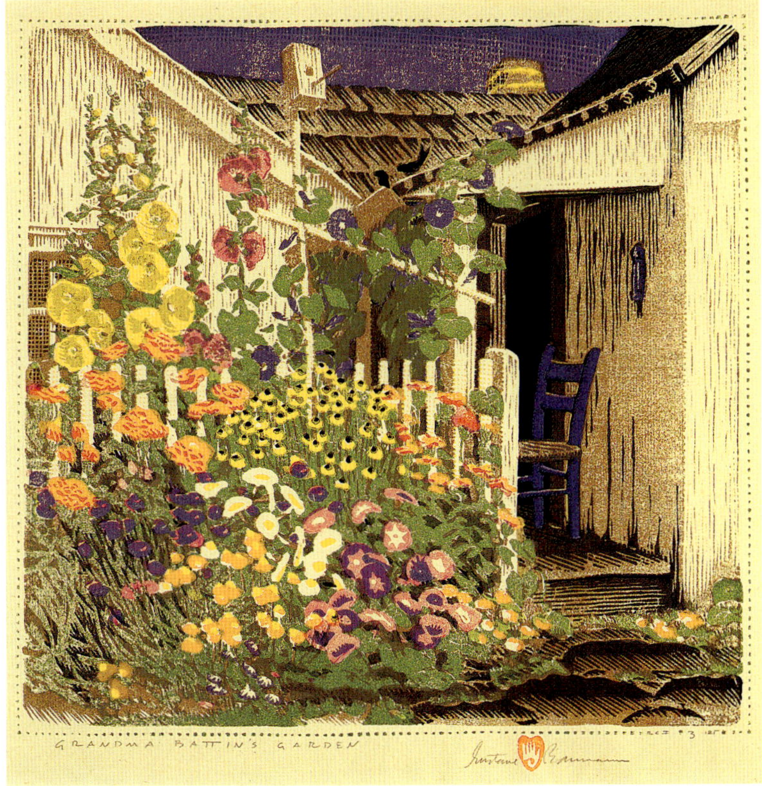

GUSTAVE BAUMANN
Grandma Battin's Garden, 3/125,
ca. 1915
Color woodcut print
12 × 13 in.
Gift with funds raised by the School of American Research, 1952–53

EXECUTED WHILE Baumann was living in Nashville, *Grandma Battin's Garden* depicts a vibrant, sunlit garden scene and a mood of quiet intimacy. It was first rendered as a gouache sketch, then traced in reverse onto a block of basswood, then carved. The block acted as a key from which six to eight subsequent blocks were carved, one block for each color. His hand-ground pigments were applied to the blocks with a press or rubbed on with the back of a spoon.

Baumann alone did all the sketching, cutting, coloring, and printing of his woodblocks, often varying colors within the edition and sometimes recutting the blocks for different effects. Generally, he produced only a few prints initially (from six to twenty-five), often waiting several years before completing an entire edition.

The Museum of Fine Arts' extensive collection of over 1,500 Baumann objects includes prints, sketches, commercial art, paintings, and hand-carved marionettes.

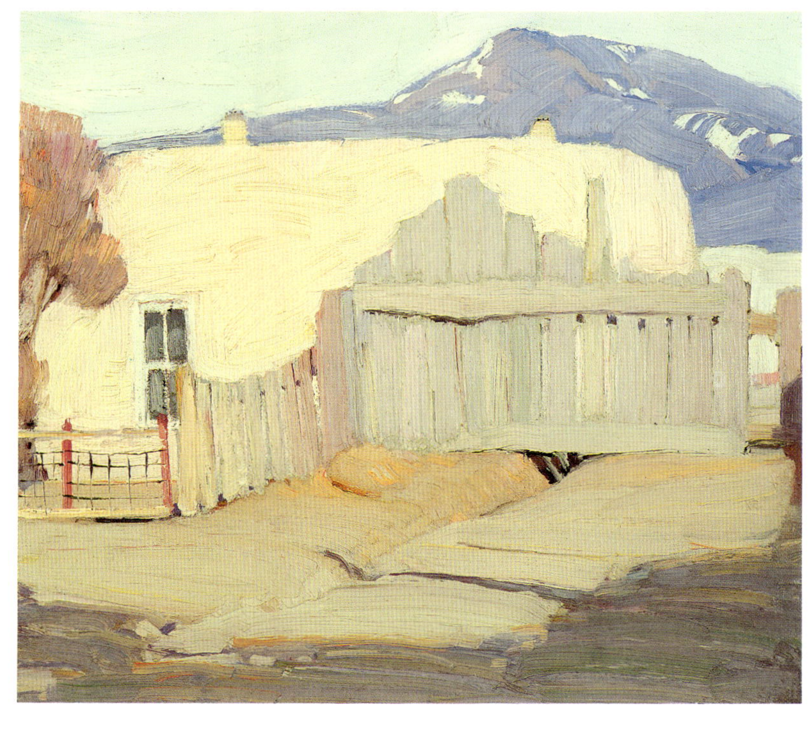

UNLIKE THE OTHER members of the Taos Society of Artists, Higgins was never a commercial illustrator, and the major influences on his painting were German, not French. He studied at the Royal Academy of Munich at a time when realism was encouraged, and he continued to embrace the German method throughout his life, a method characterized by a spontaneous reaction to the subject with no preliminary drawing. Although Higgins gained early recognition painting portraits of Native Americans, his artistic fulfillment came with painting the landscape and natural forms. In this, he became a major transitional figure linking realism with modernism.

Higgins's propensity for using heavy brush-strokes and profuse paint is clearly seen in this small, untitled scene of the adobe house and fence. Twenty such oil sketches on canvas were found unstretched and stacked among the artist's papers after his death, a quiet but significant body of work.

VICTOR HIGGINS
Untitled (Adobe House and Fence),
ca. 1920
Oil on canvas
12 × 14 in.
Bequest of Joan Higgins Reed, 1984

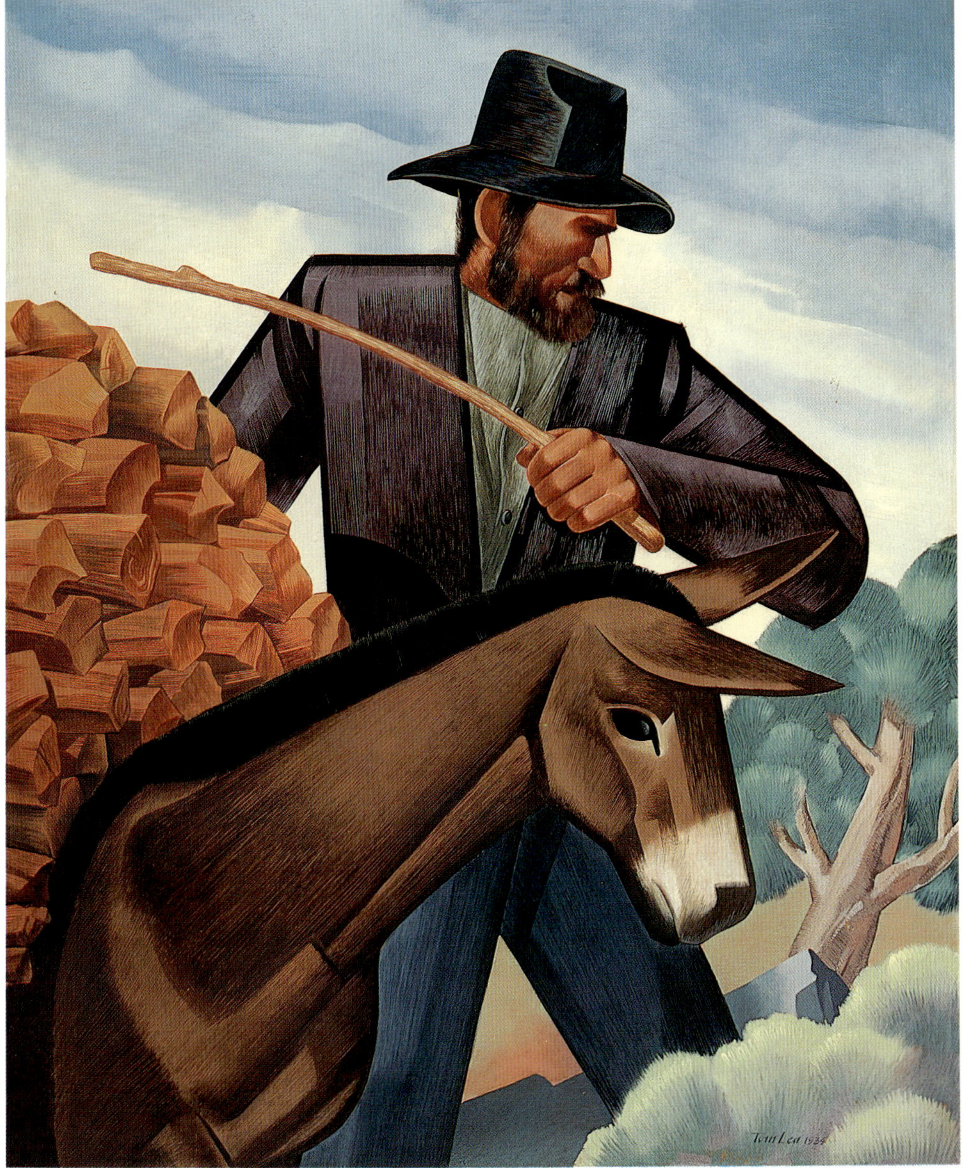

TOM LEA
El Leñador, 1934
Oil on canvas
36 × 30 in.
Gift of the Public Employees
Retirement Agency, 1972

AFTER STUDYING in Chicago and Europe, Texan Lea settled briefly in Santa Fe. Like most artists of the depression era, he encountered a limited market for his art. The Federal Art Project, which provided artists a monthly stipend with no conditions on the paintings they produced, enabled Lea to develop what became a successful career as a chronicler of the West. He simultaneously produced a series of popular novels about western culture, including *The Brave Bulls* (1949) and *The Wonderful Cowboy* (1952).

El Leñador (the woodman) is a product of the depression era. Although the painting is small, it is executed in the monumental style of mural painting so prevalent during the period. On the surface, the work refers to the men who sold firewood to homes and shops throughout Santa Fe. However, on another level, the painting effectively symbolizes the dignity and nobility of the workingman.

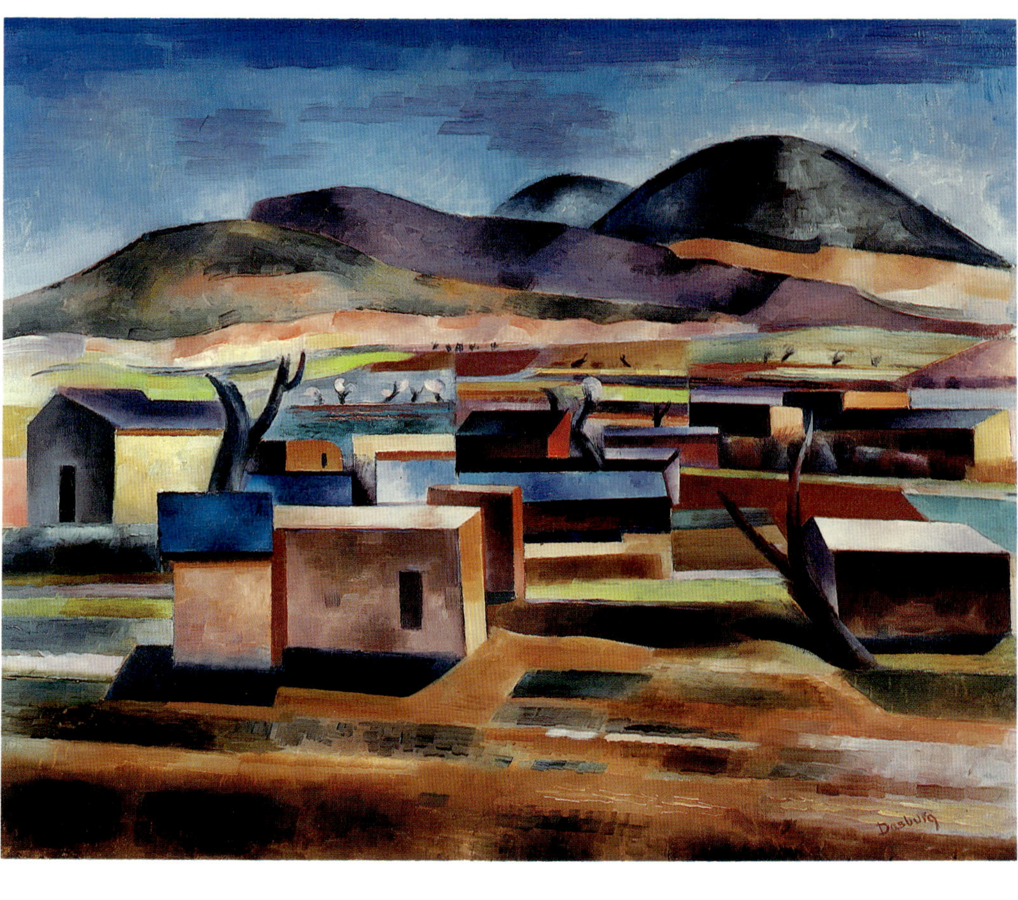

DURING HIS early career, Dasburg was exposed to a variety of theories of art. Although he studied the academic arts at the Art Students League and the New York School of Arts, notably under Robert Henri, his real enthusiasm came from learning about the modernist ideas of French painters at Ambrose Vollard's gallery in Paris and from the American artists with whom he exhibited at the 1913 Armory Show in New York. This diverse background helped Dasburg become one of the most influential progenitors in America of a modern art based on the ideas of cubism.

Invited to New Mexico in 1916 by Mabel Dodge Luhan, whom he had known in New York, Dasburg brought with him the excitement and turmoil of European art. Although he was at first overwhelmed by the vast spaces of the Southwest, as other artists had been, he soon began to employ his modified, personalized form of cubism to find structure in the landscape. In *New Mexican Village*, for example, Dasburg tipped the middle ground up so that it aligns with the picture plane, bridging the gap between near and far. This painting expresses the beauty of the contrast between the rectilinear buildings and the diagonal mountain forms of the New Mexico landscape.

ANDREW DASBURG
New Mexican Village, 1926
Oil on canvas
24 × 30 in.
Gift of Mrs. Cyrus McCormick, 1952

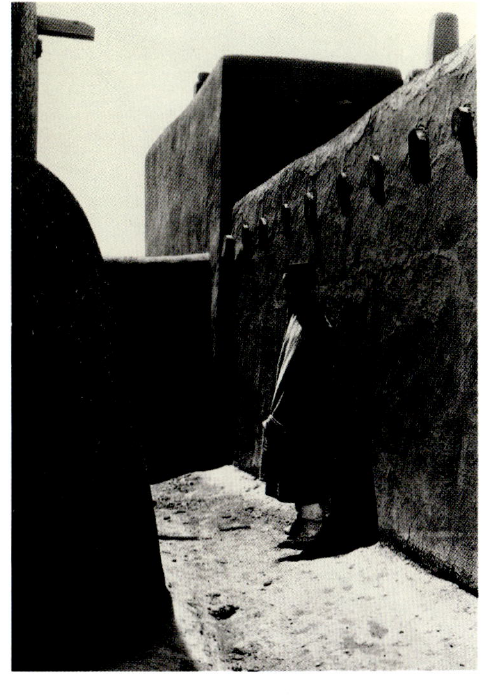

ANSEL ADAMS
At Taos Pueblo, ca. 1929
Gelatin silver photograph
8⅞ × 6⅜ in.
Anonymous long-term loan

ADAMS'S 1930 meeting with Paul Strand in Taos redirected the artist in the recognition of photography's potential as a fine art medium. After viewing Strand's negatives, Adams was confirmed in his shift from a soft-focus pictorial approach to the sharper, more direct modern approach that would become a hallmark in the history of photography.

Albert Bender, who traveled with Adams to New Mexico in 1927, helped to finance the publication of the photographer's first book, *Taos Pueblo*, which included twelve original photographs and an essay by Mary Austin. Although *At Taos Pueblo* is a photograph made during this period, it was not selected as one of the twelve original Dassonville photographs for the limited edition publication. However, it is an image that illustrates Adams's declining interests in soft-focus pictorialism and his increasing concern for a modern distillation of form.

Adams gained access to remote pueblo life through Tony Luhan, who was governor of Taos Pueblo and the husband of arts patron Mabel Dodge. In this photograph, Juanita Luhan, Tony Luhan's first wife, stands classically composed amid architectural details. The curved adobe form of the foreground echoes the shape of the woman's traditional dress. The image expresses a feeling of equilibrium. Modern in its formal approach but traditional in its cultural propriety, this photograph suggests Adams's mature style.

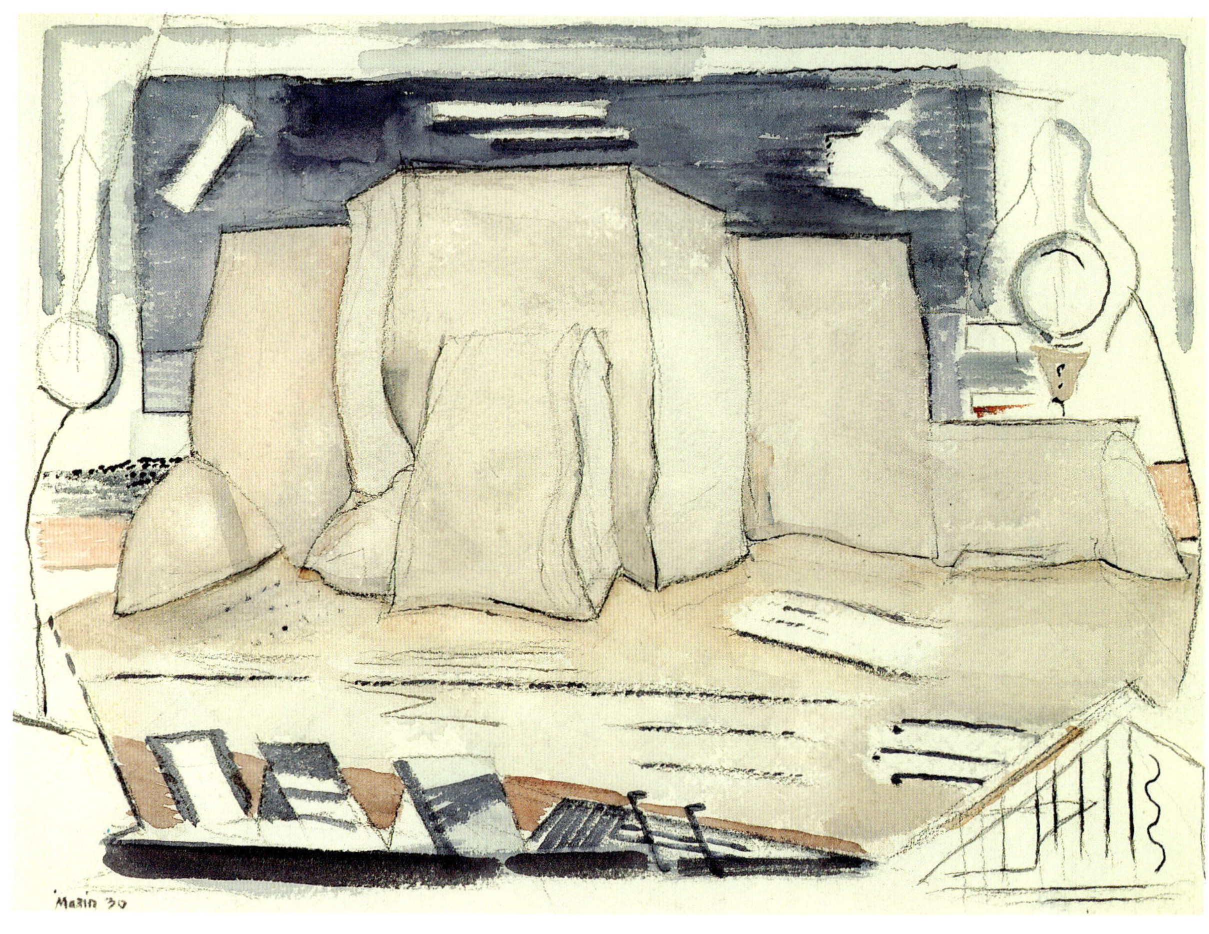

MARIN HAD been hailed as the successor of Winslow Homer, America's finest watercolorist, long before visiting Taos in 1929 and 1930. Although the austere New Mexico landscape differed radically from New England's lush scenery, Marin found it to be well-suited to his distinctive yet delicate cubist style. While in New Mexico, he painted more than one hundred watercolors of the area and disseminated information about modernist ideas and techniques to local artists who came to his studio on Sunday mornings. Marin's influence in the Taos art colony was tremendous.

Back of Ranchos Church, one of several views he painted of the famous church at Ranchos de Taos, is his only view of the apse. The same view was painted by Georgia O'Keeffe the previous year when both were guests of Mabel Dodge Luhan. Although the rendering of the church itself is quite literal, the emphasis on its soft, curving lines in contrast to the thrusting rectangular forms of the foreground, and particularly the geometrically shaped clouds in the sky, is a distinctive modern interpretation. Marin keeps the eye circling this composition by creating a complex frame consisting of a simple line across the top that breaks into a jumble of abstract forms and lines on the sides and bottom, suggesting Pueblo pottery fragments. The image of the church remains a serene vision within this restless, chaotic perimeter.

JOHN MARIN
Back of Ranchos Church, 1930
Watercolor on paper
15 × 20½ in.
Bequest of Helen Miller Jones, 1986

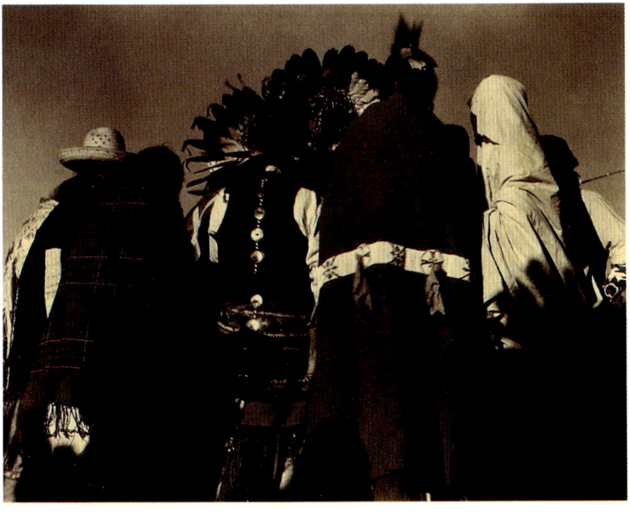

PAUL STRAND
Apache Fiesta, 1930
Platinum photograph
$3\frac{1}{2} \times 4\frac{11}{16}$ in.
Purchased with funds raised in honor of Beaumont Newhall and Eliot Porter, with a special gift from Edna and Bela Kalman, 1989

IN 1916, while living in New York City, Strand began working with abstraction, becoming one of America's earliest modernists. He visited northern New Mexico for the first time with his wife, Rebecca, in 1926, returning to work for increasingly longer intervals in 1930, 1931, and 1932. The area's rich cultural heritage and semiarid landscape provided new challenges beyond his former urban subjects.

These years were Strand's most prolific in New Mexico and were extremely important ones for his development as an artist. In this period, he found a new freedom within the photographic medium, breaking from past artistic convictions and from his mentor, Alfred Stieglitz. Abstraction mixed with an uncompromising literal realism often characterized Strand's work of the time.

Apache Fiesta presents a visual paradox. The inner sanctum where rituals are being performed and the identity of the Indians are concealed by the anonymity of ceremonial dress and by reversing the conventional viewpoint of the portrait, eliminating the faces of the individuals. At the same time, the essence of a culture has been distilled through the juxtaposition of individual forms, and the angle and force of these abstract forms strongly suggest the power and mystery of Indian ritual on a deeper level. There is a tension here between concealment and revelation. Strand's interest at the time with mobility of the reflex camera was inspired by working with both the Akeley film camera and the 4 × 5 Graflex. This picture combines the sense of a film still with the feeling of formal composition characteristic of Strand's earlier work.

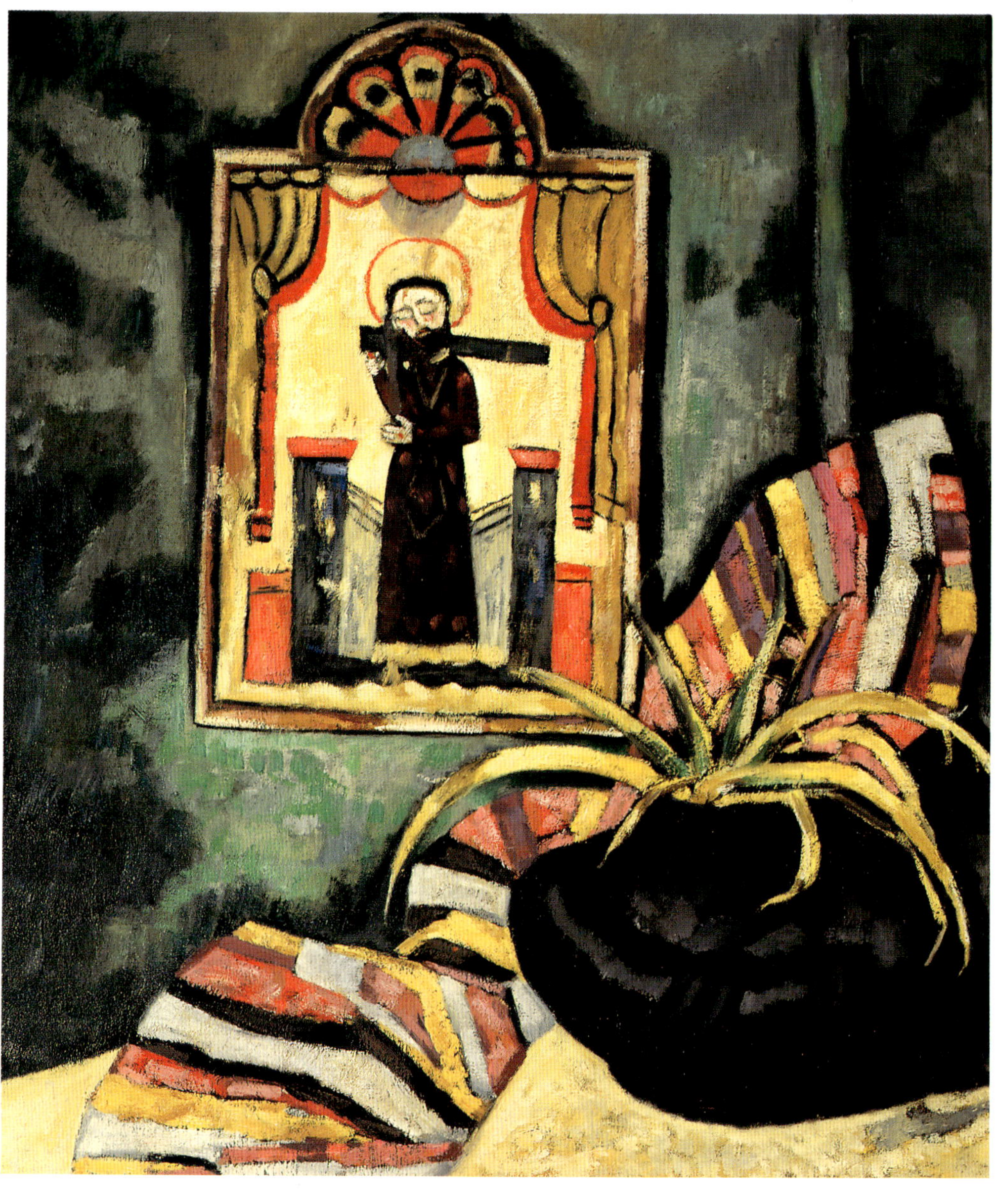

MARSDEN HARTLEY
El Santo, 1919
Oil on canvas
36 × 32 in.
Gift of a friend of Southwest art, 1919

HARTLEY'S art training at the Cleveland School of Art led to scholarships in New York City at the William Merritt Chase School of Art and the National Academy of Design, but it was Alfred Stieglitz, Hartley's dealer, supporter, and mentor, who had the greatest impact on him, sending Hartley to Europe in 1912, where he met Gertrude Stein and was influenced by the German expressionists and the Blaue Reiter artists.

After Hartley came to New Mexico in 1918 and 1919, his work, which had previously been abstract and personal, became more realistic and objective. His naturalistic landscapes, first executed in a new pastel medium, became, years later, a series of oil paintings titled "Reflections of New Mexico." In addition to these, Hartley executed a group of still lifes while in New Mexico that incorporated the religious folk art of Hispanic Catholicism. While these devotional objects were most often painted in a flat, symmetrical fashion against a monochromatic background, *El Santo* departs from this treatment.

ALFRED STIEGLITZ
Equivalent, 1929
Gelatin silver photograph
$3\frac{1}{2} \times 4\frac{1}{2}$ in.
Bequest of Rebecca Salsbury James, 1968

DURING THE 1920s, many of the American modernists around Stieglitz, including John Marin, Marsden Hartley, Georgia O'Keeffe, and Paul and Rebecca Strand, began searching for new challenges and subjects. Their travels took them to northern New Mexico, where the semiarid landscape provided simple, clear forms that were compatible with modernist sensibilities.

Although Stieglitz was impressed by his friends' discoveries, he rarely left his own environs of New York City and Lake George. Nevertheless, he produced seminal bodies of work in the 1920s that were not unrelated to the works of other artists in his circle. The collective portrait of O'Keeffe, composed of hundreds of negatives made over twenty years, and the series of cloud pictures he called "equivalents" were pinnacles of his own artistic achievements.

In 1923, after forty years of photographing, Stieglitz set out to distill the lessons he had learned. He told O'Keeffe that he would photograph clouds to prove that the success of his work had little to do with having any power over his subjects. He considered *Equivalent*, 1929, among his finest. He infused these metaphorical pictures with personal dimensions, extending ideas through abstraction.

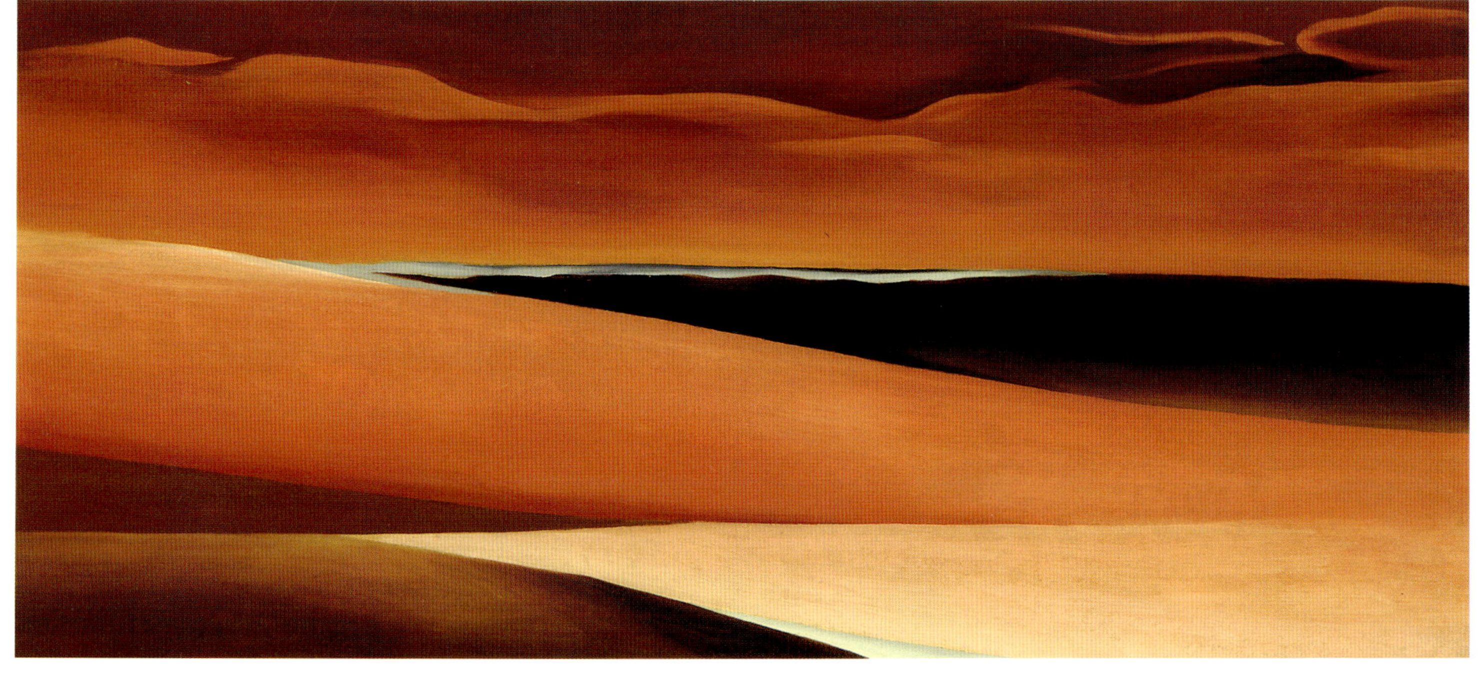

O'KEEFFE'S first extended trips to Taos beginning in 1929 generated paintings that herald the emergence of a unique artistic vision. Those early works, far removed from the cityscapes and country scenes of her New York life, tended to the stark and monochromatic, emphasizing subtleties of form and soft gradations of light. The velvety paint surface of *Bear Lake* reflects O'Keeffe's refined sensitivity to the nuances of this grandiose landscape, but it is a style she would begin to change as she focused more on the pictorial qualities of the high desert.

Bear Lake, located in the mountains north of Taos, was the subject of numerous canvases during O'Keeffe's summers at the Dodge estate. She exhibited at least five such paintings at Stieglitz's An American Place gallery in New York. *Bear Lake*, 1931, was purchased from the exhibit of the following year and remained privately held until 1984, when it was purchased for the museum.

GEORGIA O'KEEFFE
Bear Lake, 1931
Oil on canvas
$15\frac{1}{2} \times 36\frac{1}{2}$ in.
Purchase, Museum of New Mexico Foundation, 1984

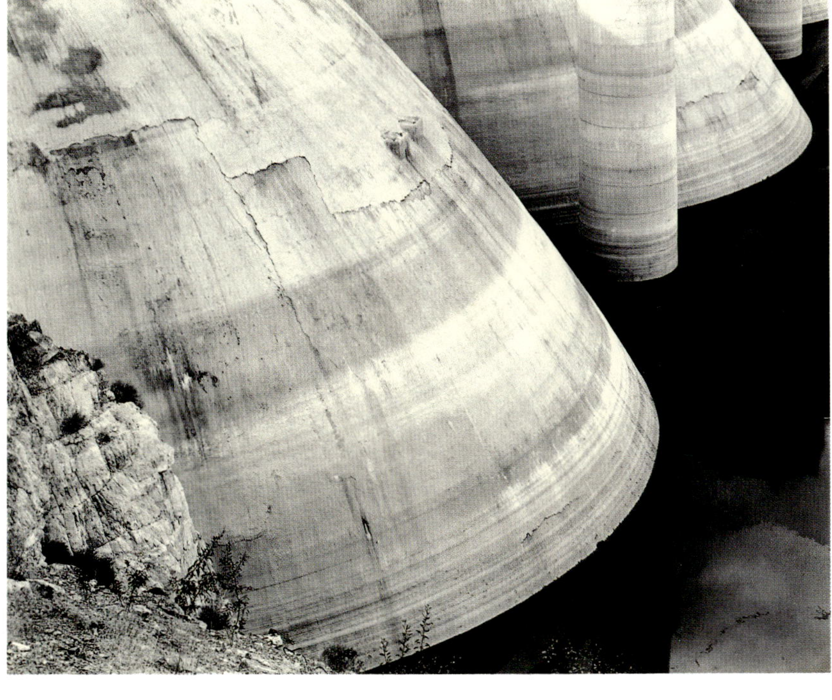

EDWARD WESTON
Coolidge Dam, Arizona, 1937
Gelatin silver photograph
$7\frac{1}{2} \times 9\frac{1}{2}$ in.
Anonymous gift, 1987

DRIVING FROM New Mexico to California with his companion Charis Wilson, who was writing about their travels, Weston stopped late one day at Coolidge Dam. Wilson described the extraordinary scene at San Carlos Lake: "The violent contrast of elements, the age of nature's desert mountains, the shiny newness of man's lake—gave the somber landscape a disquieting aspect of unreality."

Weston had written his younger friend, Ansel Adams, a few years before about photography's potential for illuminating a world beyond normal human vision, emphasizing that the medium could be used toward expressive ends: "Photography is not at all seeing in the sense that the eyes see . . . ; we carry on our willful distortion of fact . . . which give[s] results quite different from the scene or object as it was in nature." His idea of creating pictures from the *unreality* of photography, in the view of preeminent art historian Beaumont Newhall, was his most important statement. By the time Weston visited Coolidge Dam, these ideas were being incorporated into his art.

This image of Coolidge Dam was Weston's favorite among several photographs he made there. It melds his understanding of primary form found in earlier photographs with his strong interest in the landscape. The darkened water, reflecting architectural fragments and clouds, causes the curved geometric forms to float, transforming them into abstract forms detached from mundane reality. Writing to Adams about photography's creative possibilities, Weston commented: "Nature has all the 'abstract' (simplified) forms Brancusi or any other artist can imagine."

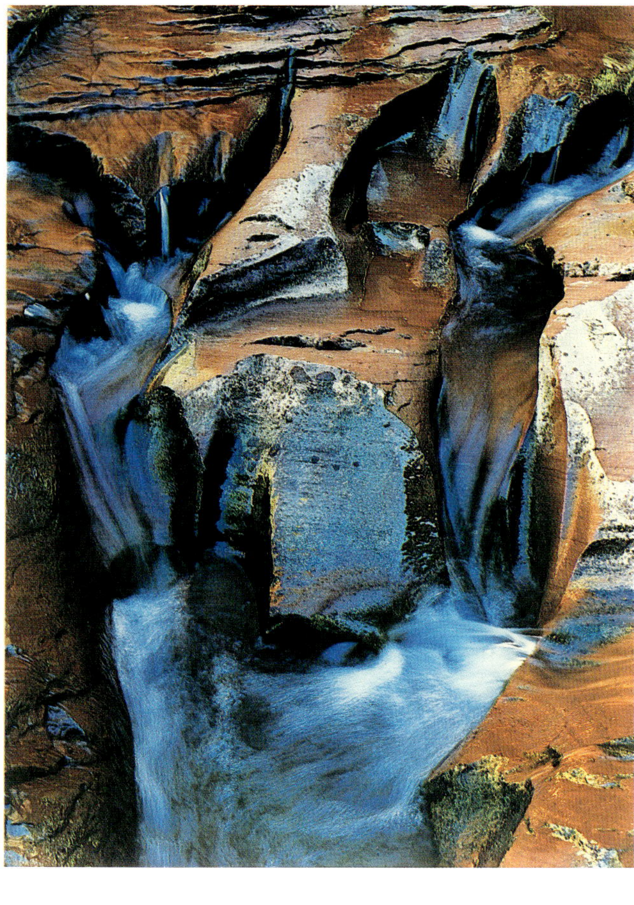

PORTER FIRST encountered the art of photography through meeting Alfred Stieglitz and seeing the early black-and-white work of Ansel Adams. Although he was initially influenced by their work, he soon developed his own style, working primarily with landscape and architecture. A few years later, in 1938, Stieglitz held an exhibition of Porter's successful black-and-white photographs at his An American Place gallery.

Porter's visits to New Mexico beginning in 1939 provided fresh challenges. In 1940, the Museum of Fine Arts gave him his first museum exhibition. It was during this period that Porter began dedicating his career to color photography.

Light, color, and form are inseparable components of Porter's vision of the world. His color photographs are filled with a spirit of discovery beyond our everyday, conditioned responses. The order inherent in nature's chaos is revealed by the artist's keen articulation of color. In *Stream Erosions, Coyote Canyon, Glen Canyon, Utah*, nature's blend of rock and water is transformed into a powerful abstraction with primeval undercurrents. The splendor of nature's creation is paralleled by the limitless bounds of human perception.

ELIOT PORTER
Stream Erosions, Coyote Canyon, Glen Canyon, Utah, 1971
Dye transfer photograph
10 × 8 in.
Bequest of Eliot Porter, 1990

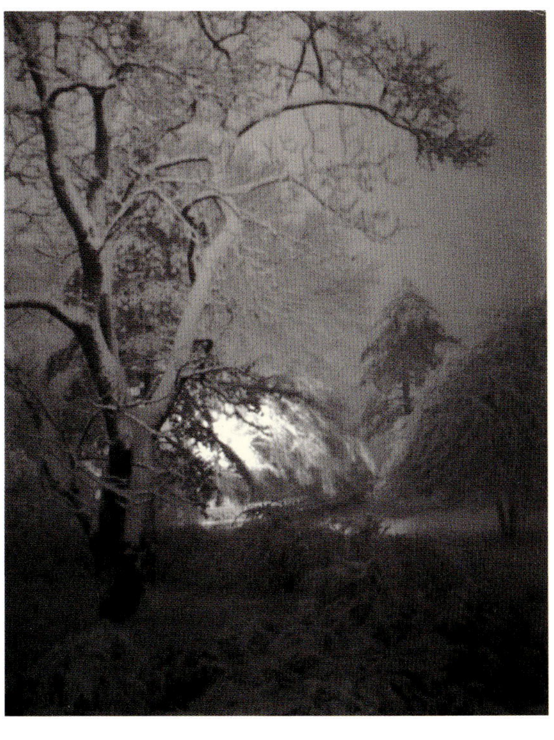

LAURA GILPIN
Central Park, New York City, 1917
Gelatin silver photograph
8×6 in.
Intended gift of Edna S. Kalman

AS A STUDENT at the Clarence White School in New York City in 1916–17, Laura Gilpin began her explorations into photography. With her first visit to New Mexico in 1921, Gilpin directed her understanding of the medium's potential and its challenges to subject matter that would absorb her for nearly six decades to come.

Central Park, New York City, part of a photographic study made at Clarence White, presented the photographer with a complex problem. Beyond the technical challenge of photographing at night, Gilpin drew on considerations of form to transform a superficially elementary choice of subject into a sustaining work of art.

The photograph contains two of the primary elements that remained central to Gilpin throughout her life as a photographer: the landscape and her mastery of light. Through photography, Laura Gilpin discovered the grace of everyday life. Her genius as an artist resides in how she continually found ways to use the commonplace to reveal the splendor of the world and its people.

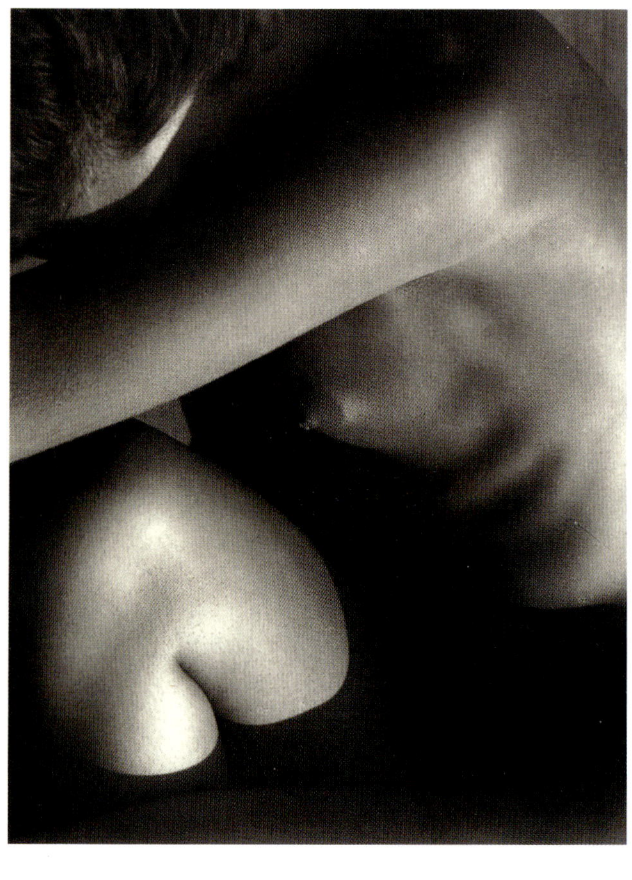

THROUGHOUT HER CAREER, Bernhard has expounded upon the idea of photographing nudes enclosed within simple structures. The idea germinated during the time of her first important commission for the Museum of Modern Art in 1934, when she photographed a large stainless steel bowl for the exhibition "Machine Art."

Although *Triangles* is not, strictly speaking, an example of this motif, the camera's rectangular frame in effect functions like an enclosing container. The frame creates additional triangles that amplify the triangular aspects of the human form that are repeated throughout the image. The figure appears to be simultaneously contained and self-contained, perfectly balanced in its architectural structure. The fundamental elegance of this picture conveys a quality one associates with the canvases of seventeenth-century French painter Nicolas Poussin. This geometric interpretation combines the classic proportions of design with a distillation of human contours. It communicates beauty, harmony, and a special sensitivity to light.

RUTH BERNHARD
Triangles, 1942
Gelatin silver photograph
11 7/8 × 9 1/16 in.
Future gift of Cindy Ewing to the Jane Reese Williams Collection

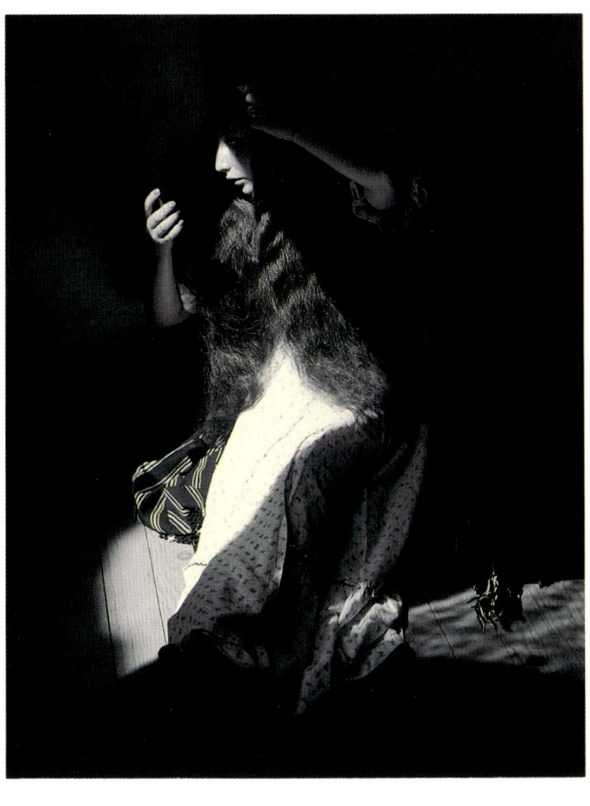

MANUEL ALVAREZ BRAVO
Retrato de lo Eterno (Portrait of the Eternal), ca. 1935
Gelatin silver photograph
$9\frac{1}{4} \times 7\frac{3}{16}$ in.
Gil Hitchcock Collection, 1983

MANUEL ALVAREZ BRAVO was the first major artist in Mexico to recognize photography's potential as an art form. The style of his early photographic and film works of the 1920s and 1930s reveals the diverse influences of French cubism, Edward Weston and Paul Strand in photography, the printmaking of Mexican artist José Posada, and the filmmaking of Sergei Eisenstein.

Although the ideals of these postrevolutionary years affected Bravo, especially through his association with Mexican artists and intellectuals, he never embraced the ideology of socialist realism for political purposes in his photography. However, the themes of life and death, so prevalent in the arts and culture of Mexico, remained an ongoing concern throughout his career.

In *Retrato de lo Eterno*, a young woman, surrounded by the enveloping darkness of a quiet room, looks intently into a small hand mirror; a minimal human gesture, elevated through dramatic light and form, takes on universal significance. Is the pervasive capacity of this photograph gained from what the photographer created with a minimum of circumstance or is it in the transcendence of acting beyond an artificial scene? Light is used sparingly to stress fundamental symbolic forms, such as the cameolike portion of her face that only she sees in the mirror. Universal levels of meaning often amplified the direct simplicity of Bravo's art, and here the photographer suggests in this unassuming scene the ageless virtue of beauty and the essence of mortality.

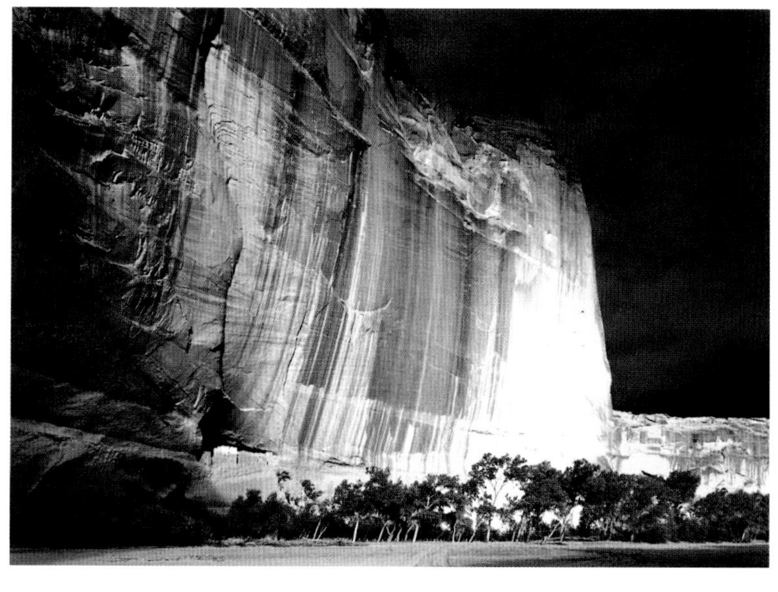

WORKING WITHIN established artistic traditions is one of the foremost challenges for photographers. What can be added, through style, content, or personal expression, that has not been exhausted by past masters of the medium? The genre of landscape, one of the oldest in art history, poses the question another way: What can photography add to a landscape already abundantly interpreted by painters, printmakers, and others of the two-dimensional medium?

In part, the answer may lie in what nature itself has to offer, an answer reflected in Clift's *White House Ruins, Canyon de Chelly, Arizona.* Many other major photographers have made the architectural splendor of these ruins their subject. Laura Gilpin photographed their unique qualities beginning in the 1930s. During Clift's first visit there with her in the fall of 1974, the silence of the canyon made a distinct impression. "The protective and awe-inspired walls of the canyon give . . . the sense of home," he later recollected. "Overall it is a place somehow not only of nature but of a certain kind of human spirit."

In this horizontal view of the ruins, the grand vertical cliffs are less emphasized than in more typical vertical renderings. Clift also inverts the sense of light, illuminating the massive wall against a mysterious dark sky and creating a "negative" image. The waning daylight allows for a precision of detail uncommon in any medium. His fine print, made with remarkable concern for nuance, aids the photograph in transcending the realms of geologic or cultural time.

WILLIAM CLIFT
White House Ruins, Canyon de Chelly, Arizona, 1975
Gelatin silver photograph
$6\frac{3}{4} \times 9\frac{5}{8}$ in.
Anonymous gift, 1984

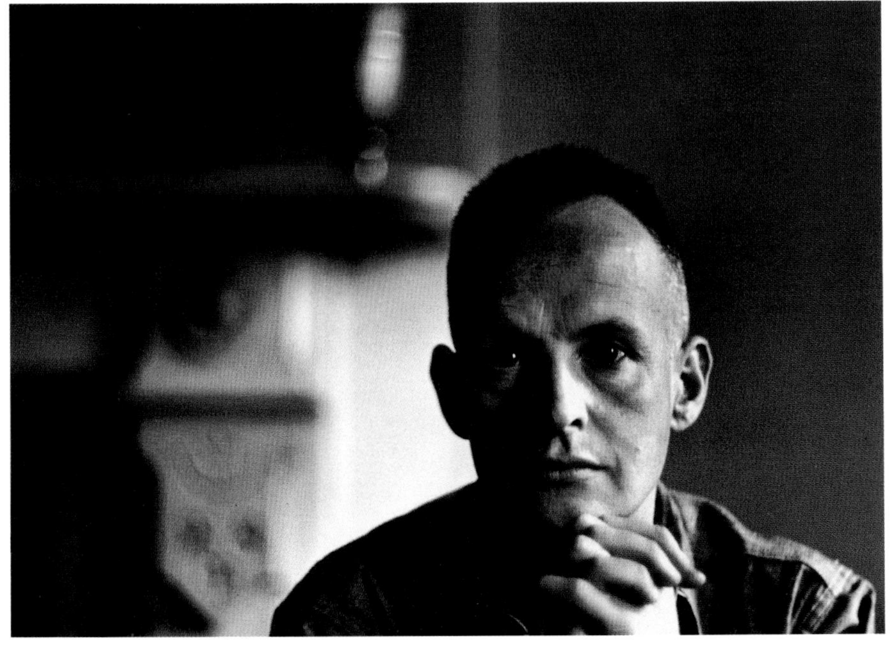

BEAUMONT NEWHALL
Henri Cartier-Bresson, 1946
Gelatin silver photograph
$8\frac{3}{4} \times 12\frac{3}{4}$ in.
Museum purchase, 1984

THE DEVELOPMENT of ideas about photography through his own use of the camera has been a significant means of exploration for preeminent art historian Newhall. The fruits of such a method–the thorough understanding of the artistic potentials of the medium in this century–were presented in his monumental study, *The History of Photography*.

Newhall met Henri Cartier-Bresson in New York in 1946 while the French photographer was on assignment for *Harper's Bazaar* and preparing for an exhibition at the Museum of Modern Art. Cartier-Bresson's emphasis on intuitively grasping the relationships of subjects within the camera's frame was a pioneering achievement. It suggested that the artist could, with a small and mobile camera, participate in determining through his vision the order of the transitory world.

The connection between photographer and subject is emphasized in this straightforward portrait of Cartier-Bresson, taken during an interview with Newhall for *Popular Photography*. Here the predominance of eyes and hands reflects with remarkable poise the photographer's vocation. The fact that Cartier-Bresson rarely allowed himself to be photographed adds to the intensity of this unpretentious portrait, made with his own lens. The camera here becomes the intermediary between this major artist and photography's greatest historian, both of whom left indelible marks on the history of the medium.

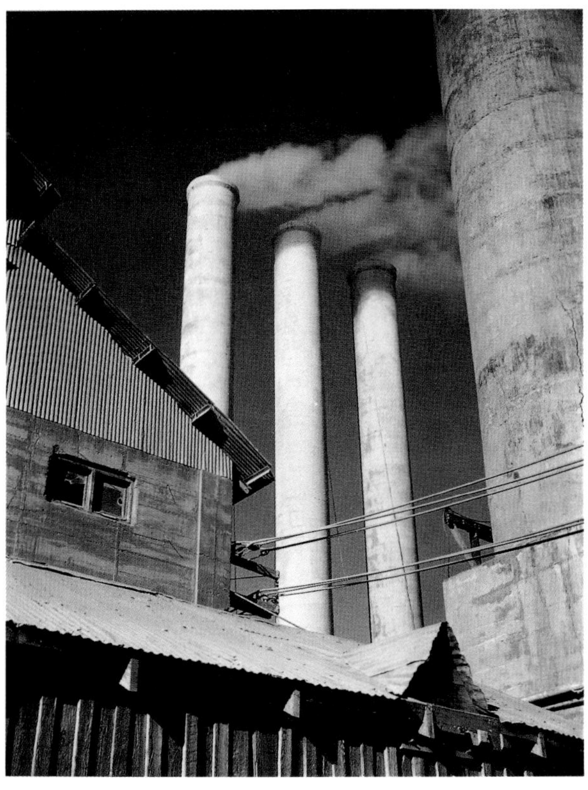

WHAT DOES a younger artist learn by working directly with a master? History reveals that the influences between protégé and teacher are often reciprocal. When Van Dyke traveled with Edward Weston to photograph California and the Southwest in the early 1930s, subjects before their large-view cameras were often the same or referred to common interests, though uniquely approached.

Weston photographed the Armco Steel plant in Ohio almost a decade before Van Dyke's *Monolith* was taken. The massive shapes of industrial pipes, vertical smokestacks, and geometric buildings were well-suited to his predilection for the essence of form. In Van Dyke's rendition, subtle dissimilarities are indicative of a different era and personal vision, yet the influence of Weston upon Van Dyke's work is apparent.

Unlike Weston's image, Van Dyke's version contains no right angles to the picture frame; instead, only diagonal lines create a dynamic interplay of forms. Blowing smoke is a prominent reminder of the human dimension of industrial production. The artist's sense of moral responsibility is in evidence.

Rather than specifying the name of the corporation, the artist identifies his subject as a *monolith*, acknowledging this structure as a living monument of modern culture. Weston and Van Dyke focused on similar associations between light and form when they visited New Mexico for the first time a year later. Van Dyke would subsequently decide that such interests in human dimensions could be explored with a broader range in another related medium—that of filmmaking.

WILLARD VAN DYKE
Monolith, 1930
Gelatin silver photograph
$9^{1}/_{4} \times 7^{1}/_{4}$ in.
Gift of Patricia Belvin, 1985

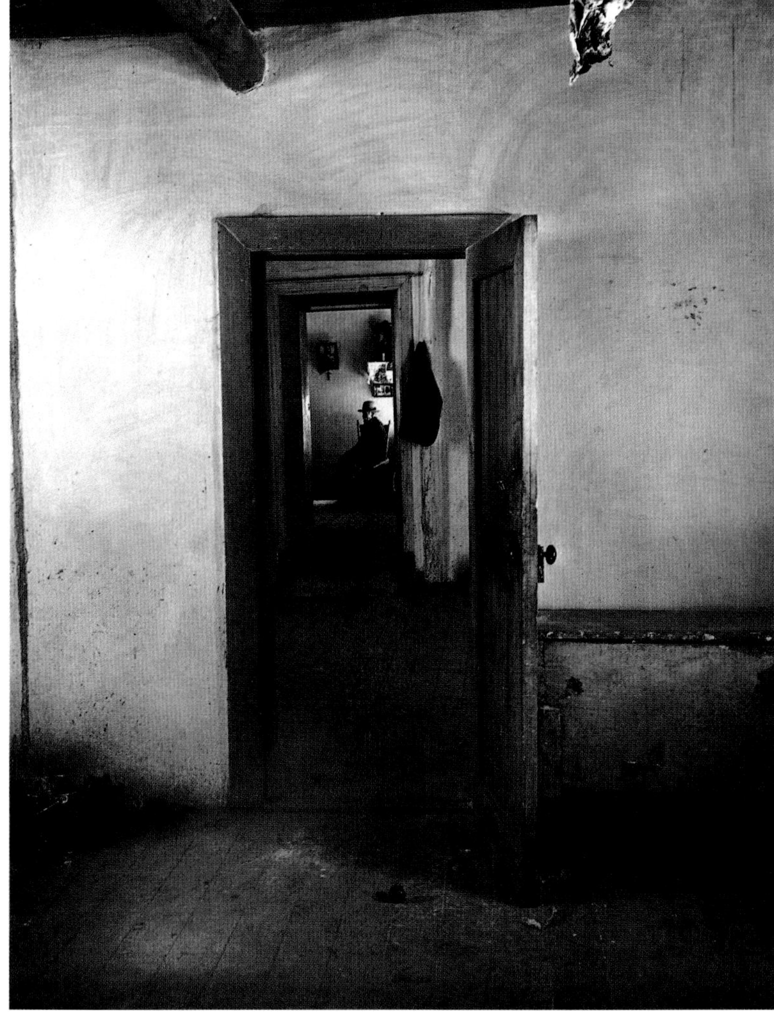

JOHN C. COLLIER, JR.
Trampas, New Mexico, Rooms in the House of Juan Lopez, the Mayordomo. Grandfather Romero Is 99 Years Old.
January 1943
Gelatin silver photograph
$17\frac{7}{8} \times 13\frac{7}{8}$ in.
New Mexico Farm Security Administration Collection, purchased with funds donated by the Pinewood Foundation, with additional support from Barbara Erdman, 1990

COLLIER WAS hired onto the team of Farm Security Administration photographers in 1941 upon the recommendation of Dorothea Lange, whom he had long admired. (Lange photographed Collier as a boy.) His initial assignment included working in little-known areas of the East, from the Erie Canal to New England, an experience that influenced his desire to photograph his native New Mexico with what he termed a "distinct knowledge." Collier convinced FSA administrator Roy Stryker to break with agency code and allow him to work in his home territory.

By 1943, he was photographing the Spanish-American culture of northern New Mexico. Having grown up in Taos, and having briefly lived at Taos Pueblo, Collier was able to reveal the daily life of rural New Mexico with a vision enlightened by deep cultural perception. In his homeland, he worked with the expediency of a filmmaker.

In 1943, he was introduced to the Lopez family; eventually, all the family members would become central subjects in his work. Here grandfather Romero awaits his eternal destiny, with doorways serving as metaphors for the stages of life. Collier's brief time photographing in New Mexico became the foundation for his later pioneering work as an artist and teacher focusing on the multidisciplinary field of visual anthropology.

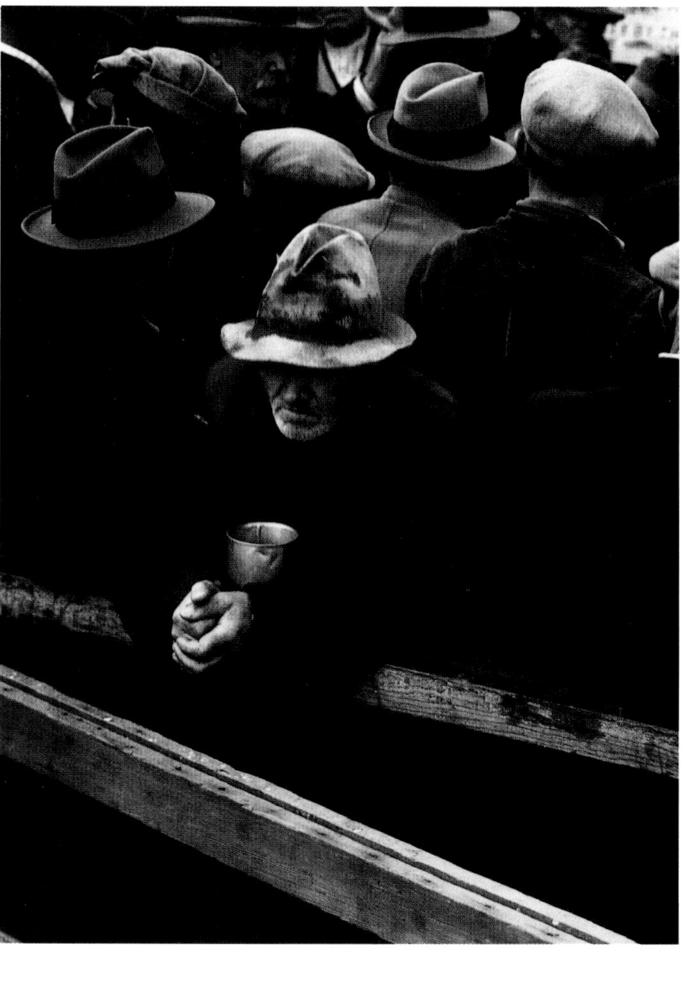

DOROTHEA LANGE
White Angel Bread Line, San Francisco, 1932
Gelatin silver photograph
13 × 9¾ in.
Gift of Mr. and Mrs. Todd Webb, 1971

LANGE'S noncommercial photography, already in process by the late 1920s, gained importance with her visit to Taos in 1931, upon the invitation of John Collier, Jr., and her part-time residency there in 1932. She photographed the Native American and Hispanic people of the area, as well as the distinctive architecture. Through her husband Maynard Dixon's painting of the growing number of homeless individuals migrating west to escape the depression, Lange approached a theme that would become central to her work. From Paul Strand, whom Lange met at the Mabel Dodge Luhan enclave, she began to understand how to effectively photograph people within their social environments, a formative lesson that would ensure her later success in documentary work. Understanding the nature of human existence and the immediate circumstances governing any given moment became essential to Lange's marked sensitivity as a photographer.

Upon returning to San Francisco, she turned her camera toward the city streets, where the turmoil of the depression was more painfully visible than it had been in New Mexico. There Lange began to photograph the links between life and events. *White Angel Bread Line, San Francisco*, her first major work, expresses, on a universal level, human determination and endurance in the face of grim and unyielding conditions.

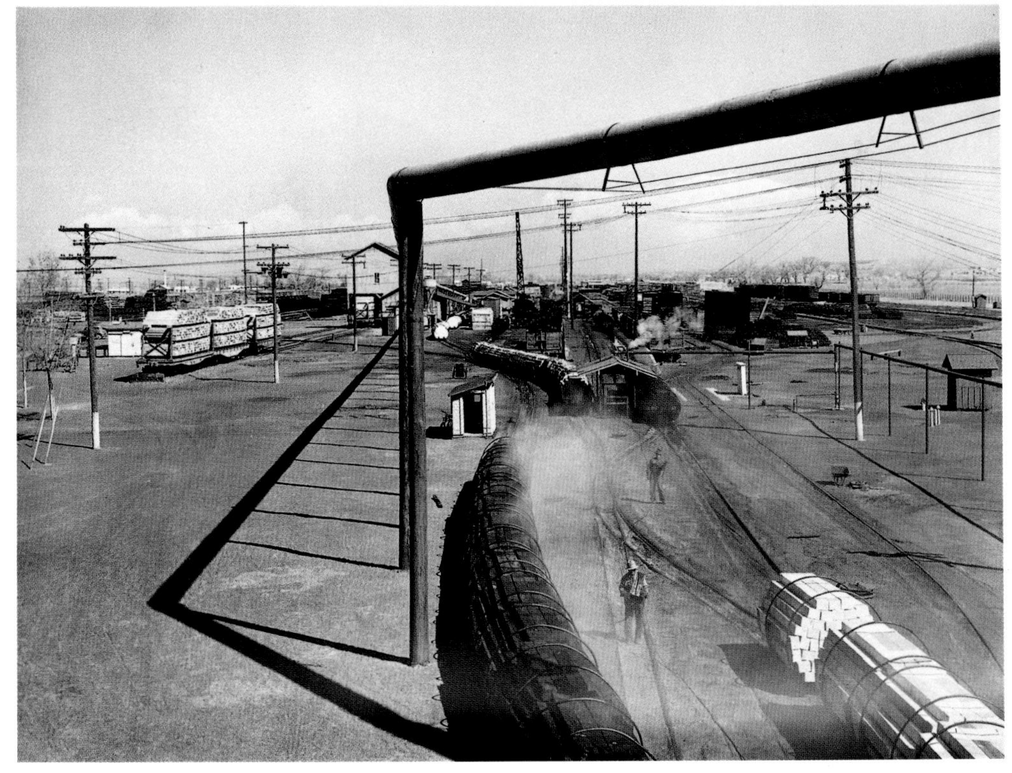

JACK DELANO
Albuquerque, New Mexico, at the Atchison, Topeka, and Santa Fe Railroad Tie Treating Plant, 1943
Gelatin silver photograph
$9\frac{1}{4} \times 13\frac{3}{4}$ in.
New Mexico Farm Security Administration Collection, purchased with funds donated by the Pinewood Foundation, with additional support from Barbara Erdman, 1990

DELANO STUDIED art and art history at the Pennsylvania Academy, where he encountered for the first time the masterful interpretations of life subjects by Van Gogh, Goya, Brueghel, and the photographers of the Farm Security Administration (FSA). He was captivated by the problem of the effect of environment and society on human lives and was intrigued by the solutions offered by these artists.

In 1940, Delano was hired by the FSA and given the assignment to photograph rural areas especially affected by the depression. With World War II, the FSA was relocated in the Office of War Information. He was assigned to photograph railroad workers and the industrial complex of the Atchison, Topeka, and Santa Fe Railway from Chicago to Los Angeles, which had become essential to the nation's military effort. During this period, he stopped in Albuquerque for a few weeks to photograph the tie- and steam-engine repair shops.

In this photograph, Delano presents a compelling relationship between the bold diagonal forms of the industrial environment and the concerns of human existence, linking the work in its social consciousness to the realist paintings of a century before.

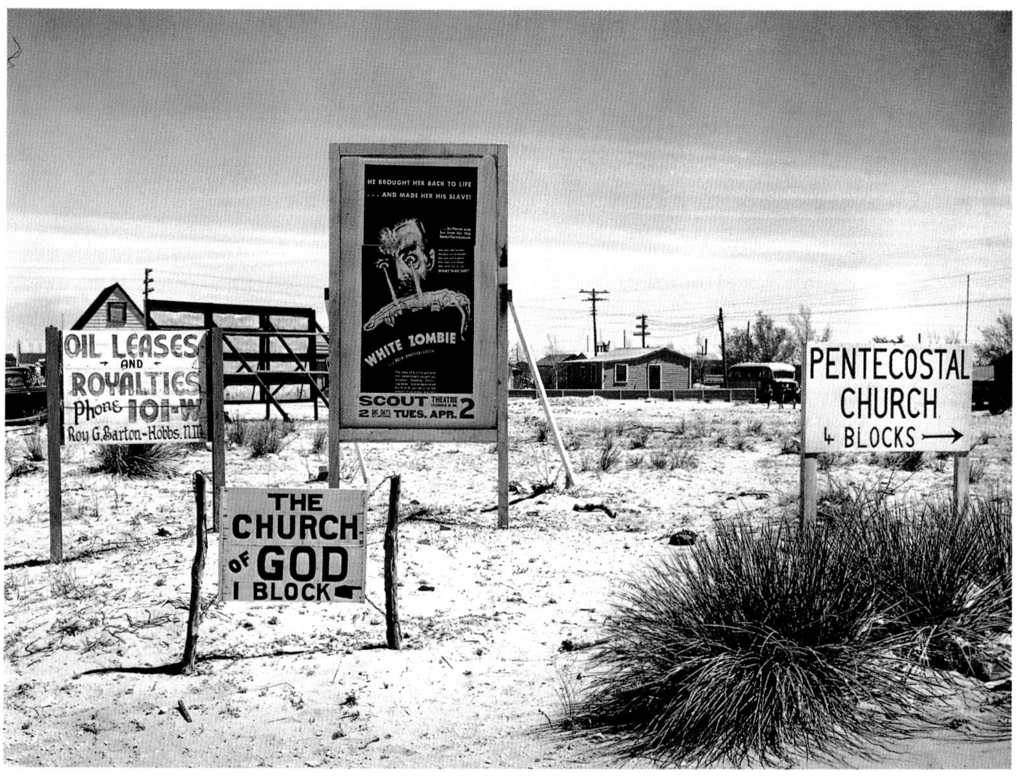

LEE WAS often considered the fundamental FSA photographer. His career, which began with chemical engineering and included a fruitless attempt at painting, was consistently devoted to the photographic expression of the human condition. Project oriented, Lee worked on assignments for Standard Oil of New Jersey and the U.S. Air Transport Command that took him around the world. His regional subjects of the coal miners in Kentucky and the political races in Texas kept him close to the working people, whom he held in high respect.

When Roy Stryker hired Lee in 1936 to photograph for the FSA, he added to his team a true humanitarian who was gifted in both the art of casual conversation and the science of photography. Complementing the staff of Walker Evans, Dorothea Lange, and Arthur Rothstein, Lee contributed a new dimension to the group with his orientation toward creating picture essays that emphasized the survival and resettlement of America's small-town folks and farmers after the depression years. He often worked on a subject for a week or more, returning again to sites, such as San Augustine, Texas, and Pie Town, New Mexico, to create a complete picture of the community. One of the most prolific photographers of the FSA, he contributed more than thirty thousand images to the files in Washington, D.C., during his tenure.

During Lee's assignment in New Mexico, concentrated in 1939 and 1940, he worked the entire state from north to south, photographing the Spanish-American weaving project in Costilla on the Colorado border and the agriculture in the Rio Grande Valley just north of El Paso, and from east to west, recording the oil boom around Hobbs and Carlsbad and the mining town of Mogollon, where he was mistaken for a German spy photographing the mines.

RUSSELL LEE
Signs in Oil Boom Town, Hobbs, New Mexico, March 1940
Gelatin silver photograph
9⅜ × 12⅞ in.
New Mexico Farm Security Administration Collection, purchased with funds donated by the Pinewood Foundation, with additional support from Barbara Erdman, 1990

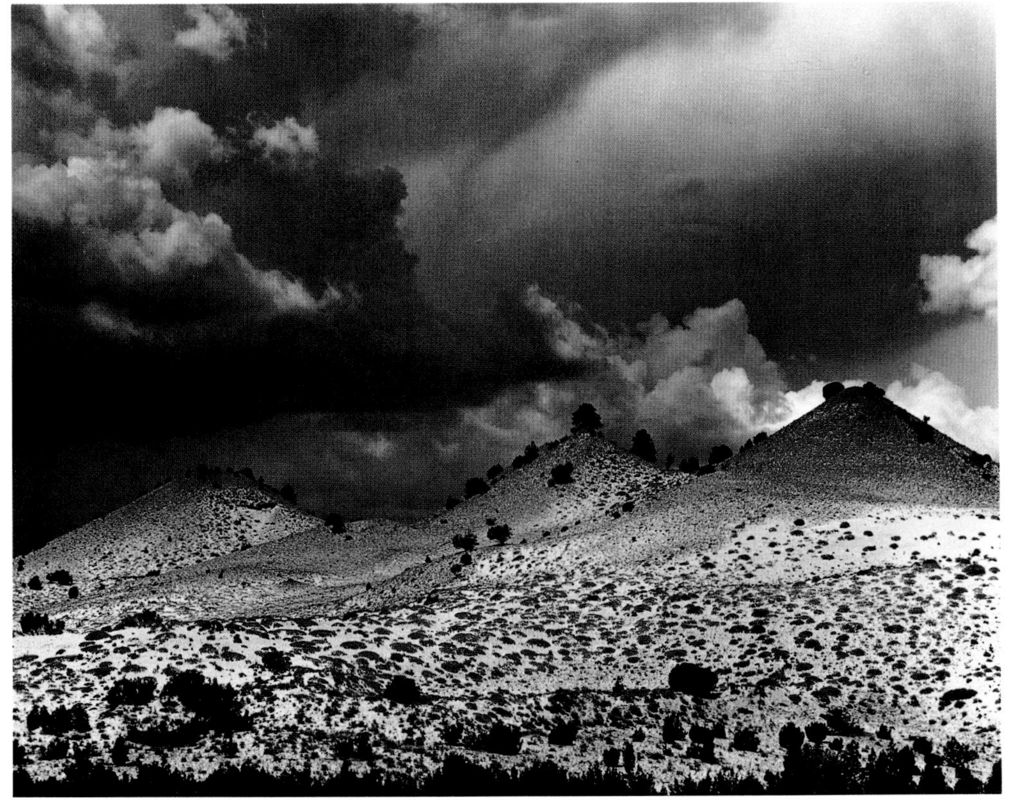

ERNEST KNEE
Sand Hills near Abiquiu, New Mexico,
1935
Gelatin silver photograph
$10\frac{1}{4} \times 13\frac{1}{4}$ in.
Museum purchase, Fine Arts Acquisition Fund at the Museum of New Mexico Foundation, 1988

KNEE MOVED to Santa Fe in 1933, purchased an 8×10 camera, set up a darkroom on Camino del Monte Sol, and joined the ranks of an art community that included John Sloan, Randall Davey, Andrew Dasburg, Gustave Baumann, and Will Shuster. He met Edward Weston upon his first New Mexico visit, and when Weston returned to New Mexico with Charis Wilson in the late 1930s, their artistic friendship deepened. Knee's landscape work of that decade remains a primary achievement in New Mexico's photographic history.

Knee and Weston photographed together in and around Santa Fe, and Knee was clearly influenced by Weston's technique and approach, though in choice of subject the two remained distinct.

Commenting on his first trip to New Mexico, Weston wrote in his *Daybooks* that "in New Mexico the heavens and earth become one." Knee's landscapes seem to embody this observation. In such photographs as *Sand Hills near Abiquiu, New Mexico*, the components of light, terrain, and sky are never subordinate. Each is an equally dynamic part of the composition. In his photographs, Knee transformed the region's topography into the spirit that dwells in place.

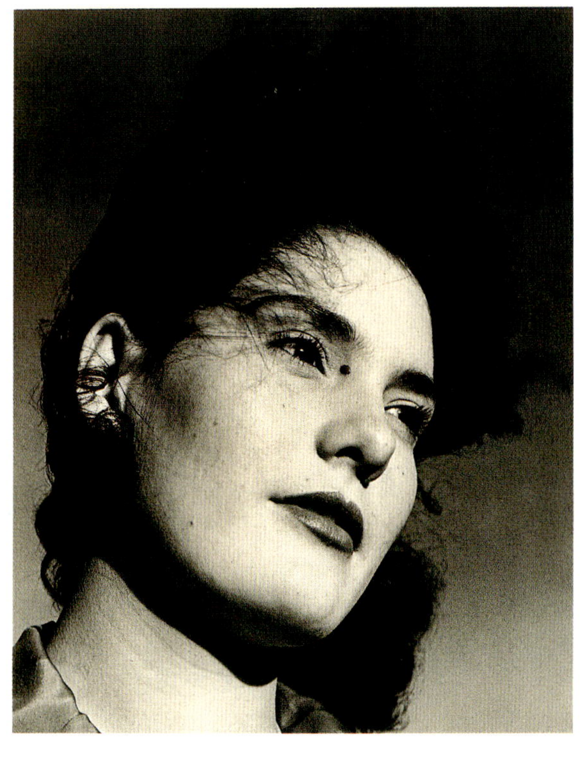

SANTA FE NATIVE Candelario often photographed in northern New Mexico in the company of other photographers, Edward Weston among them. He participated in the artist circles in Taos that surrounded Mabel Dodge Luhan, Rebecca Salsbury James, Millicent Rogers, and Frieda Lawrence. Several of his portraits were included in Luhan's *Taos and Its Artists*, and Georgia O'Keeffe helped to have his photographs included in a group exhibition at Stieglitz's An American Place in 1939–40.

In *Lupita*, Candelario has spontaneously portrayed a Sunday in New Mexico. The portrait was created with a hand-held camera from a low angle, and only a couple of negatives were made. Lupita's profile is boldly accented by the dark, neutral sky. The power of her arresting features is heightened by the photographer's intuitive response to the intensity of the moment, yet the beauty of form here transcends the place and the event.

JOHN CANDELARIO
Lupita (Santa Cruz Girl), 1938
Platinum photograph
$9\frac{3}{8} \times 7\frac{1}{2}$ in.
Museum purchase, Fine Arts Acquisition Fund at the Museum of New Mexico Foundation, 1989

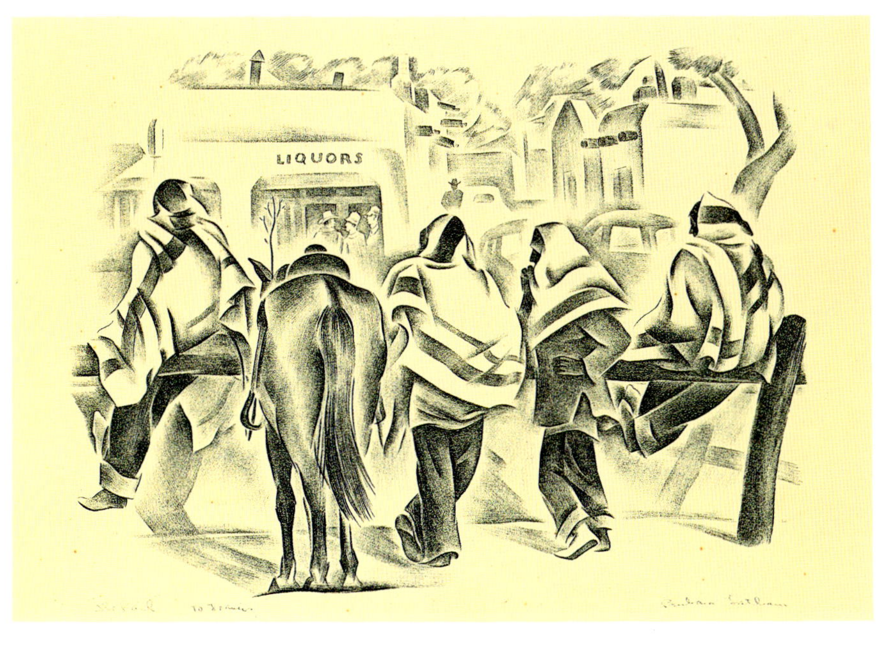

BARBARA LATHAM
The Rail, ca. 1940s
Lithograph
10 × 14¾ in.
Gift of Mr. and Mrs. Ford D. Good, 1969

LEAVING BEHIND a successful career in commercial art in New York, Latham came to Taos in 1924 as a guest of Mabel Dodge Luhan and there met and later married artist Howard Cook, also an accomplished and prolific graphic artist. At the time, Latham was also a versatile easel painter. In Taos, she met Andrew Dasburg, whom she would credit as her most influential mentor.

Her attraction to Pueblo and Hispanic life in her adopted New Mexico is presented here in a manner that is at once stylized and intimate. *The Rail* is typical of Latham's unassuming subject matter, in this example the daily gathering of Taos Indians in the town's plaza. Her unobtrusive viewpoint and the apparent ease of her subjects epitomize the artist's modest observation. With a delicate hand, she deftly captures the postures of her Indian neighbors.

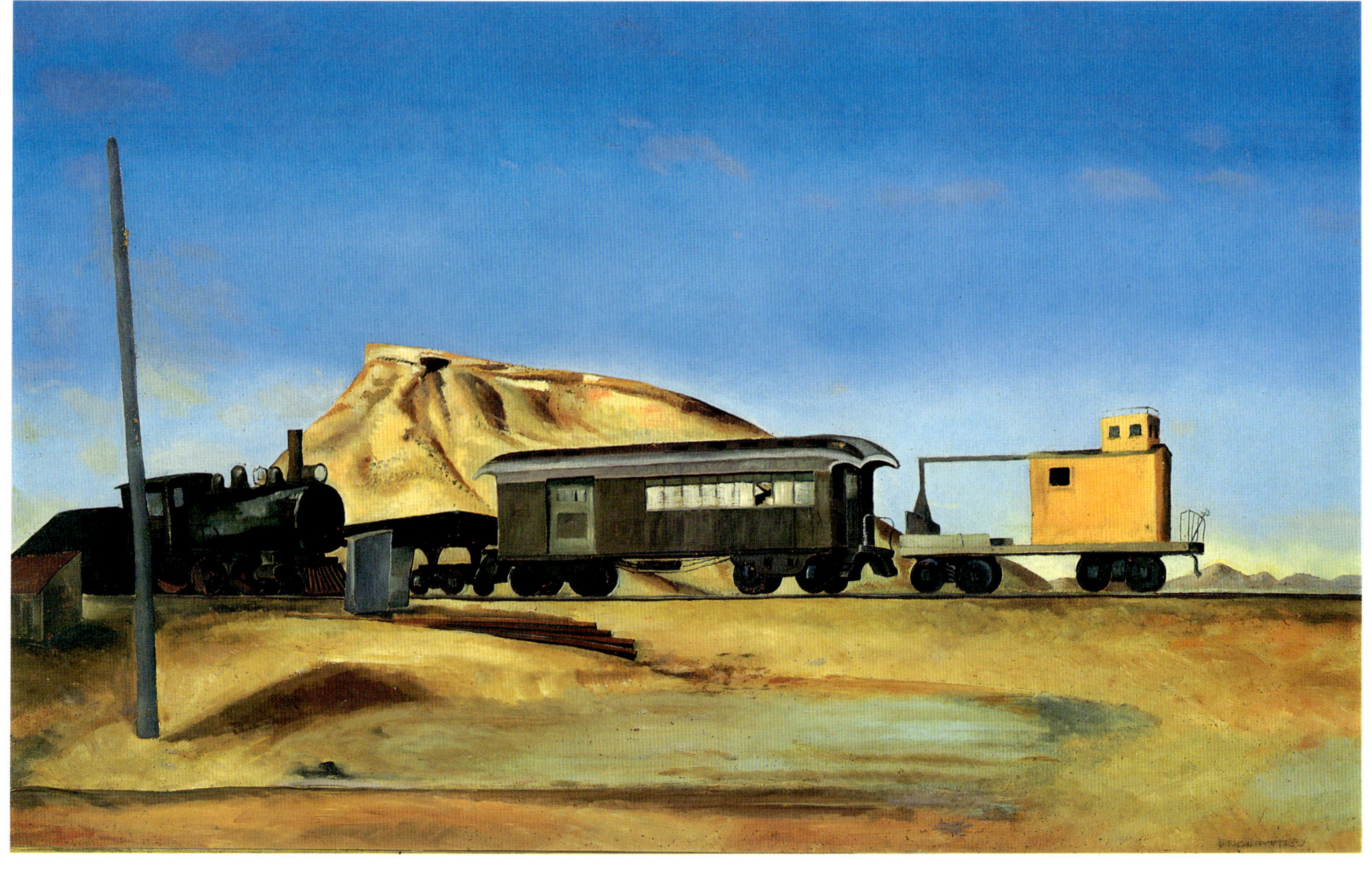

HUNTER STUDIED at the Art Institute of Chicago in 1921 and later with Slanton McDonald Wright, the leader of the School of Synchrony in Los Angeles. After this decade of studying and designing, he executed a series of mural commissions in Amarillo, Texas, and in Clovis and Fort Sumner, New Mexico, during the early 1930s. From 1935 to 1942, Hunter served as state director of the Works Progress Administration. It was during this time that he painted *The Chili Line*, a depiction of the narrow-gauge Denver and Rio Grande Railroad that operated between Santa Fe and Tres Piedras. Hunter painted the work only a short time before the tracks were removed and sent to Alaska. The simplicity of the forms of the train engine and cars, one with a shattered window, juxtaposed against the barren landscape and the cloudless sky conveys a feeling of desolation and emptiness prevalent in Hunter's work.

RUSSELL VERNON HUNTER
The Narrow Gauge (The Chili Line), ca. 1936
Oil on canvas
24 × 39 in.
Gift of the artist, 1952

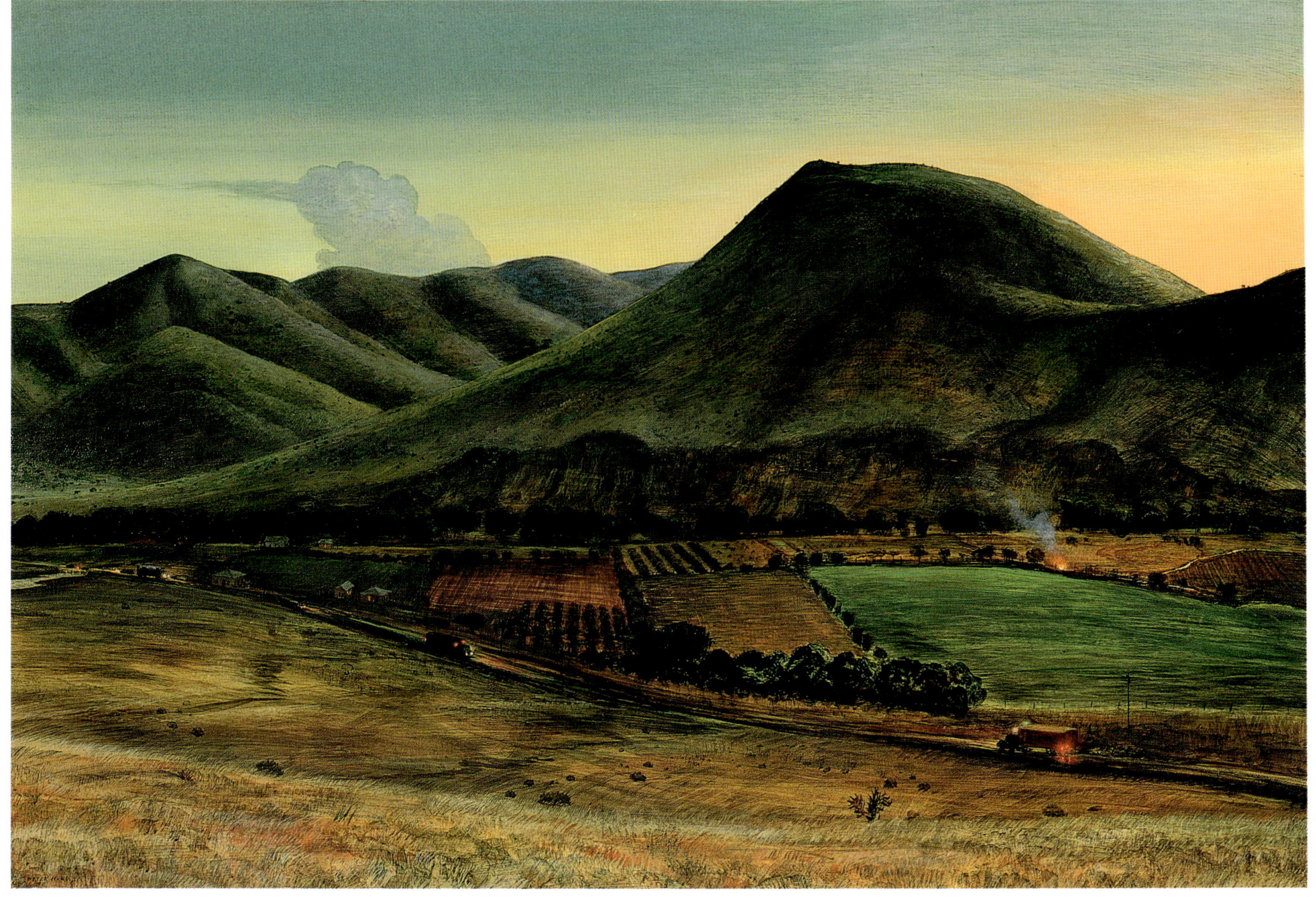

PETER HURD
Highway at Dusk, 1955
Egg tempera on Masonite
$31\frac{3}{4} \times 47\frac{7}{8}$ in.
Gift of the artist and private contributors, 1966

HURD STUDIED under the famous illustrator N. C. Wyeth and became a well-known portrait painter whose reputation suggested him to paint the official, but ultimately unacceptable, portrait of President Lyndon B. Johnson. His fascination with southwestern landscape was an extension of his love of the land in Hondo Valley, his lifelong home in southern New Mexico.

Hurd most often painted in egg tempera, a demanding medium that was commonly used by fifteenth- and sixteenth-century painters before oil painting was well developed. This opaque medium dries quickly, allowing for little error. It is said that Hurd and his wife, Henriette Wyeth, also an accomplished painter, agreed to have this painting displayed in the museum alongside a box requesting donations to the museum's acquisition fund. With the help of contributions from hundreds of visitors, the Museum of Fine Arts was eventually able to add the painting to the collection.

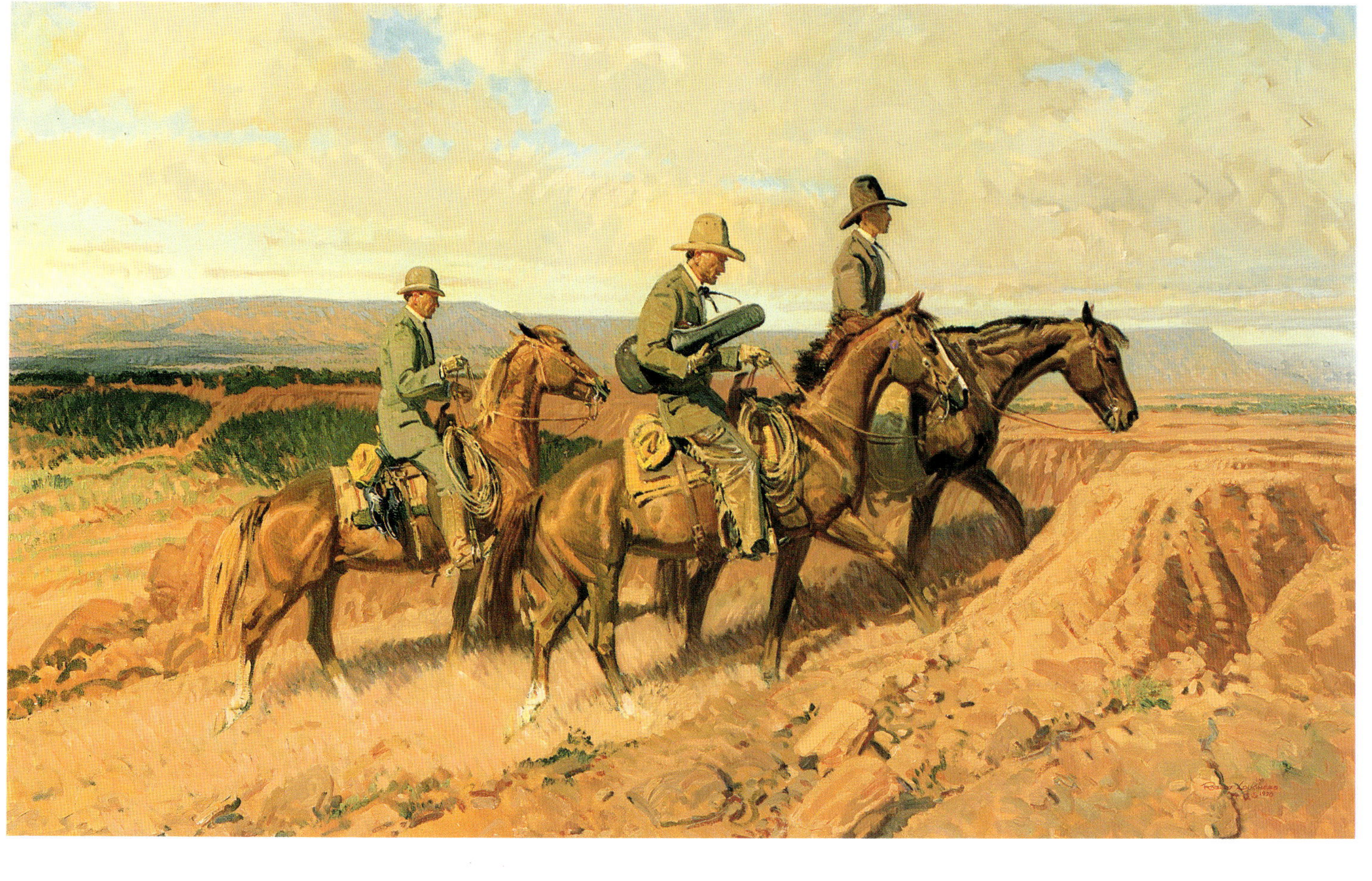

THE PAINTING *Ten Miles to Saturday Night* epitomizes an aspect of the life of the 1940s and 1950s working cowboy in eastern New Mexico. Against the vast, empty landscape, Leo Turner, the wagon boss, carries his fiddle and rides closely with two cowhands as together they travel the last ten miles to the dance hall. Lougheed once commented, "The subject of the painting is the history of the country. I understand it so well because my father was a farmer and a fiddle player."

Born in Canada, Lougheed, a former student of Frank DuMund in New York, devoted his attention to studying, drawing, and painting ranch life. His particular interest in horses led *National Geographic* to commission a series of thirteen paintings illustrating various breeds of horses. To complete his studies of the quarter horse, Lougheed went to the Bell Ranch near Tucumcari, the scene of *Ten Miles to Saturday Night*, where he returned every fall until 1970. An influential teacher and a member of the Cowboy Artists of America and the National Academy of Western Art, Lougheed was the recipient of numerous awards of merit.

ROBERT LOUGHEED
Ten Miles to Saturday Night, 1975
Oil on canvas
30 × 50 in.
Gift of Mrs. Robert Lougheed, 1986

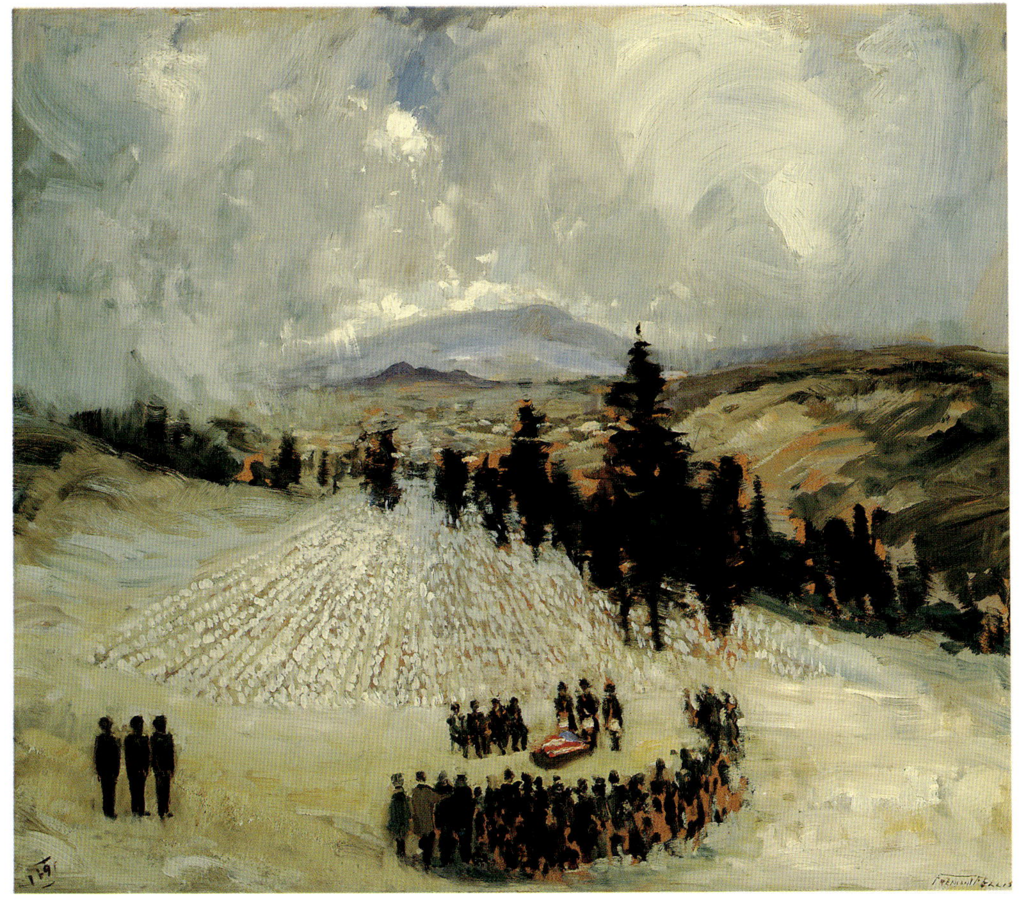

FREMONT F. ELLIS
Adios Amigo–Hasta La Vista, 1969
Oil on Masonite
25 × 29 in.
Gift of the artist, 1969

ELLIS JOINED the art colony at Santa Fe in 1919 and two years later became a founding member of Los Cinco Pintores.

The painting *Adios Amigo–Hasta La Vista* commemorates the funeral of Ellis's friend and fellow "Cinco" member Will Shuster, who died in 1969 in Santa Fe and was buried in the National Cemetery on a snowy February day. Ellis's daughter is depicted at the far left of the group, standing next to his son, who has his arm around his father. The influence of American impressionism is evident in Ellis's prominent brushwork, lack of detail, and arresting sense of light.

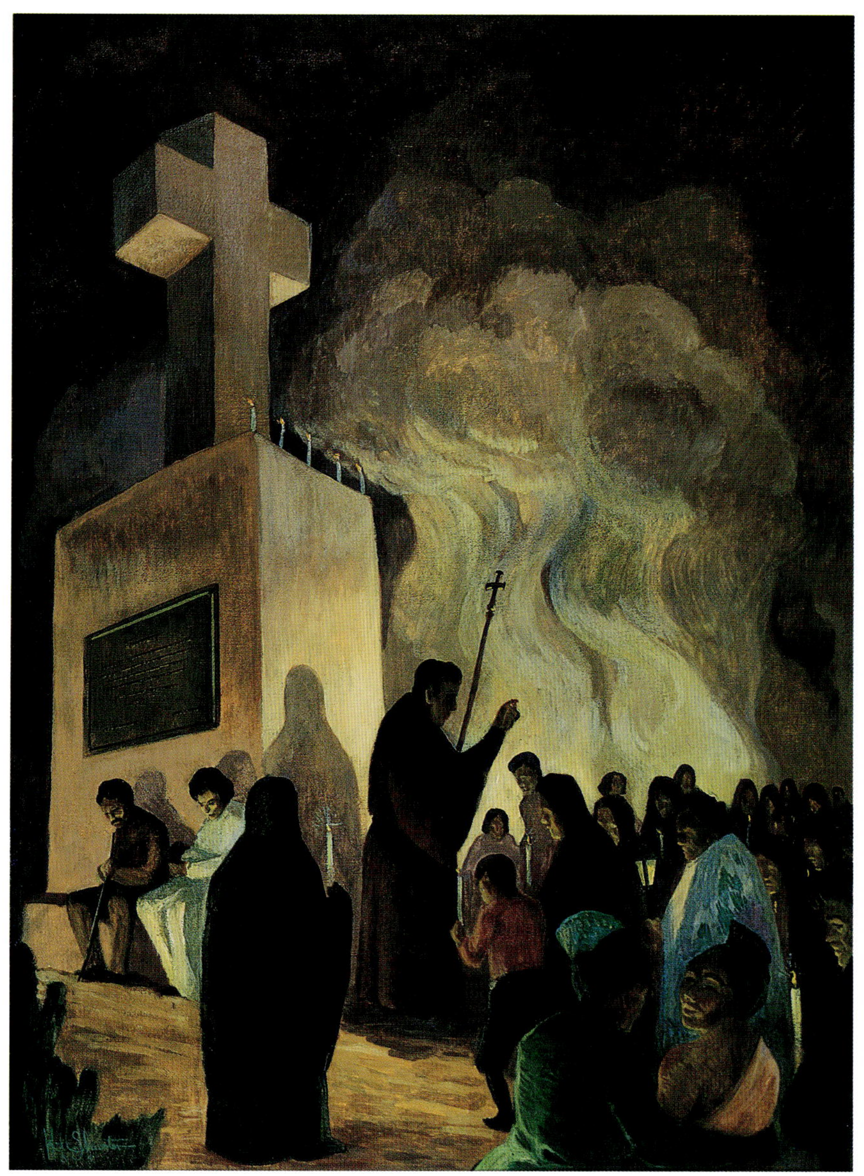

WILL SHUSTER
Sermon at the Cross of the Martyrs, 1934
Oil on Masonite
48 × 36 in.
Donated in memory of Helen H. Shuster
by her family, 1972

IN 1920, as a cure for his tuberculosis, Shuster gave up his native Philadelphia for Santa Fe. There he entered the world of a swelling art scene and was befriended by John Sloan, who led him toward the serious study of art. Over the next forty-nine years, Shuster drew heavily upon local customs and ceremonies as subjects for his art. His zeal for community manifested in an annual involvement beginning in 1926 in the town's fiesta, for which he created the giant puppet effigy "Zozobra," whose torching banishes evil and gloom.

In *Sermon at the Cross of the Martyrs*, Shuster depicts the closing ceremony of the Santa Fe Fiesta, a candlelight procession to the Cross of the Martyrs, the monument that commemorates the priests who were killed by Pueblo Indians in their revolt of 1680. The subject held sufficient significance for the artist to have rendered it in three media—a drawing, completed in the early 1930s, an aquatint in 1932, and the oil in 1934.

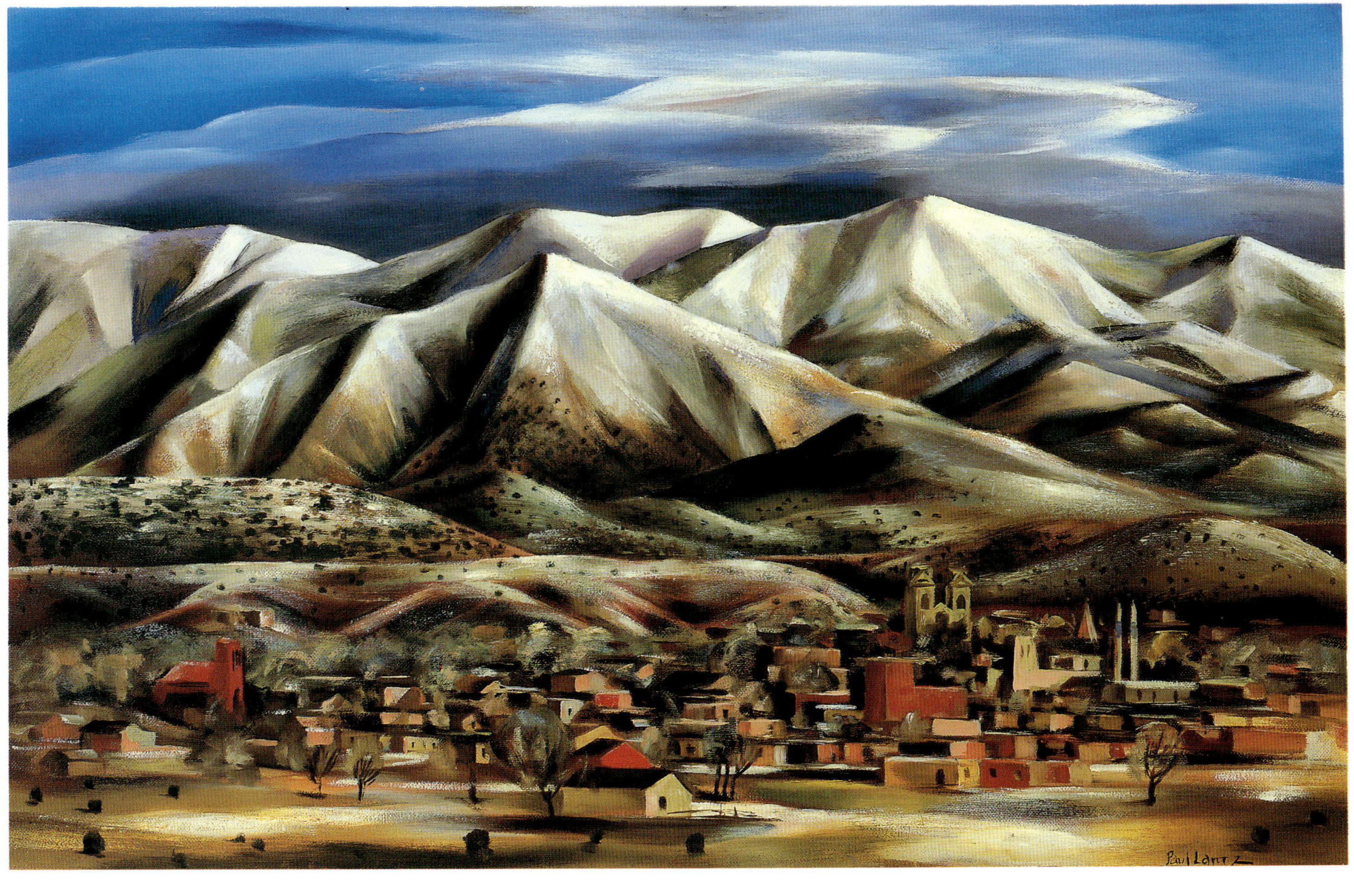

PAUL LANTZ
Snow in Santa Fe, ca. 1935
Oil on Masonite
30×40 in.
Gift of the Public Employees
Retirement Agency, 1972

AT THE TENDER AGE of seventeen, Lantz moved from Montana to New York to study at the Art Students League. Supporting himself through odd jobs, he remained in New York for four years until the stock market crash motivated him to board a freight train for Santa Fe. There he received commissions for portraits and, through local hotels like La Fonda, for murals.

Lantz's artistic career divides into two distinct stylistic categories: the earlier, softer work completed before he left Santa Fe in 1939 and the crisper, almost superrealist work created in upstate New York and during his self-imposed exile in rural northeast New Mexico.

Snow in Santa Fe, a work painted during Lantz's association with the WPA, belongs to the earlier period in both the artist's career and in the life of a small but growing town. The religious and secular buildings bear the distinctive mark of the cultural influences surrounding them, though the monumental power of the snowcapped mountains and an expansive sky charged with sweeping clouds dwarf even their rightful prominence.

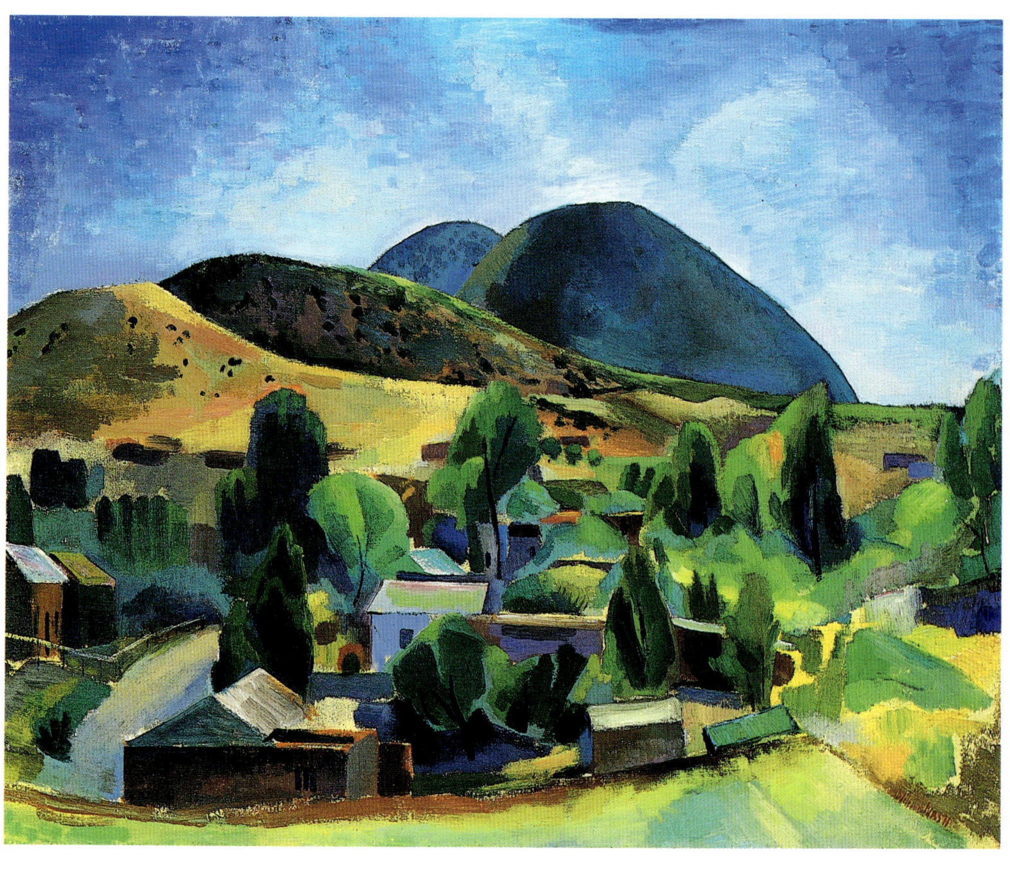

AFTER LIVING and studying in Detroit, Nash first visited Santa Fe in 1920, returning there the following year to live. He was readily accepted by Santa Fe's artistic community, where he painted and worked until 1936, and became a member of the painters' group Los Cinco Pintores. Besides being a nationally known painter, Nash was a noted singer, a commercial artist, an amateur middleweight boxer, and an accomplished pistol and rifle shot.

Nash was often referred to as "the American Cézanne" because of the influence the French painter had on his work. In 1931 the Mexican muralist Diego Rivera, after jurying Nash's work into an exhibition, declared him one of America's best painters.

Santa Fe Landscape exemplifies the painter's intellectual and formal approach to his subject. A superb colorist, Nash rendered the simplified and abstracted shapes of the landscape in a contrasting and visually exciting application of lights and darks. This combination results in a harmonious geometric and rhythmical composition that ratifies Nash's belief that "art is not concerned with the outer aspect of things. Art is concerned with the true inner spirit which determines the outer form. . . ."

WILLARD NASH
Santa Fe Landscape, ca. 1930
Oil on canvas
24 × 30 in.
Gift of Anton V. Long, 1958

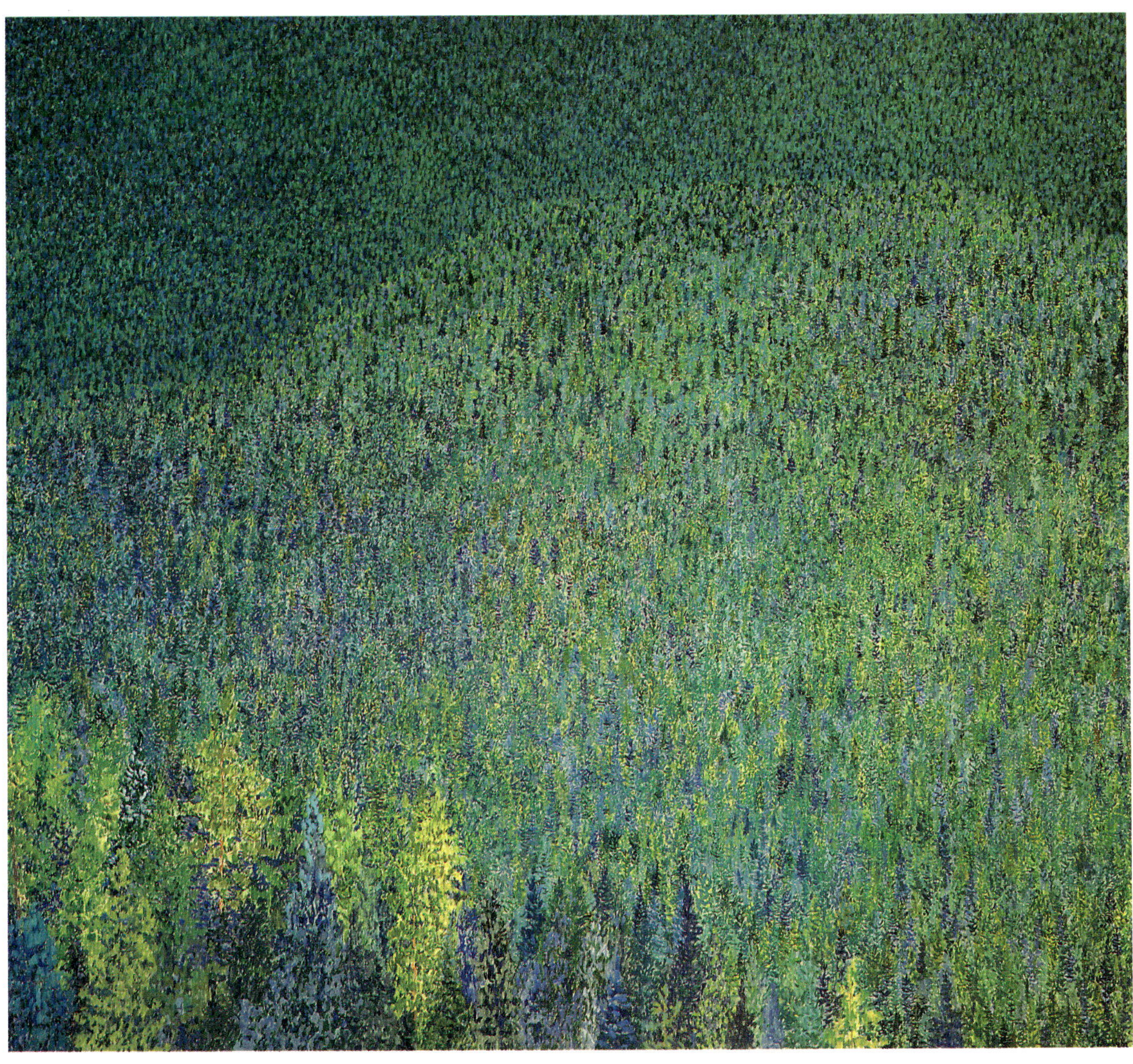

ELMER SCHOOLEY
Mixed Conifers, 1971–72
Oil on canvas
$80\frac{1}{16} \times 90$ in.
Purchased from the 1972 Southwest Fine Arts Biennial by the Museum of New Mexico Foundation

IN 1947, Schooley joined the faculty of New Mexico Highlands University in Las Vegas, New Mexico, where he established one of the first lithographic workshops in the state. During his thirty-year tenure there, he created the area's only art library, as well as opening an art gallery. In 1977, Schooley retired from teaching to become a full-time painter in Roswell, New Mexico.

Mixed Conifers was painted during Schooley's last years in Las Vegas, in a studio overlooking a hillside forest. The monumental scale, typical of his work, reflects the artist's lifelong interest in the preservation of the environment. In this painting, the western landscape is rendered without conventional perspective as a textural field that arouses a visceral response to the numinous quality in nature. Schooley's paintings, with connections to the tradition of landscape painting and to post–World War II field abstractions, are simultaneously referential and reverential.

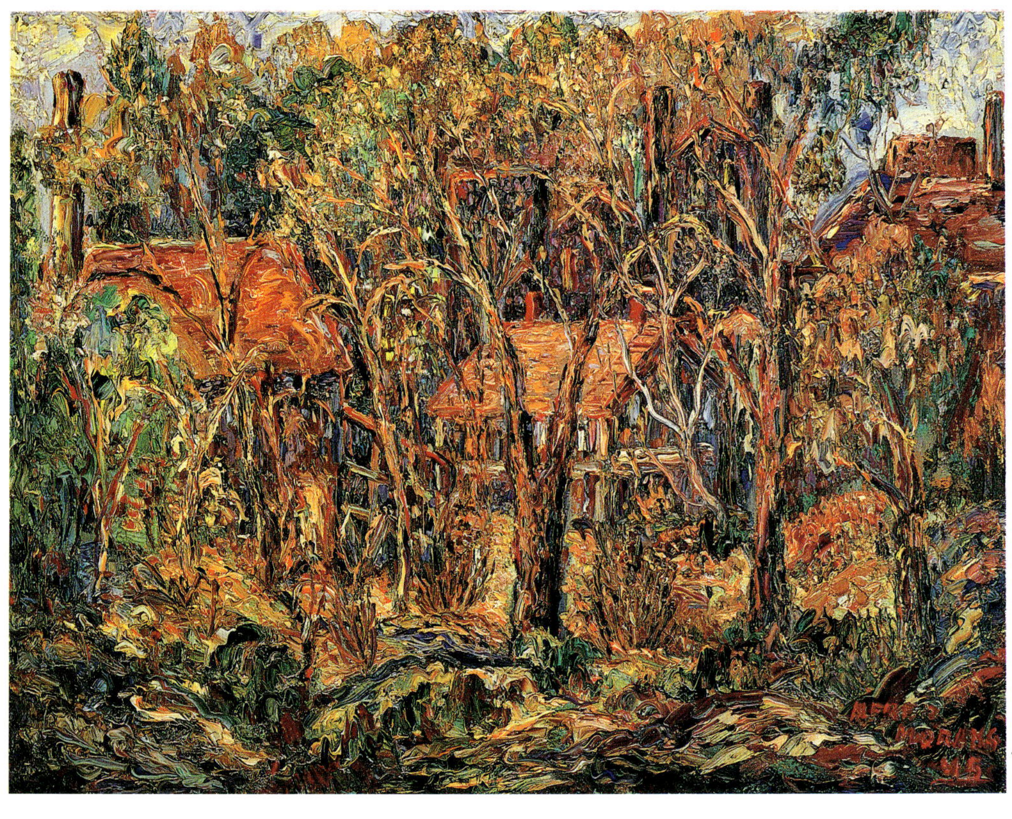

IN MORANG'S short life (1901–1958), he painted highly individualistic canvases that brought a sense of mystery and quiet intrigue to what were scenes from the everyday world around him. After moving to Santa Fe from Portland, Maine, in 1937, for reasons of health, Morang joined the local art scene as a painter, writer, and musician.

Many of his paintings illustrate the artist's favorite Santa Fe scenes, including this familiar view of Canyon Road. In Morang's day, Canyon Road was the residential and studio center of the art colony. It featured several bars brought to prominence by the characters who kept the small community even with its less isolated counterparts. In this painting, Morang's technique of heavy brushwork is reminiscent of Van Gogh's.

ALFRED MORANG
Untitled, 1945
Oil on canvas
18 × 24 in.
Gift of Mr. and Mrs. Bill L. Gill, 1985

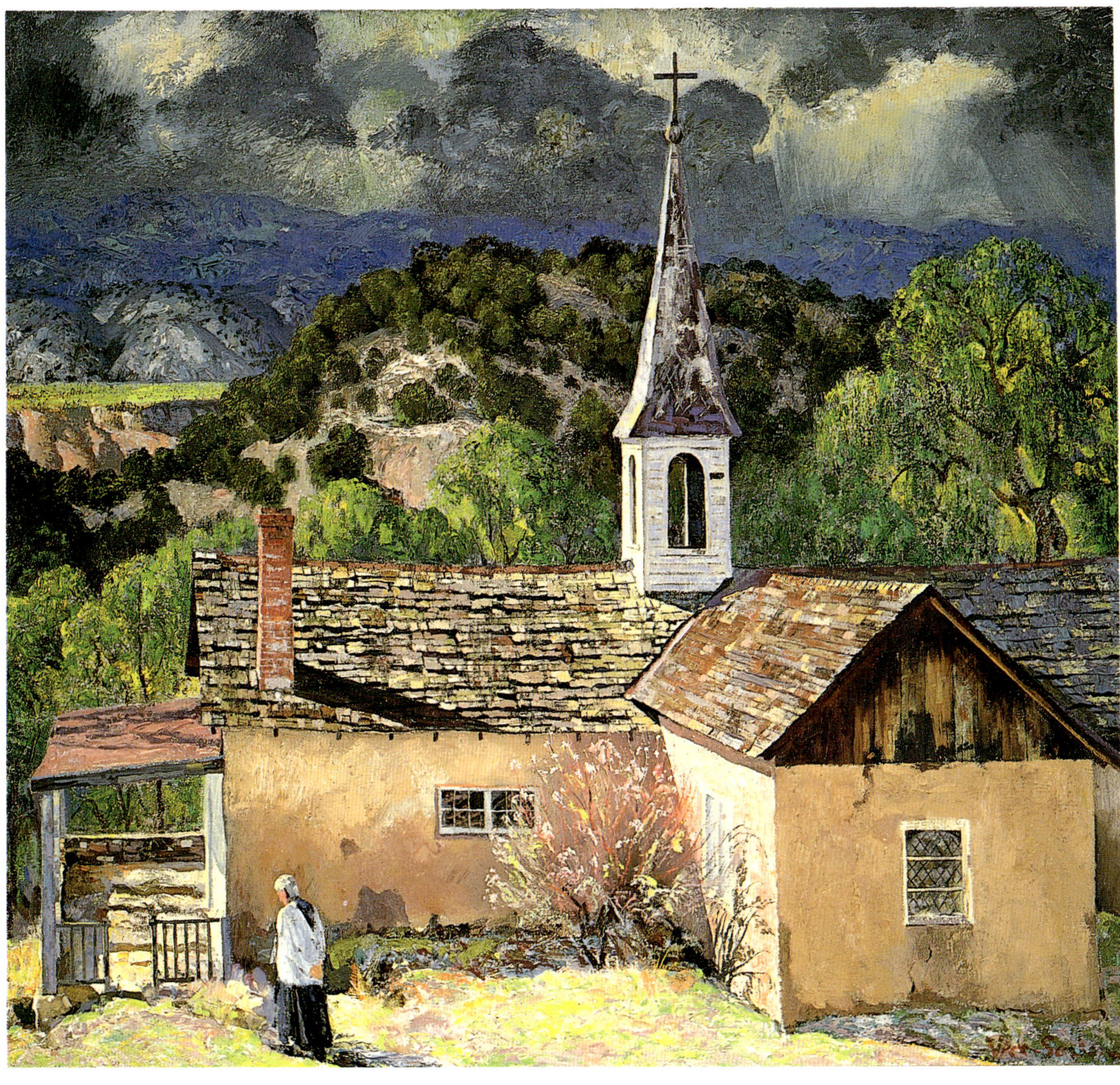

THEODORE VAN SOELEN
The Bishop's Chapel, ca. 1928
Oil on canvas
$36\frac{1}{8} \times 40\frac{1}{4}$ in.
Gift of Henry Dendahl in memory of his father, John Dendahl, 1943

PRIOR TO his relocation to New Mexico in 1916 on account of ill health, Van Soelen had toured Europe, studied at the Pennsylvania Academy of Fine Arts, and in 1910 driven a mule train for the construction crew of the Western Pacific Railroad. In New Mexico, he worked for a time as a ranch hand, becoming familiar with cowboys and ranch life–themes that he frequently incorporated into his drawings and paintings.

In addition to cowboy themes and portraits of his family and friends, Van Soelen painted over a long career the New Mexico landscape with its indigenous architecture. *The Bishop's Chapel* refers to French-born Jean Baptiste Lamy's rustic chapel built north of Santa Fe in the mid-nineteenth century. He frequently visited the chapel, seeking peace and solitude, as well as occasional shelter from the volatile storms of summer. The strong contrasts of light, the impending storm, and the solitary figure of Lamy create a sense of drama and expectancy.

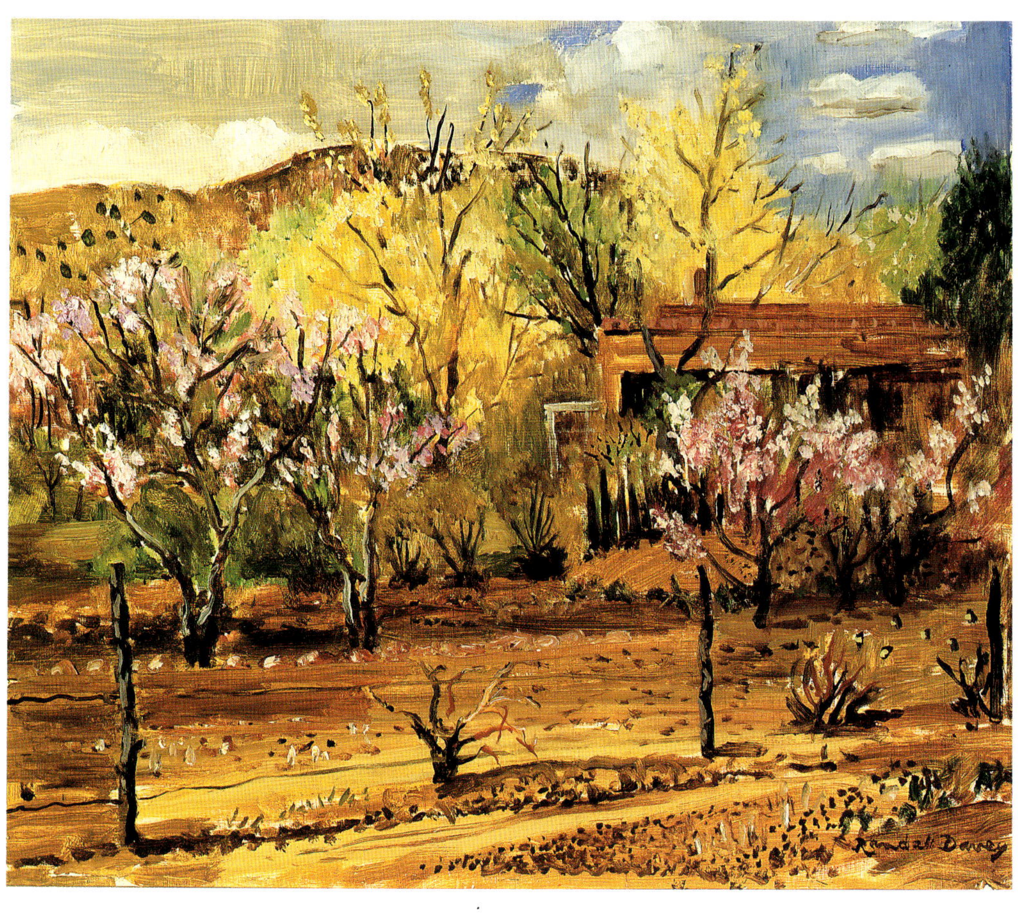

RANDALL DAVEY
Spring in Santa Fe, ca. 1950s
Oil on canvas
$21\frac{3}{8} \times 25\frac{9}{16}$ in.
Gift of Mr. and Mrs. Earl C. Kauffman, 1966

AFTER STUDYING architecture at Cornell University, Davey enrolled at the Art Students League in 1908, becoming a gifted student of Robert Henri, with whom he later toured Europe as part of his artistic training. Returning home, Davey was one of the youngest artists to exhibit in the 1913 Armory Show in New York.

Encouraged by Henri, he came to Santa Fe in 1919 with his friend and fellow artist John Sloan. Davey made Santa Fe his permanent home in 1920, purchasing an old sawmill at the end of Canyon Road, where he lived and worked for forty-four years until his death.

Davey, like Henri, Sloan, and George Bellows, believed that the source of art should be the events of daily life. However, he was not interested in social commentary, as were the others. Stylistically, the artist's early work was influenced by Henri's spontaneous approach to painting. His later, more realistic painting, though, had its roots in the work of the French impressionists, Velásquez, and Franz Hals. This is particularly true of the portraits.

Davey had a special feeling for the world of horse racing, a subject that inspired numerous paintings, prints, and pastels. A third area of concentration was landscape, which he rendered with the pastoral quality evident in *Spring in Santa Fe*.

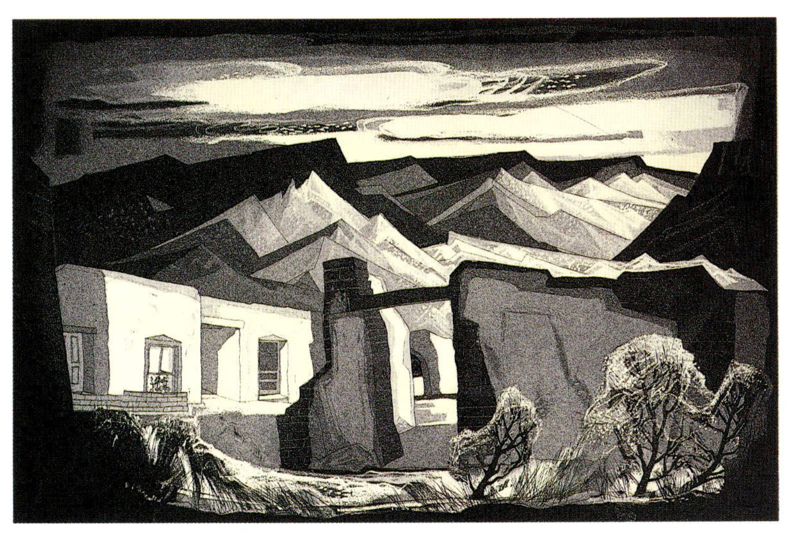

DOEL REED
Adobe and Wild Plum, 1964
Aquatint and etching on paper
$12 \times 18\frac{3}{4}$ in.
Gift of the artist, 1965

MASTER PRINTMAKER Doel Reed made a career out of producing aquatints, a direction that he forged in his youth in Cincinnati, through his teaching at Oklahoma State University, and with his visits to Taos and eventual residency there after 1959.

Originally trained as an architect, Reed often features architecture as a component of his landscapes, as in *Adobe and Wild Plum*. The themes of the work, which was commissioned by the Museum of Fine Arts, are the constancy of life and the revitalizing energy of nature. New white adobe homes appear through the portal of a dark, crumbling ruin; rising above both are eternal mountains and ethereal clouds while blossoming plum trees in the foreground amplify the sense of renewal. This work also demonstrates the rich tonality and technical virtuosity of Reed's printmaking: each shade, from the rich blacks to the glowing whites, required separate, manual pulls from the plate. Reed sketched his compositions from nature but reworked them many times in the studio, drawing a final version directly on the plate.

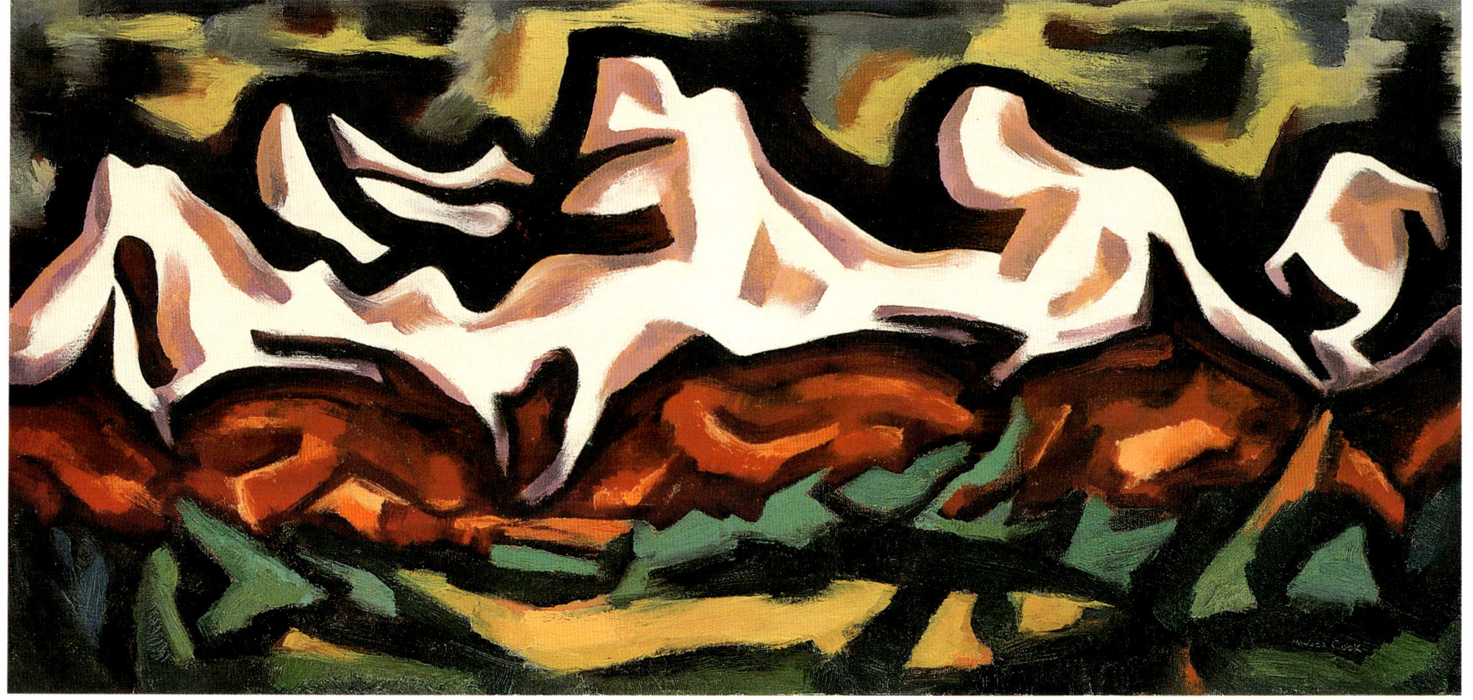

HOWARD COOK
Winter Mountain, Cycle No. 4, 1955
Oil on canvas
26 × 55 in.
Gift of the artist in memory of Dr. Reginald Fisher, 1978

COOK ARRIVED in Taos in 1925 with a commission from *Forum* magazine to illustrate Willa Cather's book, *Death Comes for the Archbishop*. While there, he met and later married the artist Barbara Latham. Before coming to Taos, Cook studied at the Art Students League in New York in 1919, where he was a classmate of Andrew Dasburg. Later he traveled extensively in Europe, Turkey, and the Orient, executing drawings and woodcuts for *Atlantic Monthly*, *Forum*, and *Scribner's*, work that won him an international reputation in the graphic arts.

Twice the recipient of a Guggenheim Fellowship, Cook, with Latham, absorbed into his art the characters and local customs that he encountered in his wide travels. This material became the basis for the murals he executed in true fresco for the San Antonio post office and the Pittsburgh courthouse; the latter was awarded a gold medal by the Architectural League of New York in 1937. In his later work done in Taos, Cook moved away from small, representational, black-and-white prints characteristic of the 1920s and 1930s to focus instead on large-scale color abstractions in watercolor, pastel, and oil.

His favored subjects of landscape, Indian ceremony, and adobe architecture were approached with increasing abstraction, though he never abandoned recognizable detail. At the same time, his cubist orientation became more pronounced and his use of color more expressionistic. A prime example of Cook's later direction is *Winter Mountain, Cycle No. 4*.

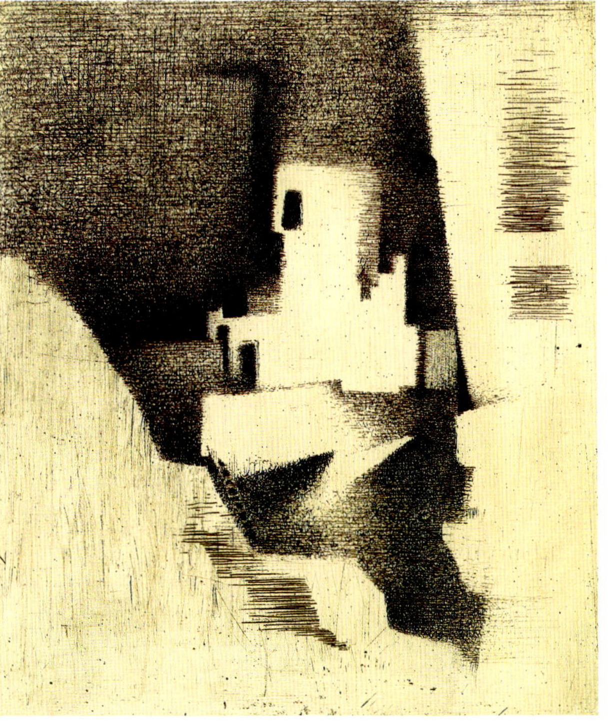

EARL STROH
Mesa Verde, 1955
Etching
11 × 9½ in.
Gift of Mr. and Mrs. Ford D. Good, 1969

STROH'S early appreciation of Cézanne extended naturally to a strong respect for the work of Andrew Dasburg, whom he befriended in the summer of his first Taos visit in 1947. His mastery of lithography encouraged Dasburg to explore the medium near the end of his life. At the same time that John Sommers was printing Dasburg's lithographs at the Tamarind Institute (1974–78) in Albuquerque, Stroh was there with master printer Lynn Baker completing his remarkable "Taos Makimono Suite" (1975–76).

The etching *Mesa Verde*, by comparison a youthful work, was printed during Stroh's first painting trip to Paris under the patronage of the Helene Wurlitzer Foundation. At the Atelier Friedlander, he developed a body of etchings that he later expanded during a second residency in Paris in 1958. These etchings share with the paintings and silver-point drawings of the same period Stroh's meticulous technique, which yields a shimmering surface texture that is evident in his finest work. Sadly, the intended edition of seventy-five prints of *Mesa Verde* was never completed due to the printer's death and Stroh's inability to recover the plates.

RAYMOND JONSON
Watercolor No. 22, 1939
Watercolor on paper
28 × 20 in.
Anonymous donor, 1954

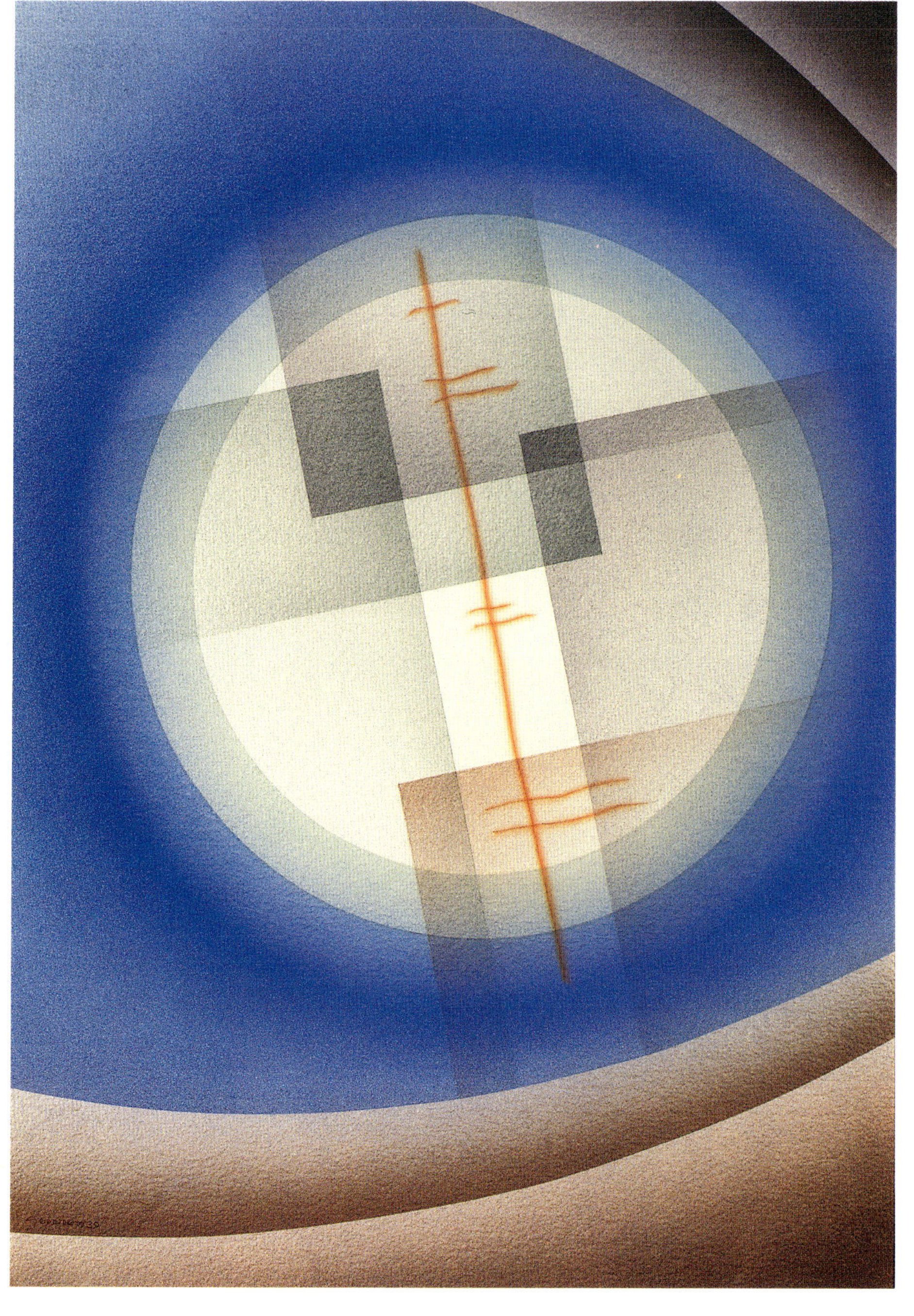

THE SON of an itinerant minister, Jonson was the first student to enroll at Oregon's Portland Art Museum School. His art education continued in Chicago at the Art Institute. There, beginning in 1911, he studied with B. J. O. Nordfeldt, Jonson's most influential mentor and his first link to Santa Fe.

After a decade of involvement in Chicago's experiment with modernism, Jonson moved to Santa Fe in 1924, where he renewed his connection with Nordfeldt and embarked on a fruitful artistic association with the similarly inclined Andrew Dasburg. An indefatigable promoter of modernism, the artist organized thirty-six exhibitions of modern art at the Museum of Fine Arts. After completing a number of murals for the Works Progress Administration, he began teaching at the University of New Mexico in 1934. With Emil Bisttram, Jonson founded the Transcendental Painting Group (1938–42); in 1950, he founded the Raymond Jonson Gallery on the campus of the University of New Mexico, the first institution in New Mexico completely devoted to contemporary art.

Watercolor No. 22 was painted the year Jonson met Archipenko and Moholy-Nagy in Chicago, two European artists whom he felt were "so much farther in the purity of form." For Jonson, the only legitimate quest of art was spiritual. He sought in works of the period to eliminate the gestural mark by adopting an airbrush technique that enabled him to achieve total nonobjectivity. In *Watercolor No. 22*, Jonson uses a vocabulary he developed as a theater designer in Chicago: architectural allusions; color promoting a sense of disembodiment; a proscenium configuration with vestigial side curtains; and spotlit shifting planes illuminating dominant central shapes.

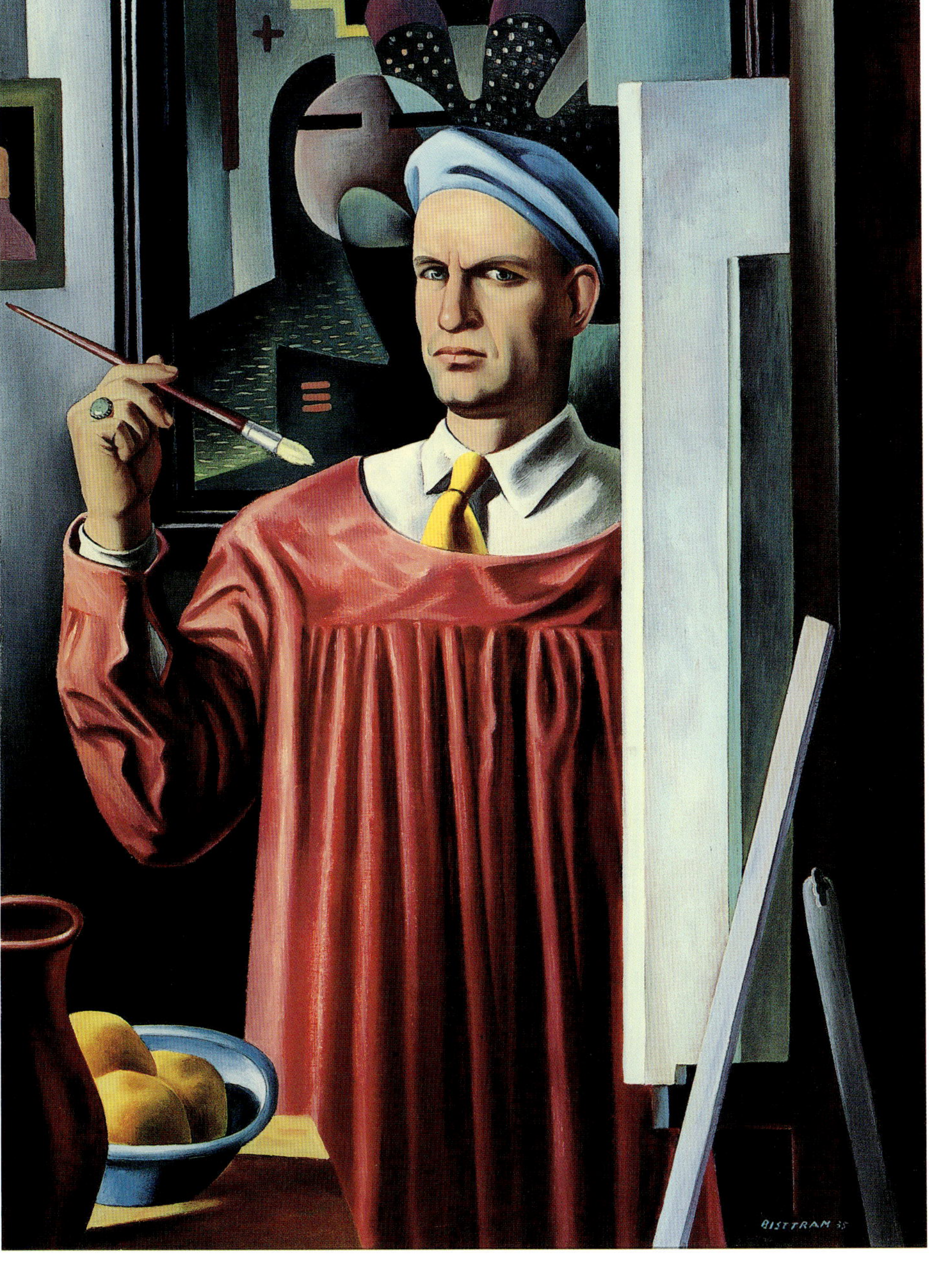

EMIL BISTTRAM
Self Portrait, 1935
Oil on canvas
$44\frac{1}{2} \times 33$ in.
Gift of Mrs. Emil Bisttram, 1978

A PROMINENT ARTIST involved in the Public Mural Projects of the 1930s and a student and exponent of dynamic symmetry typical of Diego Rivera's Mexican School of painting, Bisttram, along with Andrew Dasburg and Raymond Jonson, became one of the most active teachers in New Mexico. His first nonobjective canvases were painted in Taos in the mid-1930s, though his interest developed in the direction of mysticism and transcendental art. As he matured, Bisttram painted more and more abstractly, though no single style dominated.

A mixture of artistic styles is evident in *Self Portrait*, a painting that echoes the late renaissance in composition, with a classically robed artist standing at the easel. However, the background is comprised of abstract paintings and a stylized *koshare* while the main figure owes its style to the social realism of the Mexican muralists. Bisttram's knowledge of the works of these influential muralists is also apparent in several frescos he painted in the Old Taos County Courthouse during the federally supported projects of the 1930s.

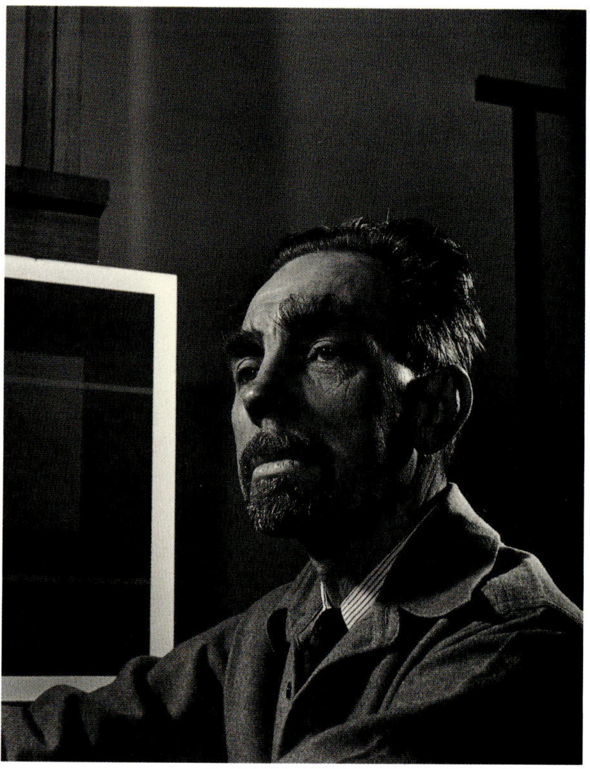

IN THE LATE 1940s, *Life* magazine began featuring articles on many of the forty-eight states, a project that was never completed. In 1947, Gene Smith, recovering from extensive injuries resulting from his coverage of the Pacific war, was assigned New Mexico for a project that never saw publication.

Although Smith's work in New Mexico was never central to his concerns as a photojournalist, he found the mixture of people—particularly the artists, writers, and musicians—of great interest. Working mainly in Santa Fe and surrounding areas, he explored the theme of the self-made individual. It was during this period that the photographer pioneered a new style of photojournalism: the photographic essay with expressive dimensions.

Smith's portrait of modernist painter Raymond Jonson embodies in its strength of presentation Jonson's career-long concern with geometric abstraction.

W. EUGENE SMITH
Raymond Jonson, 1947
Gelatin silver photograph
$13\frac{3}{8} \times 10\frac{1}{2}$ in.
Museum purchase, Fine Arts Acquisition Fund at the Museum of New Mexico Foundation, 1988

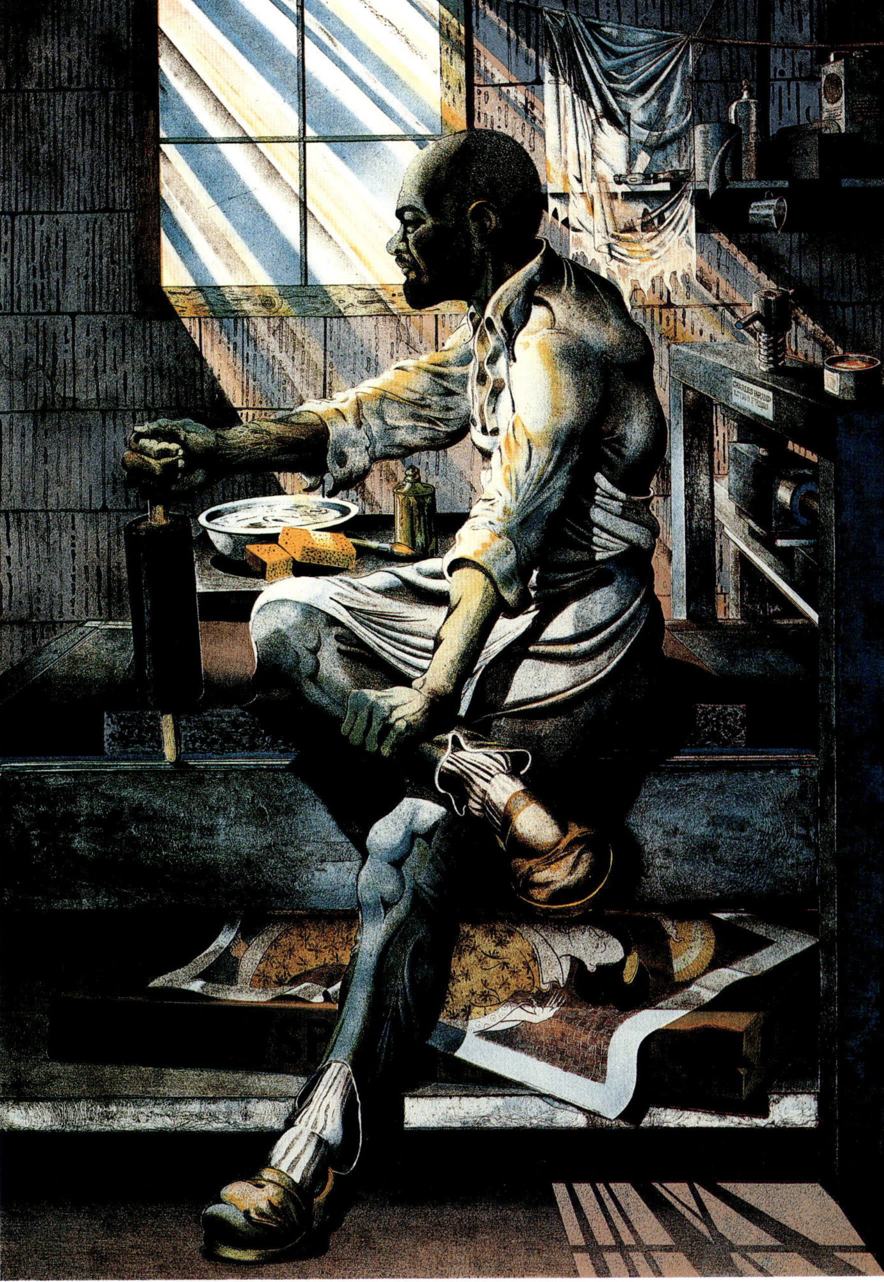

RON ADAMS
Profile in Blue, 1986
Color lithograph
42 × 30 in.
Purchase award with funds donated toward "New Mexico '87" from the Ovenwest Corporation, Frank Ribelin, and the Santa Fe Gallery Association, 1987

FOR MORE THAN a decade, Adams's print shop, Hand Graphics in Santa Fe, served as a major source for limited editions of prints, primarily lithographs. His shop was among several in the state that grew out of the influence of the Tamarind Institute in Albuquerque, helping to establish New Mexico as a major center for printmakers. Trained at the renowned Gemini G.E.L. in Los Angeles, Adams eased many major artists from their accustomed mediums into printmaking.

Profile in Blue represents the artist's first major foray into printmaking of his own. A self-portrait, it is a masterful evocation of the printer's environment: the tools of the trade; the press; the allusion to printmaking's history, with a handful of Japanese prints resting beneath the press; and the printer himself, contemplative, at center stage.

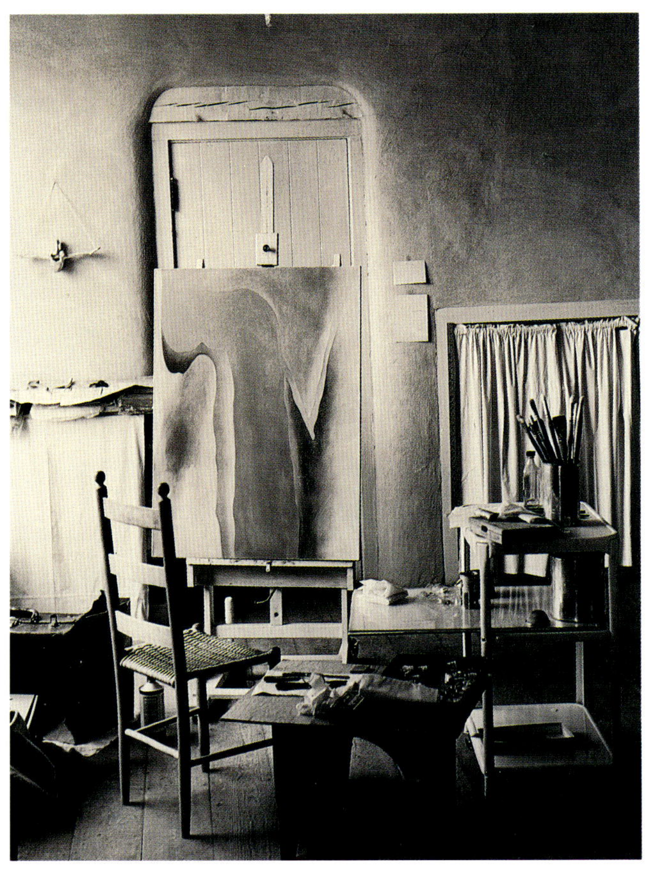

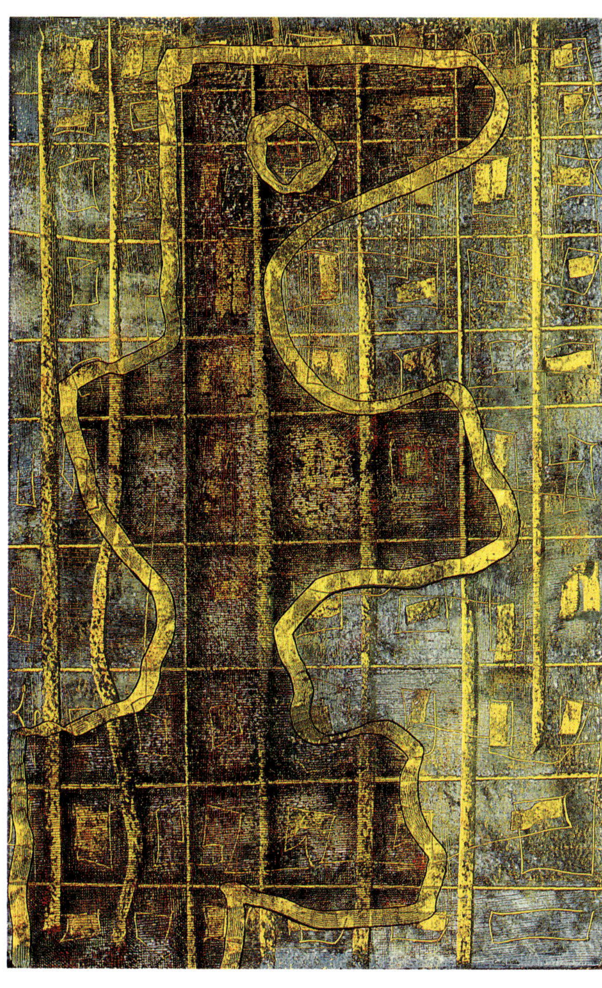

CADY WELLS
Abstraction, 1948
Opaque watercolor and ink on paper
21¾ × 14¼ in.
Purchase prize, "Fiesta Exhibition," 1948

PATRICIAN NEW ENGLANDER Cady Wells came to Santa Fe in 1932 to study with Andrew Dasburg. He found the social and intellectual milieu to his liking and by 1933 was a full-time resident of nearby Jacona. From the mid-1930s to 1940, Wells painted watercolor landscapes that were significantly influenced by Dasburg and John Marin. Upon returning to Santa Fe in 1945 after military service, he began a period of profound artistic experimentation.

Typical of this period of radical stylistic change, *Abstraction* displays a remarkable intricacy and technical control. At the time, Wells, still working primarily with water-based pigments, was experimenting with creating both simulated and real textural patterns. The content of this painting is totally abstract; the background is a golden grid containing a geometric calligraphic design. A superimposed abstract form is outlined with a carefully articulated golden ribbon, and the form's interior is an intricate mesh of meticulously drawn lines that gives an illusion of depth to the underlying grid. The color is applied in various thicknesses, from transparent washes to thick pigment, and in places, lines are scratched into the surface, providing additional tangible texture.

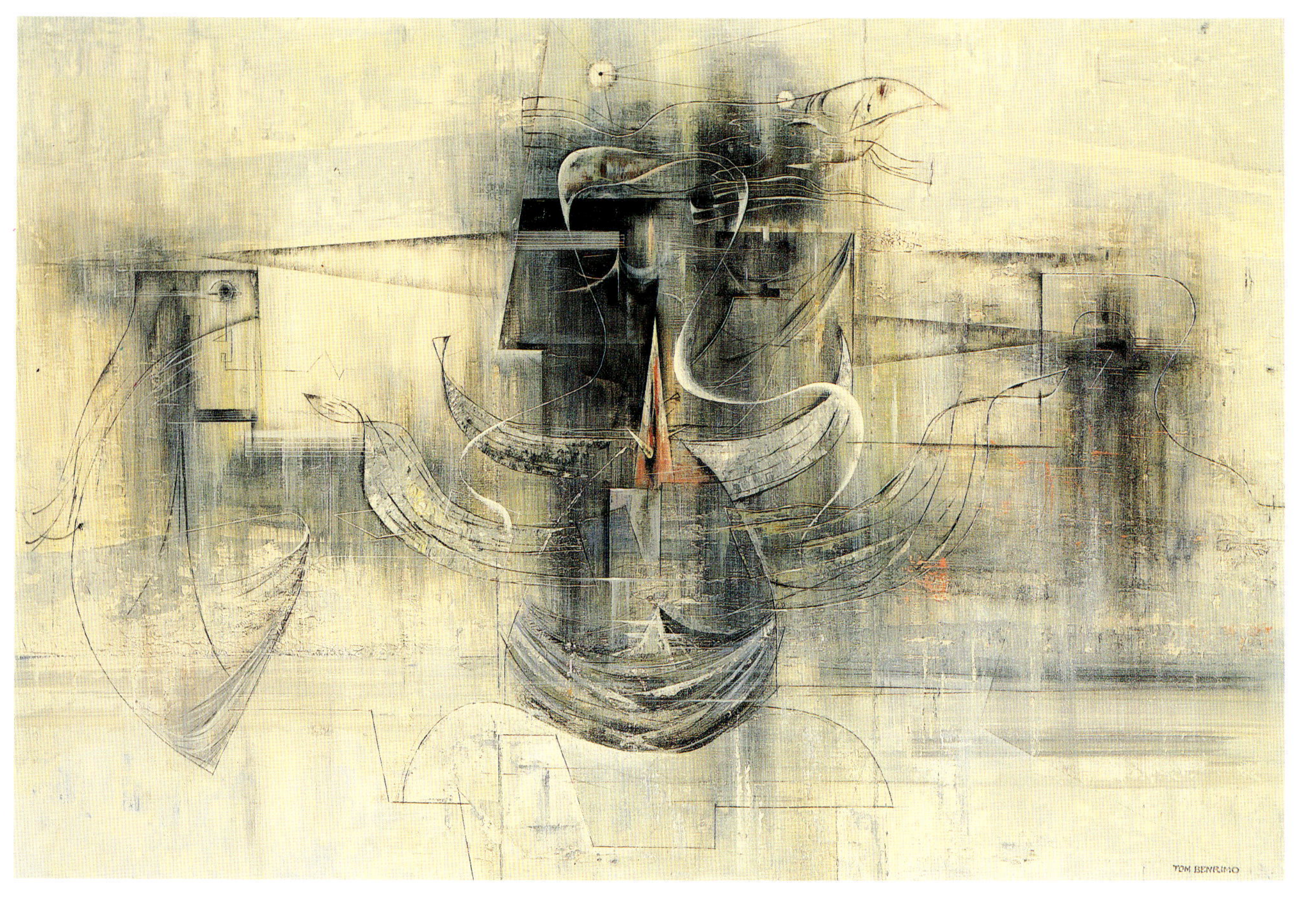

AN INFLUENTIAL teacher at the Pratt Institute and a highly successful commercial artist, Benrimo and his wife, Dorothy, a noted jewelry designer, abandoned New York's artistic circles in 1939 to pursue personal artistic development in remote northern New Mexico. A self-educated man, he was deeply interested in philosophy and physics, particularly in concepts relating to time and space perception.

Benrimo was New Mexico's preeminent surrealist. In *Dark Image*, he combined personal, surrealistic symbols, further mystified by abstraction, within a cubist space. An ethereal, curvilinear female figure is superimposed over a dark, angular male profile; a white, angular, masklike face appears in front of the female figure's knee. Gossamer veils, a recurring motif, allude to mysteries: the veil behind the shoulders of the female figure is in the shape of a crescent moon, a female fertility symbol. Each prismatic space created by line, color, and texture encompasses symbolic secrets. Both in form and content, the work is a study in contrasts: light and dark, male and female, rough and smooth, what is revealed and what is concealed.

THOMAS BENRIMO
Dark Image, 1953
Oil on Masonite
$24 \times 35\frac{3}{4}$ in.
Gift of Dr. and Mrs. R. C. Derbyshire, 1988

ADJA YUNKERS
City Lights, 1950
Color woodcut
$7\frac{3}{8} \times 15\frac{1}{2}$ in.
Museum purchase, Fine Arts Acquisition Fund at the Museum of New Mexico Foundation, 1988

BORN AT the turn of the century in Riga, Latvia, Yunkers spent his youth wandering through Europe and Mexico before settling in Sweden during World War II. There he built a reputation for his complex and dazzling prints. After a fire destroyed his studio and his entire body of work, Yunkers moved to New York City in 1947 and taught at the New School for Social Research. He first came to New Mexico in the summers of 1948 and 1949 to teach at the University of New Mexico, and there he inspired and vitalized the local art community. His hope of starting an art school in New Mexico was interrupted by a year in Rome on a Guggenheim Fellowship. He returned instead to New York, where he remained for the rest of his life.

City Lights is a fine example of Yunkers's expressionistic wood carving, whose delicate incisions and overlays were influenced by art as diverse as German expressionism and the ukiyo-e prints of Japan. Although the medium of the woodcut was often used by twentieth-century western artists precisely because of its crudeness and emphasis on the patterns of wood grain, in his use of the medium, Yunkers accomplished subtle complexity, often using as many as fifteen colors. Even though this is one of the artist's more abstract images, there is a palpable evocation of flashing lights in the city on a rainy night.

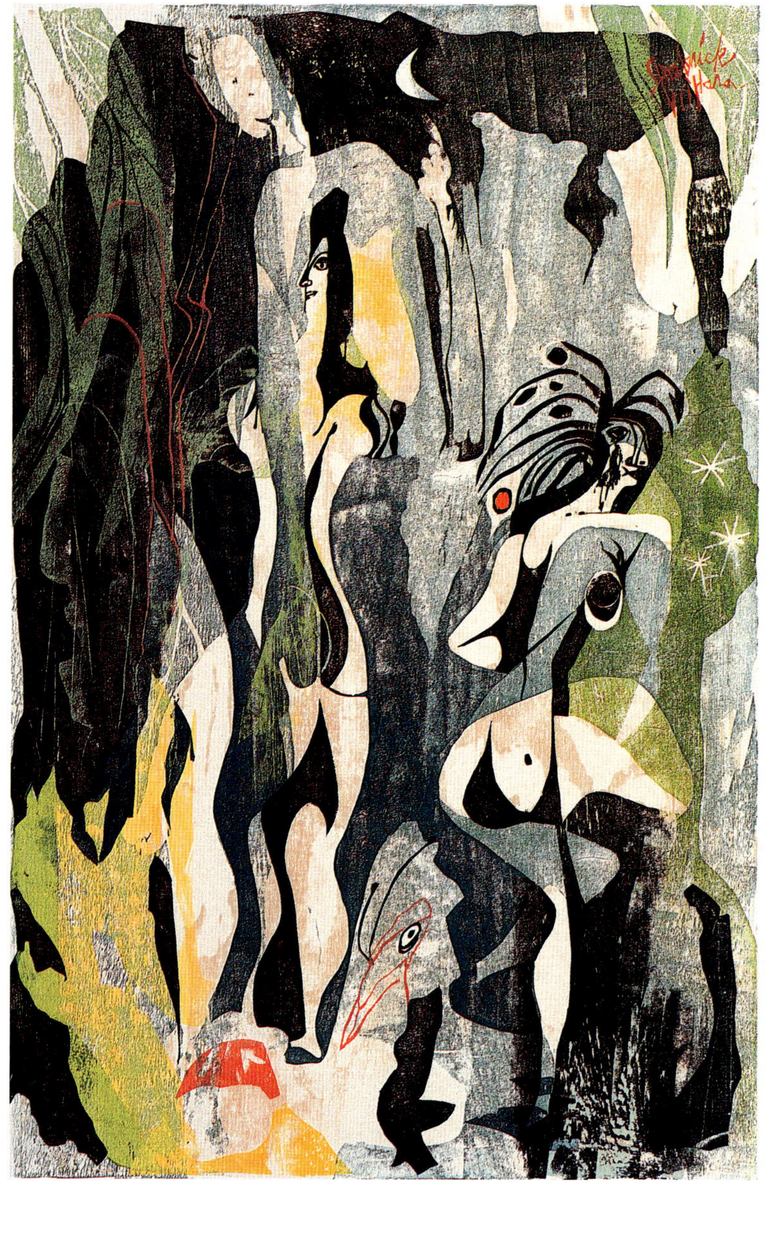

FREDERICK O'HARA
Garden of Folly, 1954
Color woodcut print
$25\frac{1}{4} \times 16\frac{1}{2}$ in.
Gift of Mary Louise O'Hara, 1980

A FORMER ARTIST for the *Boston Globe*, O'Hara traveled extensively in Europe, Africa, Cuba, and Mexico before settling in Albuquerque to work as a painter. His printmaking career began in 1949 after meeting the masterful woodcut artist Adja Yunkers. From this encounter, he began to develop the influential style of woodcut and lithography printing that is exemplified in *Garden of Folly*. O'Hara's success as a printmaker was immediate and his work was accepted into many exhibitions around the country, including several of the Graphics Annuals held at the Museum of Fine Arts during the 1950s, where he won eight Purchase Awards.

O'Hara's wife, Mary Louise, wrote that "New Mexico was the inspiration for his greatest artistic development, as is obvious for the many Indian themes, subtle landscapes, and delicate colors. He always considered himself a New Mexico artist." It was the wish of both Frederick and Mary Louise O'Hara that the Museum of New Mexico be given, after his death, a complete collection of his prints, which numbers almost one hundred.

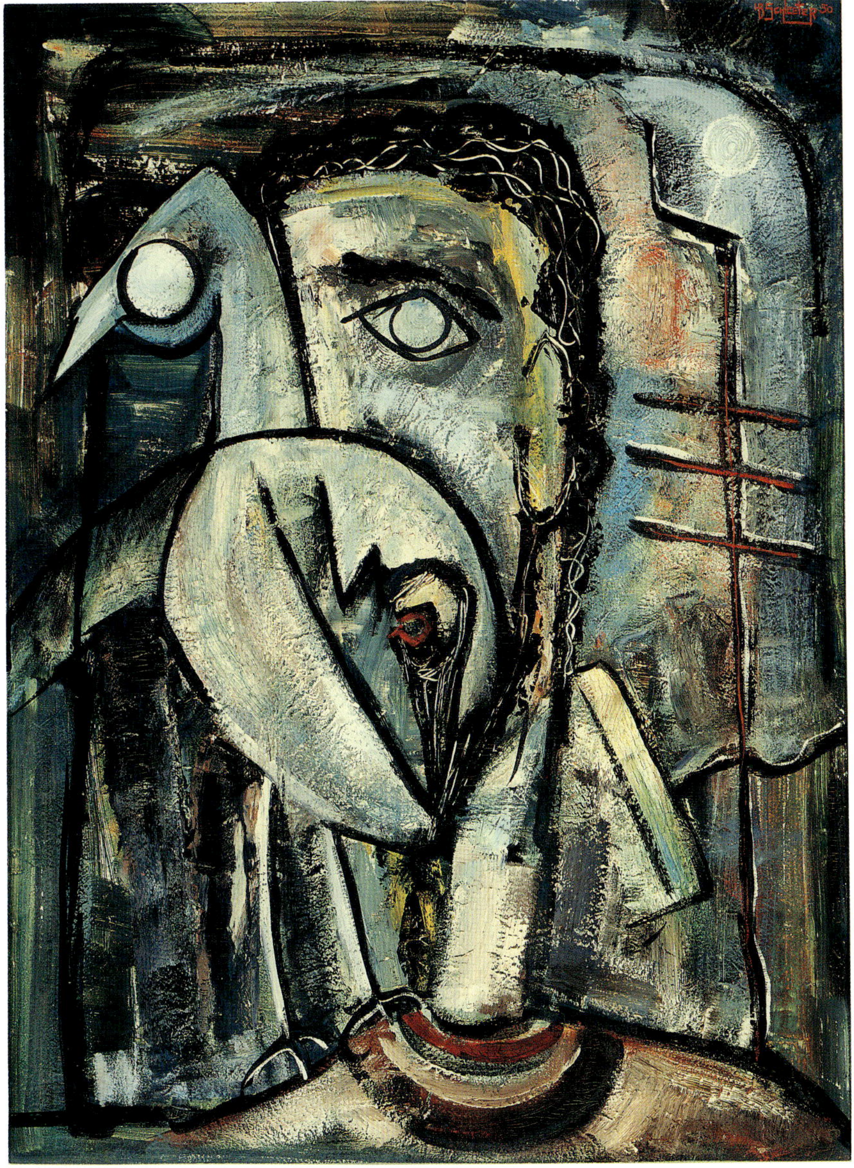

HOWARD B. SCHLEETER
St. Francis with a Bird, 1950
Wax, oil glaze, and gouache on board
$33^{1}/_{2} \times 27^{1}/_{2}$ in.
Gift of Mr. and Mrs. Bill L. Gill, 1985

ALTHOUGH SCHLEETER studied briefly at the Albright Art Institute in his native Buffalo, New York, he described himself as a self-taught artist. His brand of abstract art was slow to gain acceptance in New Mexico in the 1930s, the time of his relocation there. Such pioneering artists as Schleeter were fortunate to have access to the Raymond Jonson Gallery, established at the University of New Mexico and dedicated to local artists working in the modernist styles.

Schleeter, though not conventionally religious, frequently employed religious imagery in his work. Rather than reflecting his specific beliefs, this imagery was the key to a profound inner reality that awaited discovery. *St. Francis with a Bird* portrays the patron saint of Santa Fe, who is especially venerated in the Southwest and whose gentle spirit is admired by both Catholics and non-Catholics. Shown in profile, St. Francis's exaggerated, all-seeing eye is turned directly toward the viewer. A dove, symbol of peace and the Holy Ghost, is perched on his shoulder, sheltering his mouth with its wing. The combination of the rough texture created by the mixed media and the subdued colors creates the effect of an old church fresco.

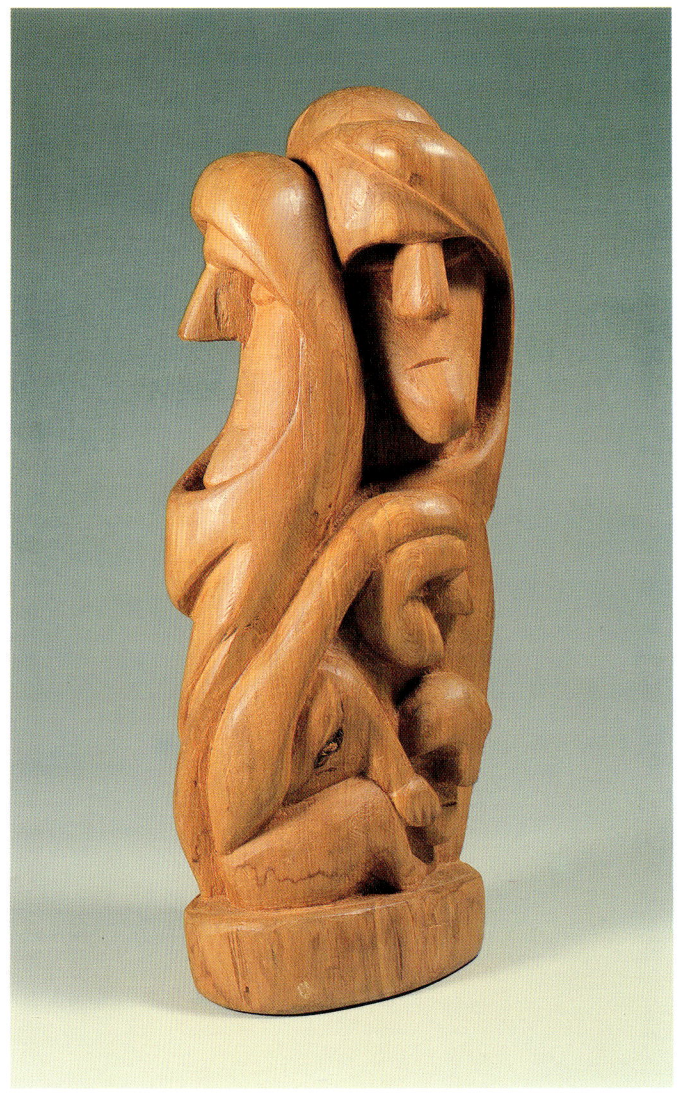

BARELA, a self-taught Taos wood-carver, did not receive any financial support for his work until he joined the Works Project Administration/Federal Arts Project in 1935 under the directorship of Russell Vernon Hunter. Freed of financial burdens, his work flowered during this period.

Barela's figurative work resulted from his deep religious beliefs, strengthened by his personal creative vision. Although his style has primitive overtones reminiscent of the art of Africa or Easter Island, it derives from a purely personal source. There is an expressiveness in Barela's carvings not found in similar work of his contemporaries, a unique quality that was recognized when his work was included in the collection at the Museum of Modern Art.

The sensuous carving of *Five Ages of Man* represents the stages of life: birth, childhood, youth, middle age, and old age.

PATROCINIO BARELA
Five Ages of Man, ca. 1940
Cedar
$18\frac{1}{4} \times 7 \times 5$ in.
Gift of Clifford Clarke, 1975

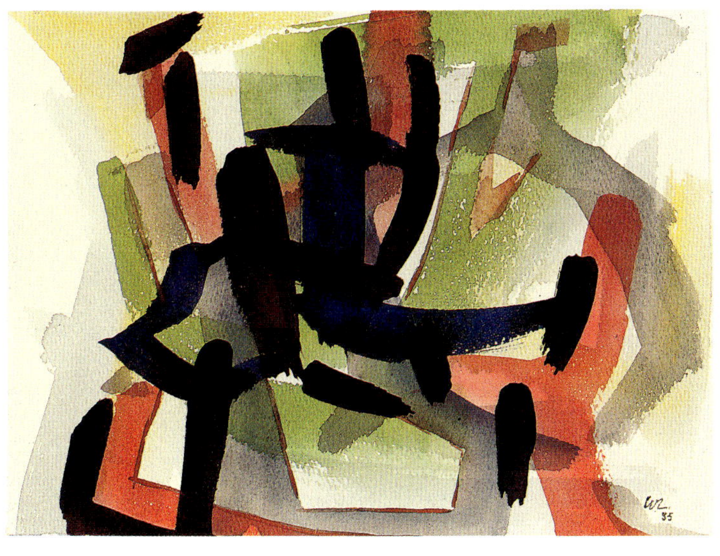

WILLIAM LUMPKINS
This Was a Breakthru, 1935
Watercolor on paper
7⅝ × 10¾ in.
Gift of the William and Norma L. Lumpkins Trust, 1989

BORN ON THE Rabbit Ears Ranch west of Clayton, New Mexico, Lumpkins' parallel careers as artist and architect have placed him in the forefront of twentieth-century arts. He began painting as a teenager with his companion Peter Hurd, whom he met in Roswell, New Mexico. From 1950 to 1967, Lumpkins lived in La Jolla, California, where he was immersed in large-scale experimental work with a group of artists teaching and working at the La Jolla Art Center. In 1984, he was one of the founders of the Santa Fe Institute, where such master teachers as Richard Diebenkorn and Helen Frankenthaler have taught, inspiring the artist to be ever more prolific.

This Was a Breakthru (also published as *Xapu*) is one of Lumpkins' most startling images from the 1930s. Thoroughly gestural and spontaneous, it was undoubtedly influenced by John Marin's paintings, which had fascinated him as a young artist in 1931 when he first studied them as abstractions and realized that watercolor was a demanding medium requiring rapid decisions. In this painting, there is a confident use of the white paper ground, a flashing attack of color, and a reliance on the kinesthetic—all resulting in a crisp and unmuddied painting. It is a harbinger of the meditative work Lumpkins created after returning to Santa Fe in the late 1960s.

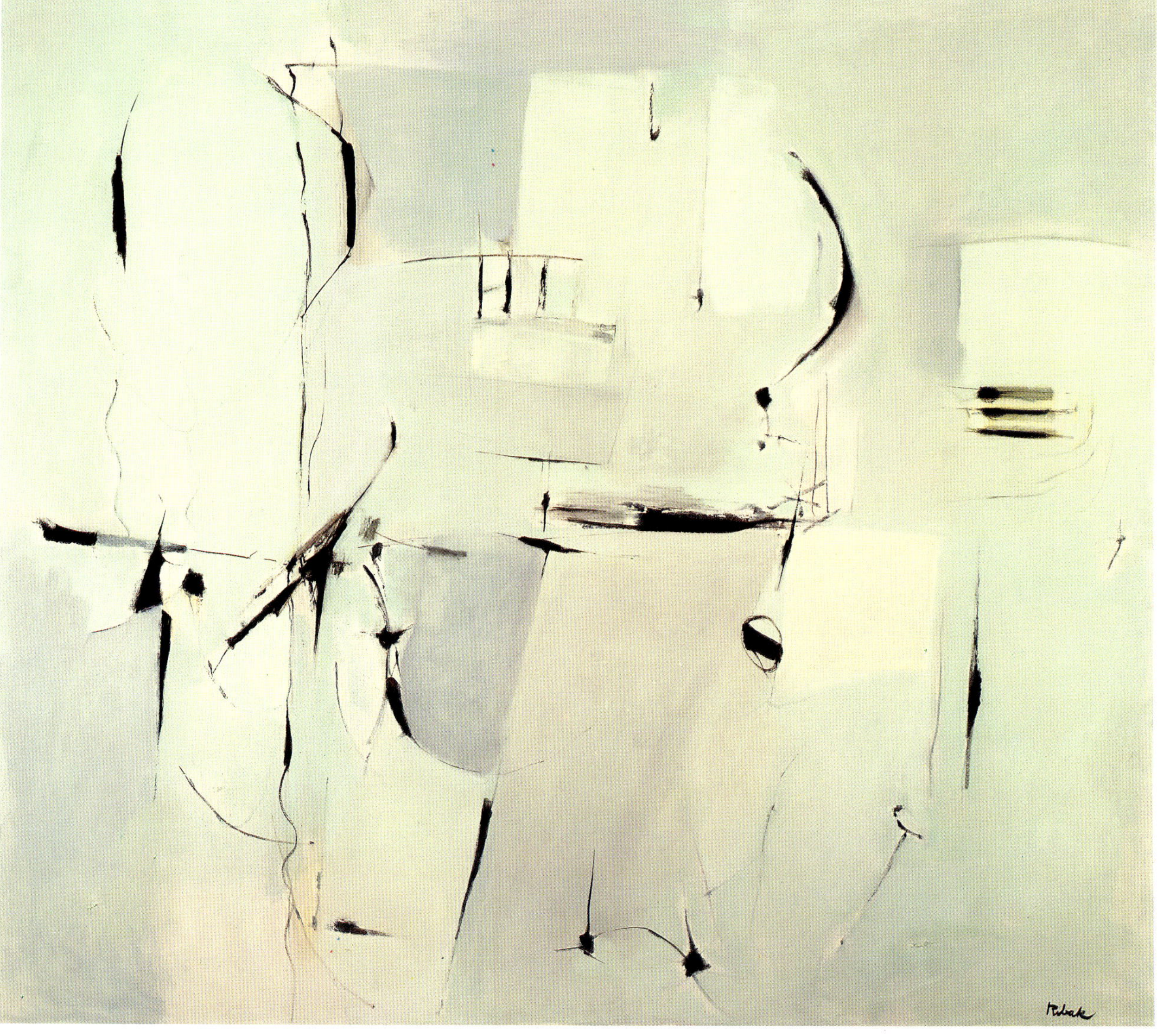

LOUIS RIBAK

Canyon with Greys, ca. 1959
Oil on canvas
60 × 70 in.
Gift of the artist, 1969

IMMIGRATING TO New York from his birthplace in Lithuania, Ribak studied at the Art Students League in New York, where his most important influence was John Sloan. The artist painted in a social realist style through the 1920s and 1930s, becoming a founding member of An American Group. In 1942, he married painter Bea Mandelman; after military service, the couple moved to New Mexico on Sloan's recommendation. Unsatisfied with Santa Fe, Ribak settled in the more remote Taos, where he lived until his death. In order to survive financially in this small town not yet known for its commercial art market, he gave private art lessons and eventually opened the Taos Valley Art School in 1947, one of the many New Mexico schools that educated GIs returning from the war. The dramatic terrain of the region around Taos was Ribak's source of inspiration, and he eventually developed an expansive and lyrical abstract style that effectively expressed the essence of his surroundings.

Canyon with Greys is a solitary, introspective work of an artist no longer concerned with the external look of things. Ribak's "Canyon" series instead seeks to elucidate an inner, kinesthetic experience. The shifting field of countless variations of warm greys suggests a page from a musical score.

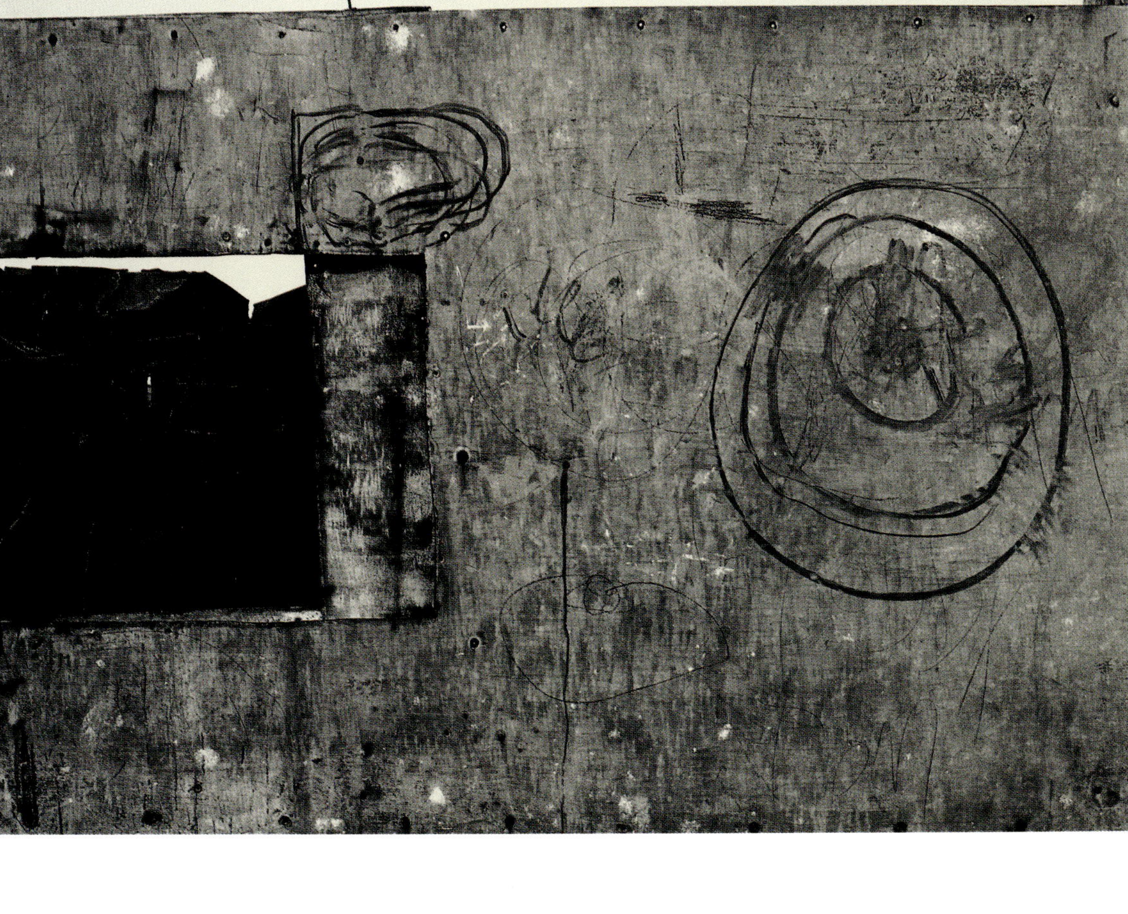

AARON SISKIND
Bronx 1, 1950
Gelatin silver photograph
36×50 in.
Future gift of Susan Crocker

BY THE LATE 1930s, Aaron Siskind began to explore ways of photographing the world from a social-documentary perspective. His projects in Harlem and New York's urban tenements with Sid Grossman and the Photo League began as studies in human relationships. Photographing life in descriptive detail ran parallel to his teaching English and literature in New York City at the time. Photographs could be used like words in creating statements that were part of a greater whole.

Working in the Methodist community of Martha's Vineyard, he further examined the expressive aspects of folk culture. The beauty of Gothic architectural details was translated into photographs that conveyed in a more confined space an individual feeling for form, structure, and relationships. Objective documentary concerns began to share in meaning with the photographer's personal perceptions. The *picture* of a given subject, Siskind realized, could also sustain a life of its own.

Siskind turned away from rendering *naturalistic* space and developed the photograph as a visual form of expression. In the 1950s he began photographing flat subjects such as walls to discover more than literal fact. This change in approach was fundamental: in New York the abstract expressionists were pursuing similar directions in their painting. "The shift," Siskind wrote, "was from description to idea and meaning." The significance was that a photograph could convey other values through the artist by the mastery of the intrinsic qualities of the medium.

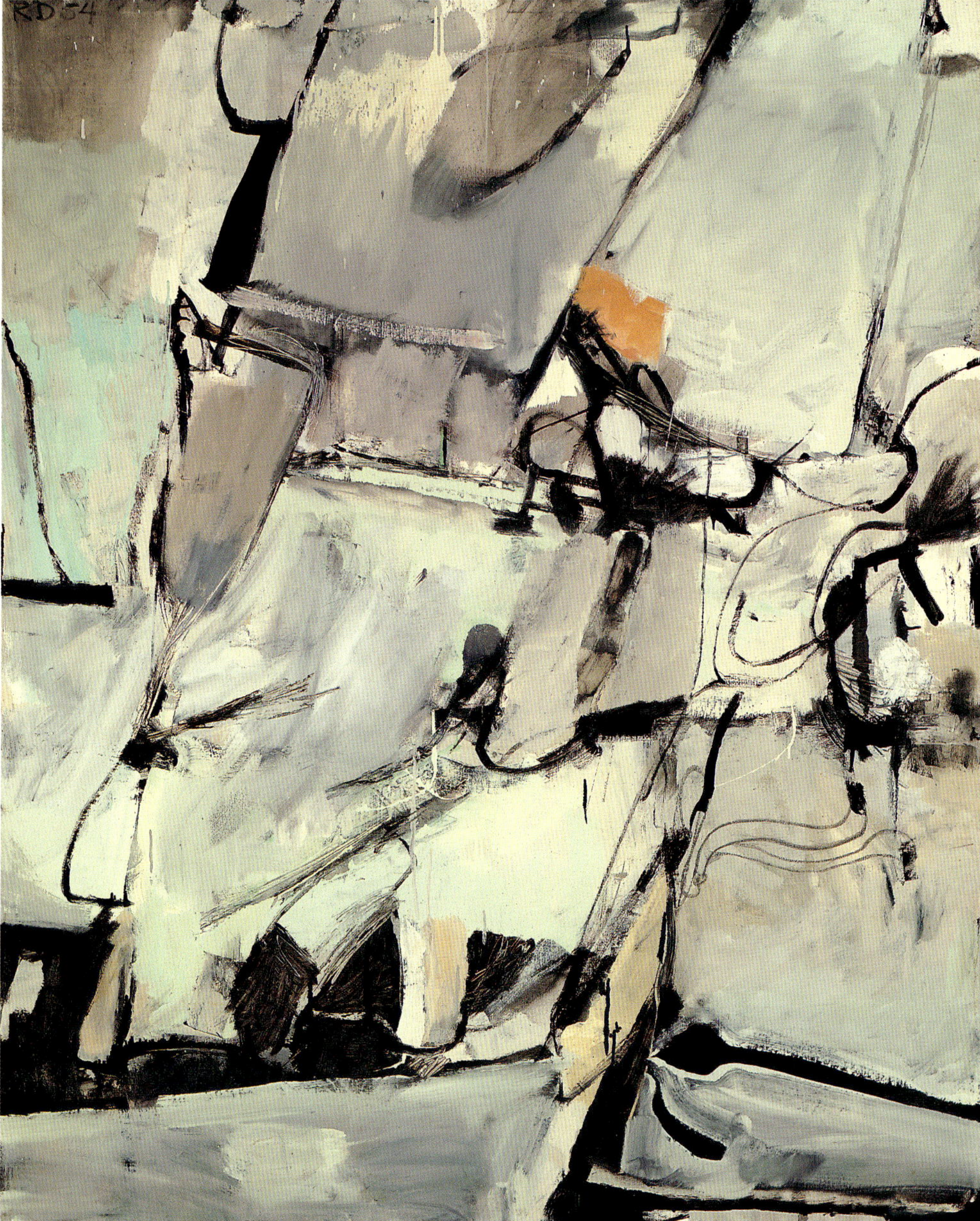

AFTER HIS academic training in northern California and his self-study of the paintings at the Phillips Collection in Washington, D.C., Diebenkorn went to Albuquerque on the GI Bill and enrolled at the University of New Mexico, where he received his master's degree. His subsequent return to northern California began a celebrated twenty-year teaching career. These years in his Ocean Park studio were Diebenkorn's most significant in yielding a series of paintings of compressed views of the neighborhood where he lived.

Berkeley No. 15, from a series made between 1953 and 1955 named for the location of his studio, is from Diebenkorn's most abstract expressionist period. It is a painting that shows how thoroughly he absorbed the work of Willem de Kooning and one that combines all of the early characteristics of his work—lush painterliness, the aerial view of the landscape, and the wiry line of George Herriman's Crazy Cat comics. Although Diebenkorn's paintings demonstrate the process of building the image with decisions and changes recorded in *pentimento*, they are distinguished from action painting by the complex thought processes combined with constant readjustments that underlie their creation.

RICHARD DIEBENKORN
Berkeley No. 15, 1954
Oil on canvas
64 × 53 in.
Gift of Joann and Gifford Phillips, 1980

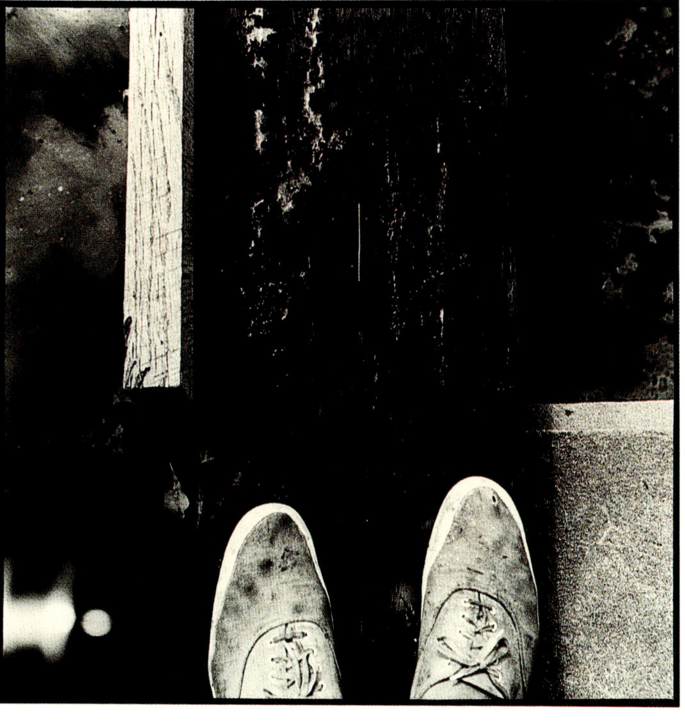

ROBERT RAUSCHENBERG
Sneakers, 1979
Gelatin silver photograph
$11\frac{1}{2} \times 11\frac{3}{4}$ in.
Museum purchase from the Eugenia Janis Fund, 1989

IN 1948, Rauschenberg briefly visited Black Mountain, the open-concept art college in North Carolina, where he was introduced by Josef Albers and Hazel Archer to working exercises in collage and photography. After only a few months, the seeds of Rauschenberg's unconventional career were sown.

Shortly afterward, he moved to New York City and began to experiment with life-size photograms on rolls of light-sensitive blueprinting paper. Human figures and forms from nature were arranged directly on the paper's surface then exposed with a hand-held floodlight. The result was a color reversal, with object images remaining white while the surrounding areas turned blue. These early formative pieces significantly alter our expectations about the worldly space of pictures. By incorporating aspects of the photographic medium into his multimedia works, Rauschenberg broke the rules that delineated individual art forms. His use of the camera helped to recast what was accepted as the shape and experience of the world. Importantly, by using various media, the artist referred to what he experienced as the dimensionless nature of contemporary life.

In *Sneakers*, we are confronted with a visual ambiguity: Are we looking down at the artist's feet, as the conventional view would suggest, or are these flattened shoes a reminder that the world is progressively a matter for technology, thus rendering the shoes obsolete?

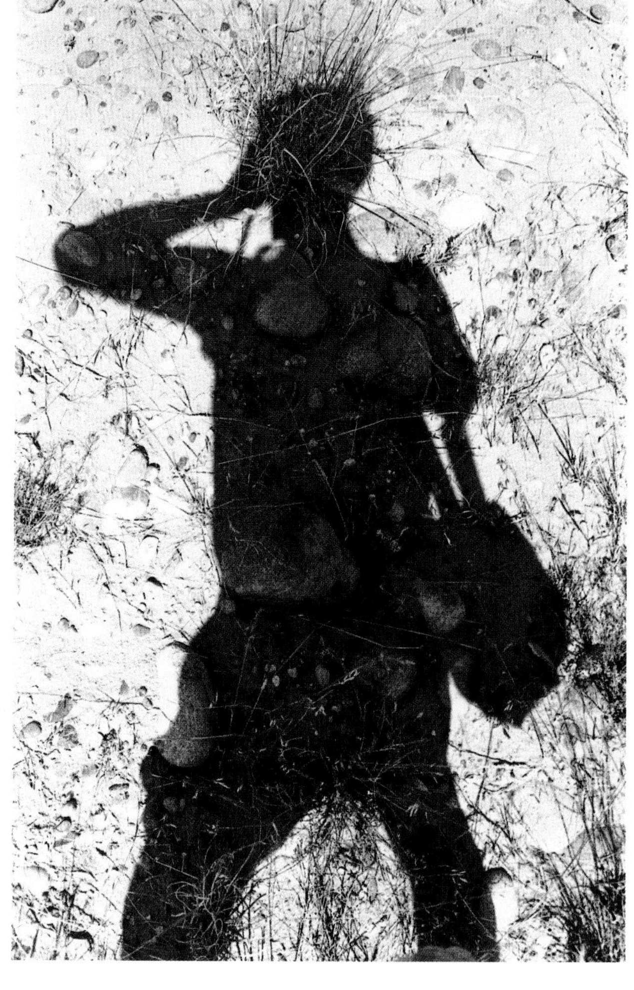

SINCE 1964, Friedlander has created self-portraits as an extension of his primary photographic work. Often these pictures include only aspects of the photographer's body or its shadow as elements within landscapes. At first glance, these photographs appear as an exercise of self-indulgence, a sight jest, or as stereotypic references to the photographer in a game of mirrors. On closer inspection, they become part of a journey of self-discovery.

In *Canyon de Chelly, Arizona,* the superimposed shadow suggests that this is a theatrical stage where the act of looking has become the subject. Perhaps the unmanipulated position of rocks and dormant grasses—now aligned within the gesture of the photographer's body, his positioned camera, and his shoulder pack—alludes to the primeval source of corporeal energy.

The delicate global balance between natural and human forces is a central concern of the twentieth century. As John Jackson writes, "If we are again to learn how to respond emotionally and esthetically and morally to the landscape, we must find a metaphor—or several metaphors—drawn from our human experience." In this sense, the photographer rendered here is a modern symbol of hope.

LEE FRIEDLANDER
Canyon de Chelly, Arizona, 1983
Gelatin silver photograph
14×11 in.
Museum purchase, Photo Group Fund, 1990

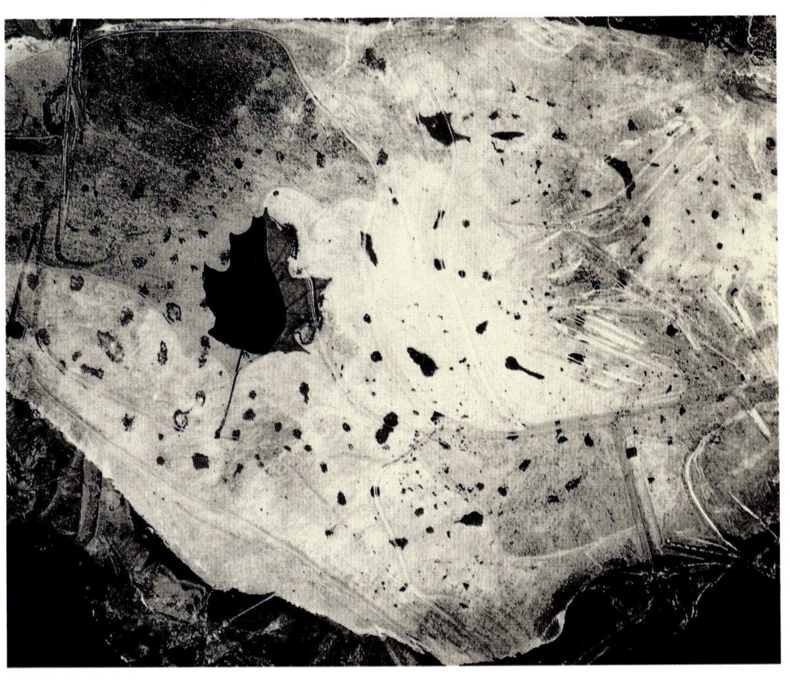

PAUL CAPONIGRO
Nahant, Massachusetts, 1958
Gelatin silver photograph
$7\frac{5}{8} \times 9\frac{3}{8}$ in.
Gift of Richard and Susan Streeper, 1991

DETAILS OF NATURE have preoccupied artists for centuries and photographers since the invention of photography in 1839. In this century, masters of photography such as Edward Weston and Paul Strand discovered the beauty of form through fundamental approaches and an uncompromising refinement in craftsmanship. Their ability to express the essential forms and qualities of subjects through the camera brought the world to the viewer with unwavering directness.

Paul Caponigro's awareness of nature's universal order has created further achievements in expressing the mystery of nature through the medium of photography. Within a continuing process of discovery, his images touch on life's most profound riddles while inviting introspection. A new landscape emerges with its own scale and meaning.

In *Nahant, Massachusetts*, visual ambiguity transforms the subject to a universal plane. Is this an image of a leaf united with nature's remnants, locked in a season's quandary of frozen order? Here found objects are transposed to a different temporal and spatial realm. This small constellation of organic fragments frozen in a labyrinth of flowing tonalities more closely resembles a much vaster domain, such as the night sky or the ocean floor. Only the leaf reminds us of our physical place in the universe, amid intimations of greater spiritual secrets.

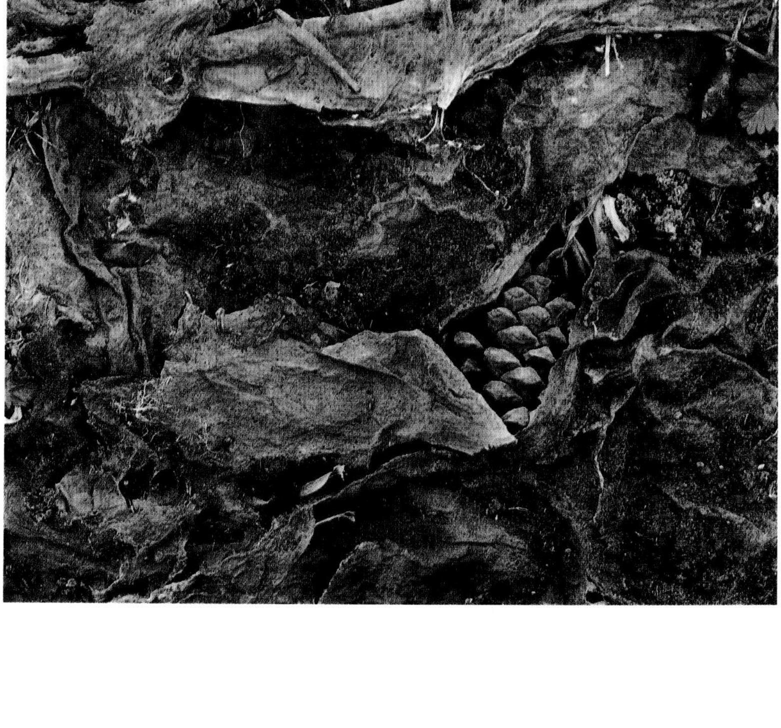

WHAT MEANING can the character or assembly of nature's fragments provide? The intricate structures in Sommer's photographs reveal through association. Like a constellation of thoughts surrounding a central idea, the correspondent parts form a matrix by which nature is revealed more fundamentally.

In *Pine Cone*, such links between mind and matter are made manifest in photographic terms. The countless minute forms and textures of nature's deposits, coupled with the rare perfection of the print's resolution, invite infinite readings of this collagelike ordering of circumstance. Does this image depict the substance of reality or of dream? Such a photograph speaks of individual discovery through metamorphosis, and in viewing it, our imagination enters realms of the fantastic.

While photographs often provide a sense that a moment in time has been captured instantaneously, in Sommer's art, a sense of time only emerges as we look more deeply. Here a pine cone sits half hidden by floating enigmatic forms from the forest that are animated by an equivocal presence. Transformations begin to take place before our eyes. "Life is the most durable fiction that matter has come up with," the artist reminds us, "and art is the structure of matter as life's most durable fiction."

FREDERICK SOMMER
Pine Cone, 1947
Gelatin silver photograph
7⅝ × 9 9/16 in.
Gift of Joann and Gifford Phillips in memory of Dina Woelffer, 1990

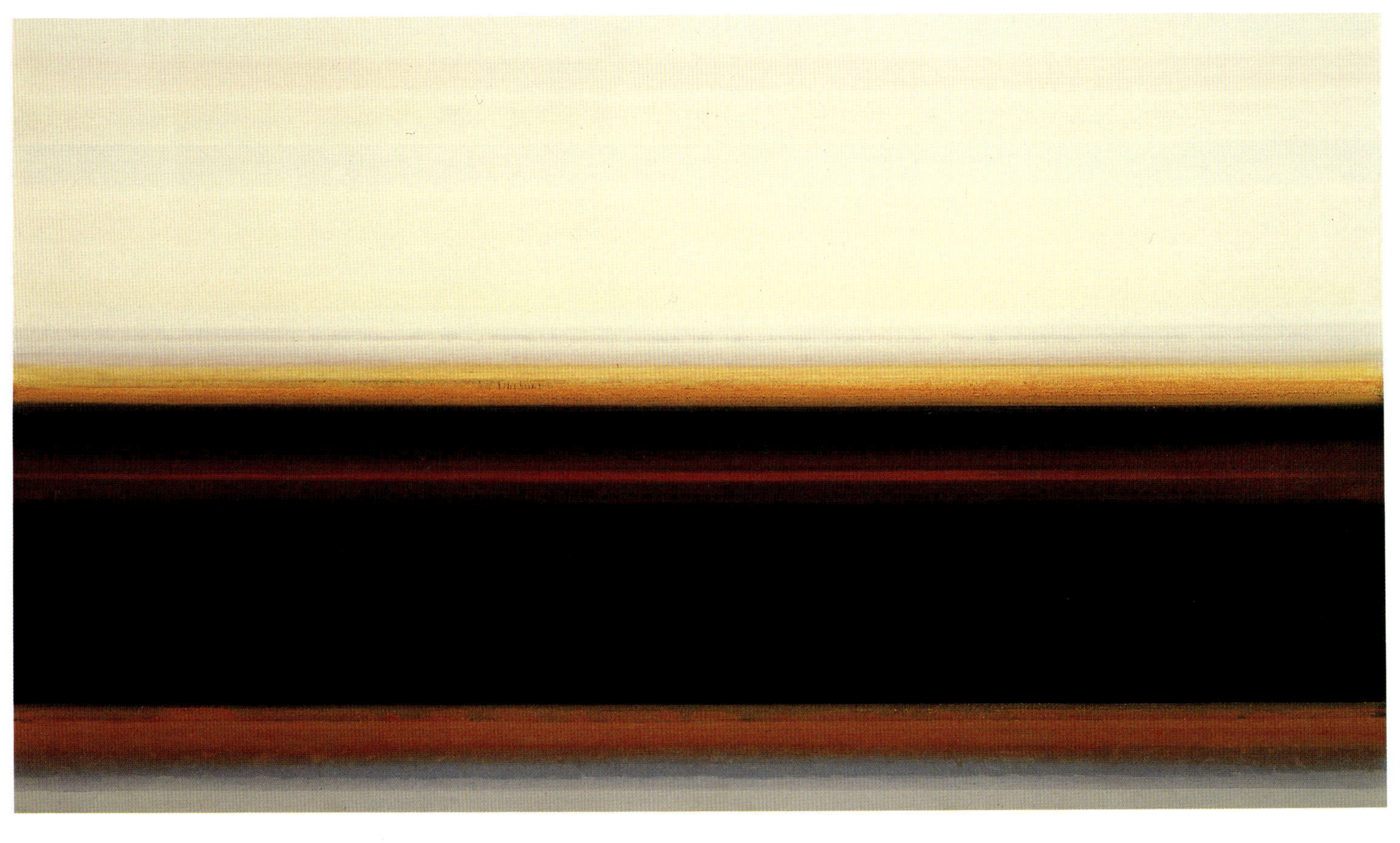

LARRY CALCAGNO
Landscape, 1970
Acrylic on canvas
48 × 84 in.
Gift of the Gallery of Modern Art, Taos, 1973

A PRIMARY CHALLENGE of a contemporary landscape painter is to interpret a natural view with personal vision through either a realistic or abstract style. New Mexico landscape painters face an even greater challenge because the physical aspects of the land are so dominant. Calcagno, who has split his residency between the natural beauties of Taos and Hawaii and the urban vigor of the lower east side of New York City, looks optimistically at the land, expressing it as bright horizontal bands that retain a spiritual dimension and evoke awe of the earth's basic elements.

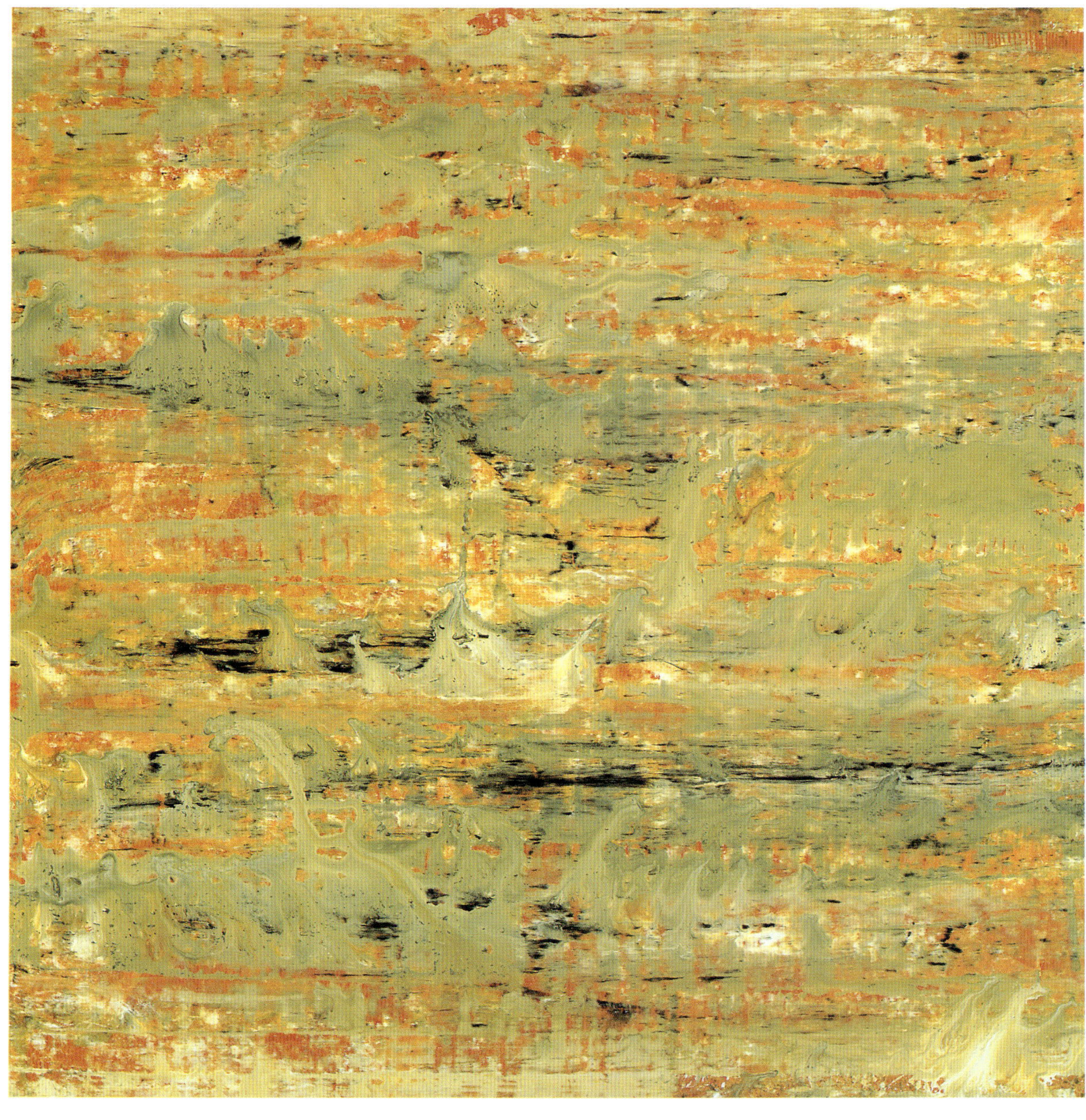

BEFORE WARREN DAVIS moved to New York in 1963 he was making active abstract expressionist paintings in the isolated Texas Panhandle community of Amarillo. By the mid-1960s Davis had rejected the violent activity of execution that typified abstract expressionism in favor of a quieter, more subdued form of nonrepresentational expression. While most large abstract paintings of the period shouted at the viewer with loud, broad strokes of angst, his work aspired to a studied silence.

Working the canvases quickly with squeegees, sponges, and brushes and adeptly moving around acrylic colors in unexpected but soothing blends, Davis created paintings full of patterns and alignments that appear perfectly realized. During his prematurely short career, the artist produced a large body of work that included watercolors, collages, and large-scale paintings that demonstrate an exhaustive commitment to pure abstraction.

WARREN DAVIS
Untitled, 1971
Acrylic on canvas
70×72 in.
Gift of Stan Sodolski and Beverly Pappe, 1981

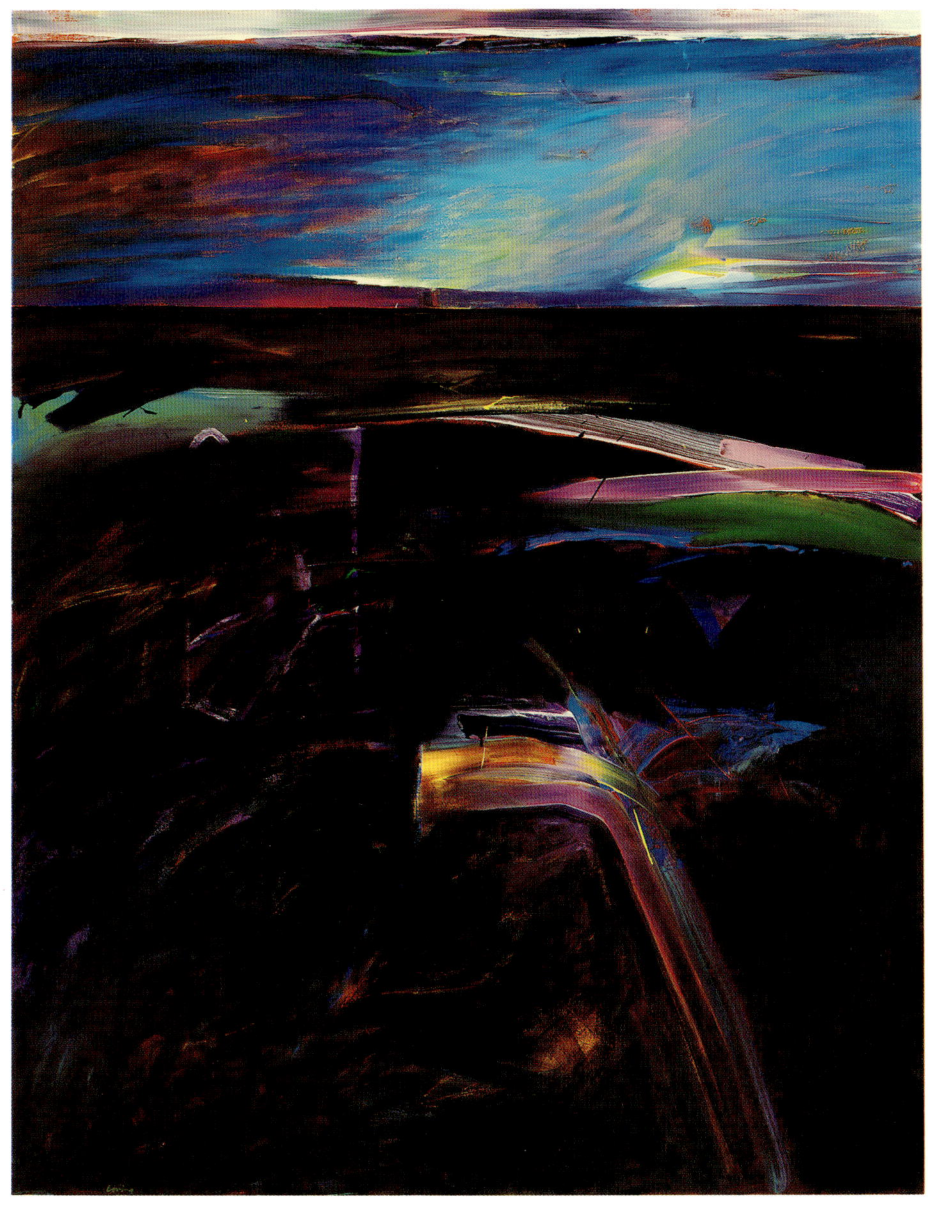

REG LOVING
Terreno, 1983
Acrylic on canvas
60 × 48 in.
Gift of Meg and Sam Heydt, 1988

WHETHER THEY refer directly to terrain and horizon, as in this work, or are nonobjective, Loving's large abstract paintings evolve from his preoccupation with the earth's mysterious hidden nature. His ongoing concern with mining and geology can be traced to his childhood. "When I was young," he has said, "I wanted to be a geologist or a mining engineer, but I was deficient in math, so I became a painter."

Terreno is part of a series on lixiviation, a term that refers to the extraction of minerals through percolation, or leaching. The artist becomes the alchemist who transforms the raw materials of his subject into paintings. "Mining and metalurgy are like alchemy," Loving wrote for a 1985 exhibition. "It is extracting raw material of ore from the earth, reducing and turning it into wealth. Extraction, extrapolation, reduction, and abstraction are also the process that the artist is involved with when producing a work of art."

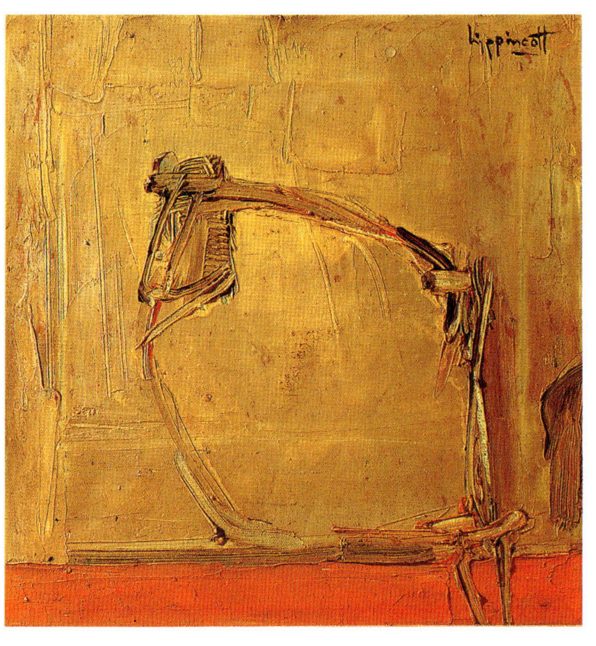

NEW YORK–BORN painter Janet Lippincott began her career during World War II while on active duty in Europe. Supported by the GI Bill, she came to New Mexico in 1949 to enroll in Emil Bisttram's art school in Taos, settling in Santa Fe at a time when abstract art was rarely exhibited. She continued her studies at the Colorado Fine Arts Center with Emerson Woelffer, who arranged her first solo exhibition in Mexico City in 1957. An abstract artist for nearly fifty years, Lippincott has identified Mark Rothko, Helen Frankenthaler, and Nicolas de Stael, along with some modern Japanese painters, as her inspirations.

In Lippincott's oeuvre, *Fossil* is unusual, both for its size and its composition. A large abstraction in a small format, it is an artifactual mystery of unknowable past events whose secrets reveal themselves under the circumstances of quiet contemplation.

JANET LIPPINCOTT
Fossil, 1968
Oil on canvas
12 × 12 in.
Gift of Mr. and Mrs. William C. Overstreet, 1984

LEE MULLICAN
Meditation on Leaves in a Pond, 1962
Oil on canvas
40×75 in.
Gift of Joann and Gifford Phillips, 1980

LEE MULLICAN first visited New Mexico in 1938 with his mother, an amateur *plein air* painter who worked in Taos during the summer months. After World War II, he moved to San Francisco, where he founded the Dynaton Group with Wolfgang Paalen and Gordon-Onslow Ford, with whom he shared an approach to automatic painting first promoted by the surrealists. After twenty years as a professor at the University of California, Mullican began to divide his time between Los Angeles, where he works on computer drawings at UCLA, and Taos, where he paints and makes ceramics.

Meditation on Leaves in a Pond is a luminous, shimmering field painting produced with machinelike precision that creates the disconcerting effect of being a handmade, protocomputer image. Made during a period when Mullican was restricting his palette to only one or two basic colors and using only strokes in one direction, it is named after the famous surrealist painting *Meditations on an Oak Leaf* painted in 1942 by André Masson. Mullican's work embodies a successful paradox: He acknowledges the influence of automatism from surrealism, expressed in the fluid surface patterns, and yet he constructs the painting according to a prescribed and conscious agenda.

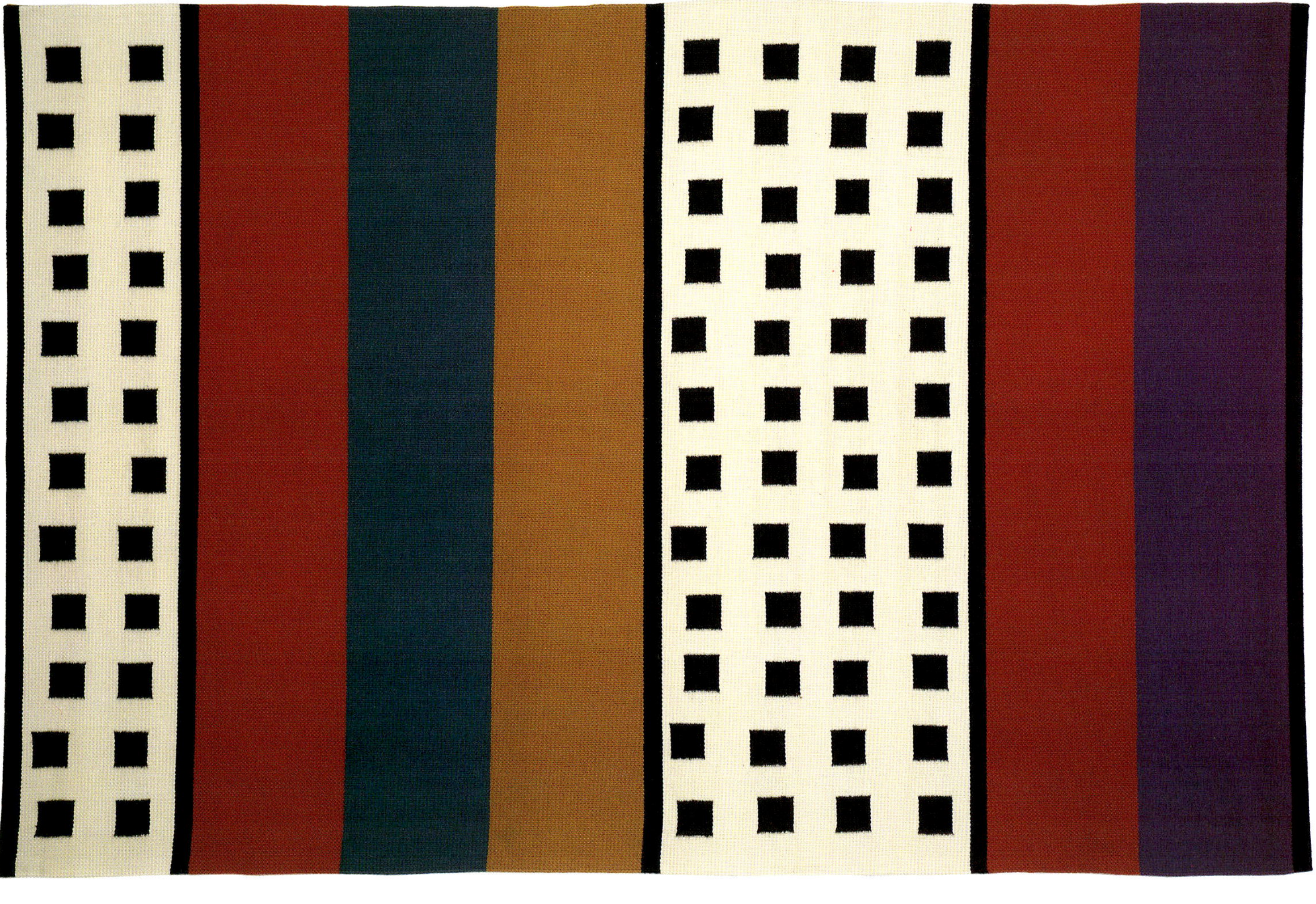

FOR MANY CENTURIES, Native American weavers have made functional pieces that were at the same time artistic masterpieces. Ramona Sakiestewa's traditional heritage is to the Hopi Indians, with whom she is linked through her father. The traditional Hopi vertical loom was her means of teaching herself to weave. She has also studied ancient Anasazi weaving techniques and worked with weavers from the Chincero area of Peru, whose tradition goes back to pre-Columbian ancestors. To this multifaceted ancient legacy, Sakiestewa has introduced modern and innovative approaches.

Starting with small maquettes, or drawings of the patterns, the artist explores solutions to design problems that are based primarily upon reduction. Like an abstract painter, she looks for the essential forms and lines that are significant to a composition. In a medium where symmetry and regularity of pattern are stressed, Sakiestewa pushes the limits of traditional design in order to imbue her weavings with both spontaneity and symbolism.

RAMONA SAKIESTEWA
Katsina/6, 1989
Fiber
50×77 in.
"Southwest '90" Purchase Prize

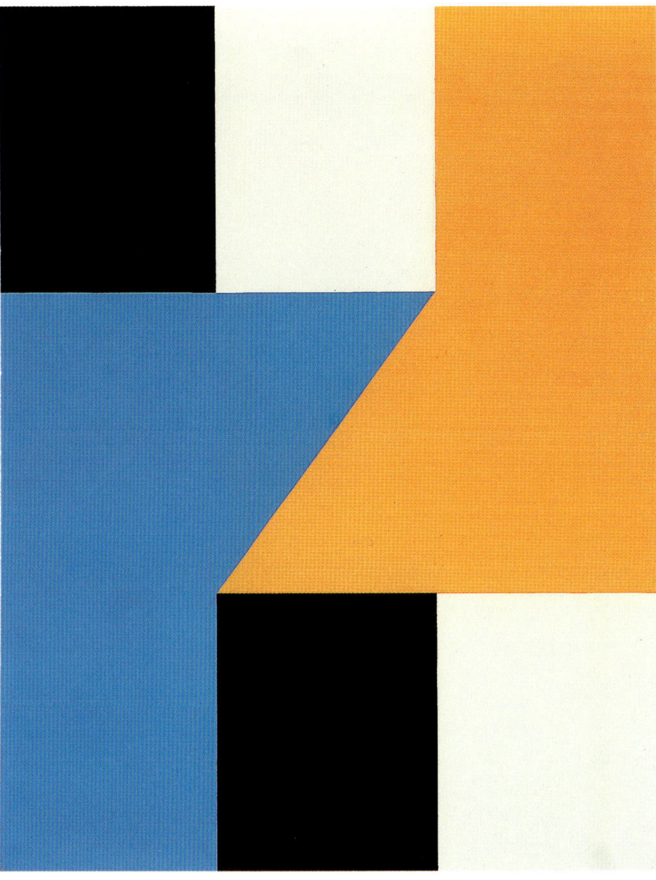

FREDERICK HAMMERSLEY
Paired, 1961
Oil on canvas
30 × 23¾ in.
Museum purchase, Fine Arts
Acquisition Fund at the Museum of
New Mexico Foundation, 1988

HAMMERSLEY'S carefully formulated paintings, with their reductive geometry and unmixed colors, have been exhibited and written about in connection with a loose confederation of artists known variously as "abstract classicists" or the "Hard-Edge Painters." While the roots of their geometric abstraction can be traced to Malevich and Mondrian, these painters of the 1960s were reacting to the gestural, rarely controlled marks of the second-generation abstract expressionists.

The methods with which Hammersley creates his paintings range from an intuitive placement of shapes and colors, at one extreme, to working out formal ideas of order and color in notebook form at the other. The final paintings, most of which are structured on a grid, still retain a fresh painterly quality and a clear sense of control that approach a classical and conclusive beauty.

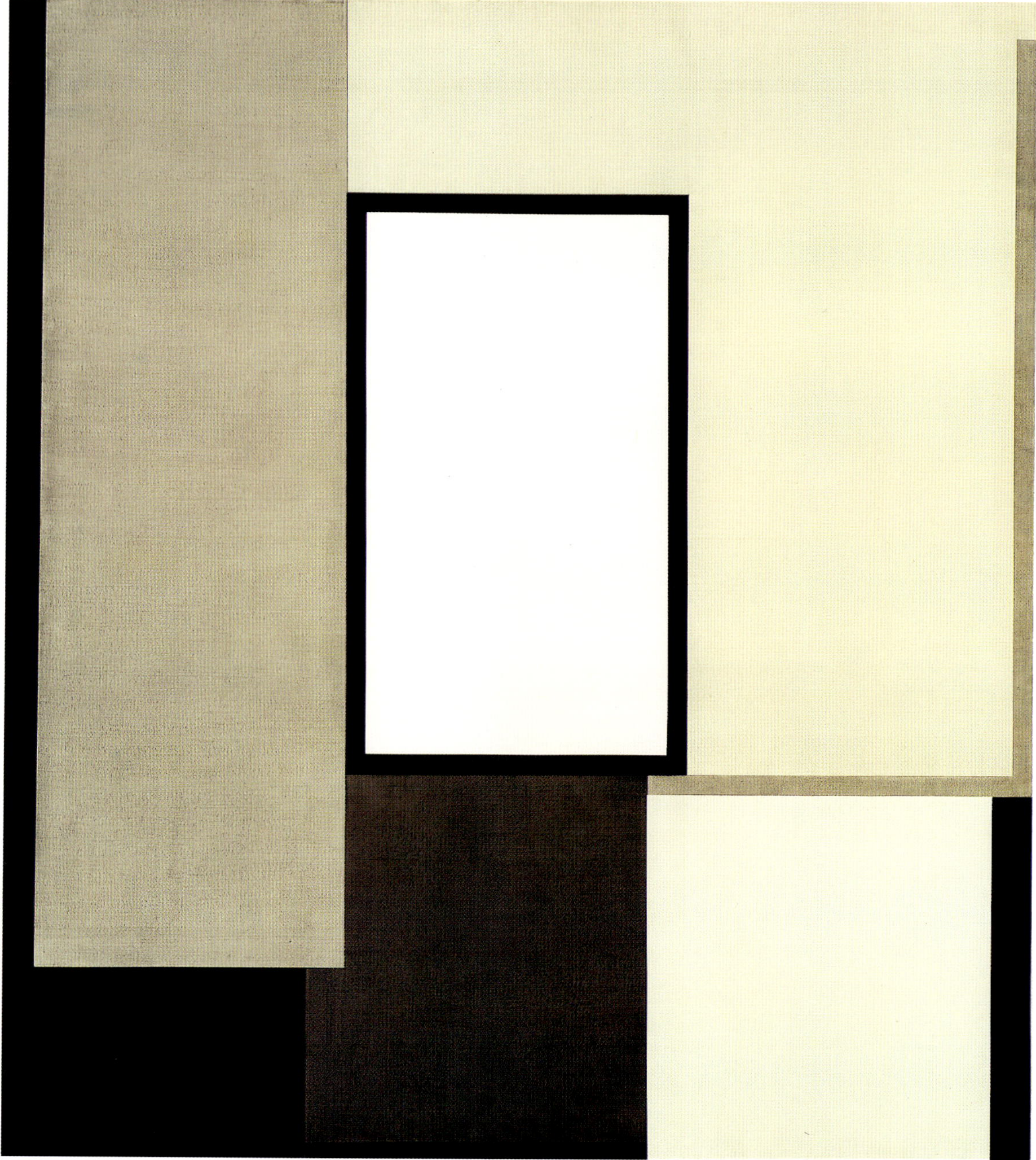

THE VIBRANCY of classical modernism is exemplified in *Platonic Sanctum*. "There are two temperaments," App has observed. "The romantics like to just start. They begin with the unknown and move toward the known. If one begins with the known [as I do], one is not without the romantic impulse." That impulse is seen in App's updating of the modernist grid, adding to it a sensitivity to space and light that has been enhanced through his experience of living in California and the Southwest.

Space, light, and rigorous control characterize his paintings, as well as the vibrancy that results from the interplay of opposites: flatness and space, presence and absence, stability and movement, light and dark.

TIMOTHY APP
Platonic Sanctum, 1987
Acrylic on canvas
72 × 66 in.
Purchase prize with funds donated toward "New Mexico '87" from the Ovenwest Corporation, Frank Ribelin, and the Santa Fe Gallery Association, 1987

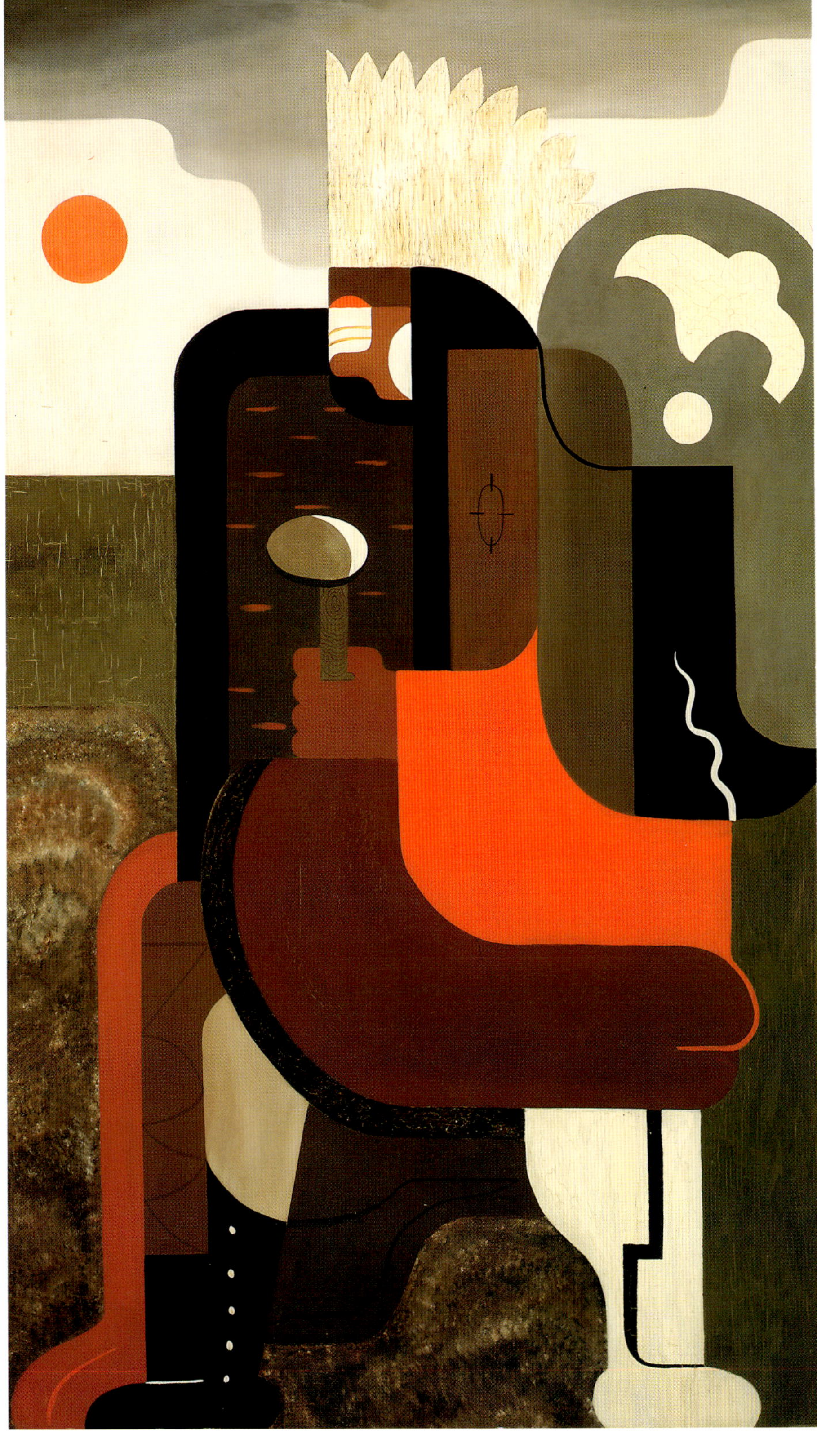

HILAIRE HILER
Chief Sits in the Spring, 1933
Oil on canvas
$64 \times 38\frac{1}{2}$ in.
Gift of the artist, 1946

A SELF-TAUGHT ARTIST, teacher, writer, and founder of the prestigious Fremont School in Santa Fe, Hiler pursued the idea of unifying art and science through the use of a design formula for producing art. His structural paintings, exhibited internationally, revealed a new method of design configuration in which nonobjective organic forms of sculpture and painting were employed in sequential relationships, an approach that likened the work to that of Fernand Léger. In *Chief Sits in the Spring*, Hiler implicitly demonstrates the inseparable relationship between art and science.

FRITZ SCHOLDER
Indian on Galloping Horse after Remington No. 2, 1976
Color lithograph
$30 \times 22\frac{1}{4}$ in.
Gift of Mr. and Mrs. Ben Q. Adams, 1979

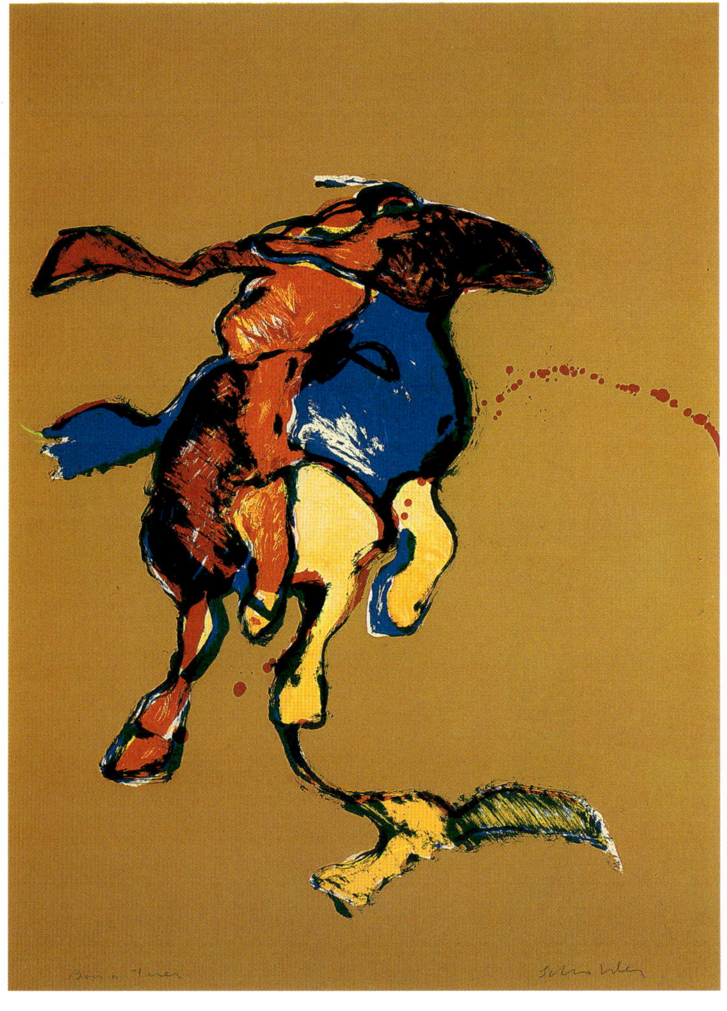

A QUARTER-INDIAN through his paternal grandmother, abstract expressionist Fritz Scholder has insistently resisted being identified as an "Indian artist" and has vocally deplored the stereotyping and commercialization of Native American culture. His first "Indian Series," painted in 1967 while he was teaching at Santa Fe's Institute for American Indian Arts, was an attempt to debunk the traditional image. It triggered a school of Native American painting in which contemporary art is used as a means of social protest and expression of cultural alienation.

In 1970, the Tamarind Institute, which had just moved from Los Angeles to Albuquerque, invited Scholder to make a series of lithographs. He found the medium suited to his bold style and produced many subsequent prints in collaboration with the institute, such as *Indian on Galloping Horse after Remington*. Loosely based on Frederic Remington's bronze *The Cheyenne*, the print's stark image of horse and rider appears to gallop forward, when viewed from the right, and to recede, when viewed from the left. Such optical games were employed by Remington in his monumental paintings.

Scholder's intentionally ambiguous title suggests that Remington led the way for such hollow, stereotypical images of the Indian brave. The artist also seems to be suggesting that the brave is pursuing Remington in revenge for his hypocritical mythologizing. In any case, this work is no tribute to the master of the Western myth.

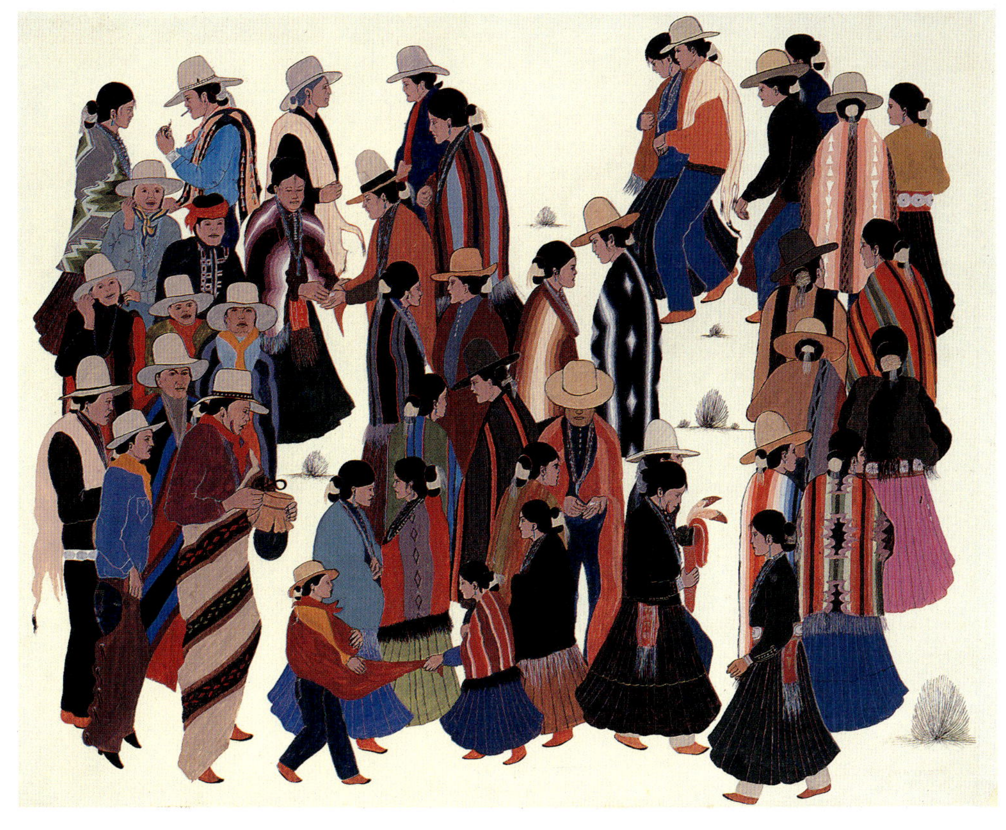

ANDY TSINNAJINNE
Navajo N'da-a', 1938
Watercolor on paper
23 × 29 in.
Gift of Dorothy Dunn Kramer, 1974

IN 1932, the Santa Fe Indian School hired Dorothy Dunn, a young woman with an art background and experience working with Navajo and Pueblo children, to teach fine art at the school—a position that prior to that time did not exist within the civil service. The following year, she established the now celebrated "Studio School" of Indian painting. It was the momentous beginning of a movement of easel painting by Native Americans. The young artists were encouraged to express aspects of their cultural heritage in their art. Paintings depicted ceremonial dances and everyday activities in a style that relied upon flat, silhouetted patterns painted with opaque watercolors. This artistic approach was passed on to generations of students who often found a market for their works among anthropologists, government agencies, tourists, and eventually art collectors.

Navajo artist Andy Tsinnajinne was a student of Dorothy Dunn and a graduate of the Santa Fe Indian School. His long career as a painter has spanned six decades and evolved through several stylistic changes. *Navajo N'da-a'* represents the artist's finest work dating from his studio school experience. It portrays the Squaw Dance, which takes place over the nine days of the Enemy Way healing ceremony.

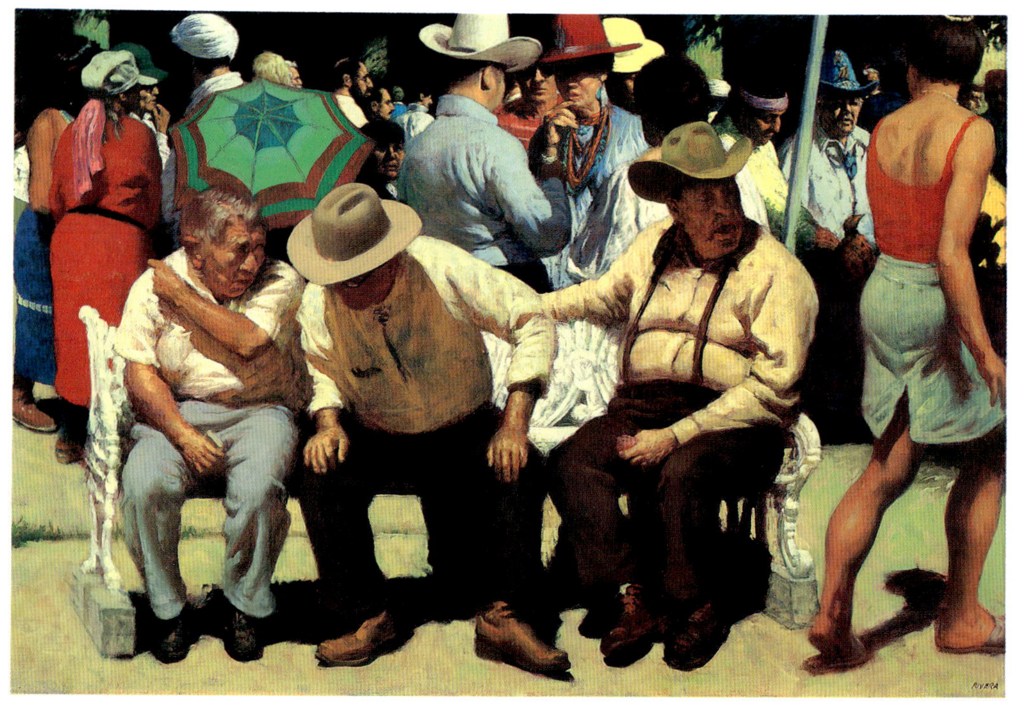

NEW YORK REALIST Elias Rivera attended the Art Students League in the late 1950s when abstract expressionism was dominating art history. However, he chose, instead, to follow the tradition of genre painting many hundreds of years old, following in the footsteps of Robert Henri, John Sloan, and so many others.

In New York, he focused his realism on subway life and street life, like a modern-day Daumier, and on occasion on distant social concerns, as in the race riots depicted in the painting *Birmingham, Alabama*.

In New Mexico, where he moved in 1982, Rivera's social realism turned to the community at hand and to the beauty the maturing artist now concerns himself with.

ELIAS RIVERA
Santa Fe Fiesta, 1984
Oil on canvas
20 × 30 in.
Gift of the Aviation Materials Management, 1987

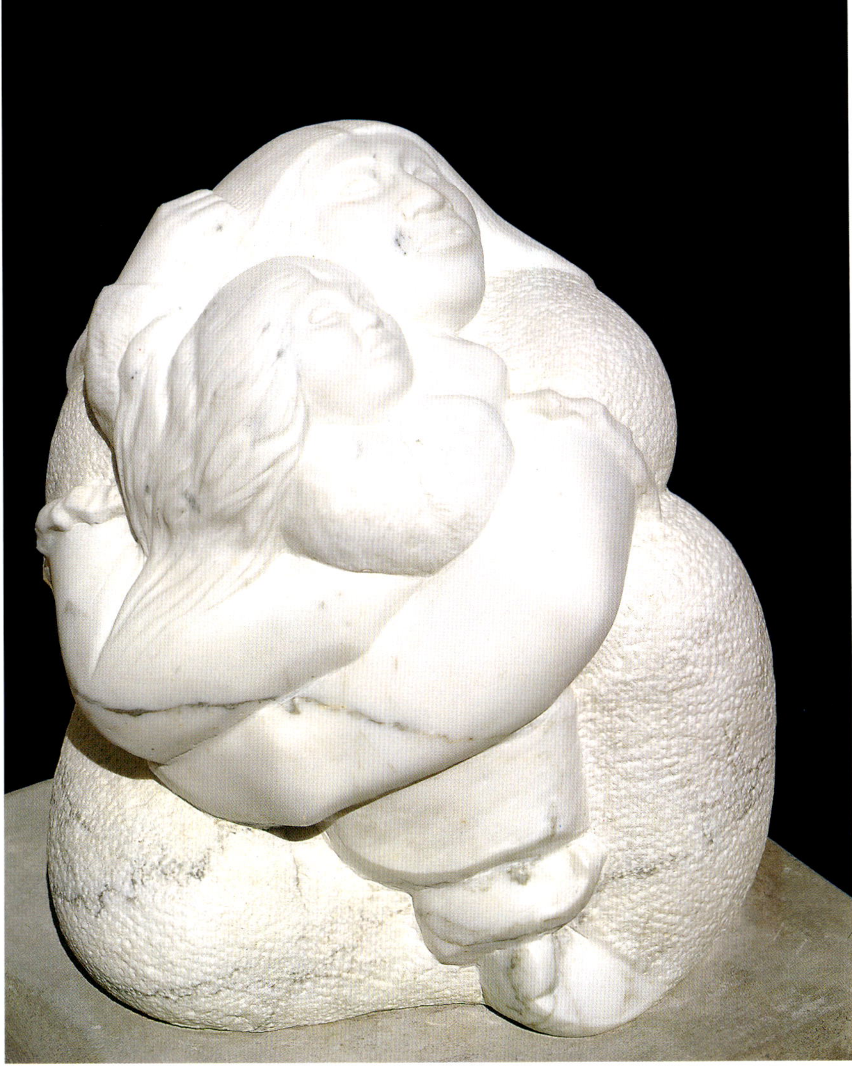

ALLAN HOUSER
Apache Mother, ca. 1970–75
Marble
20¼ × 18 × 12 in.
Museum purchase with a grant from the National Endowment for the Arts, 1975

A CHIRICAHUA APACHE born in Oklahoma, Houser established sculpture as an acceptable medium for contemporary Native American artists, elevating it beyond its regional status to the highest levels of international recognition. He began his career as a painter, trained by Dorothy Dunn at the Santa Fe Indian School. The Museum of Fine Arts hosted Houser's first solo show in 1937. In the 1940s, he began carving small wooden sculptures, receiving his first federal commission in 1948, a war memorial honoring Indian soldiers killed in World War II. By 1960, he had devoted himself exclusively to sculpture. Houser was also a dedicated and inspiring teacher, working at Indian schools in the Southwest from 1942 until 1975. He was a founding faculty member of the Institute for American Indian Arts in Santa Fe and for four years was director of the sculpture department he founded in 1971.

Throughout his career, Houser has created many variations on the theme of mother embracing child. *Apache Mother* typifies this area of the artist's work in its static quality, juxtaposition of areas of contrasting textures, and minimal manipulation of the stone's natural form. All extraneous detail is eliminated, giving the faces the archaic quality of Olmec masks. Transcending ethnicity, these figures evoke the power and pathos of a universal human bond.

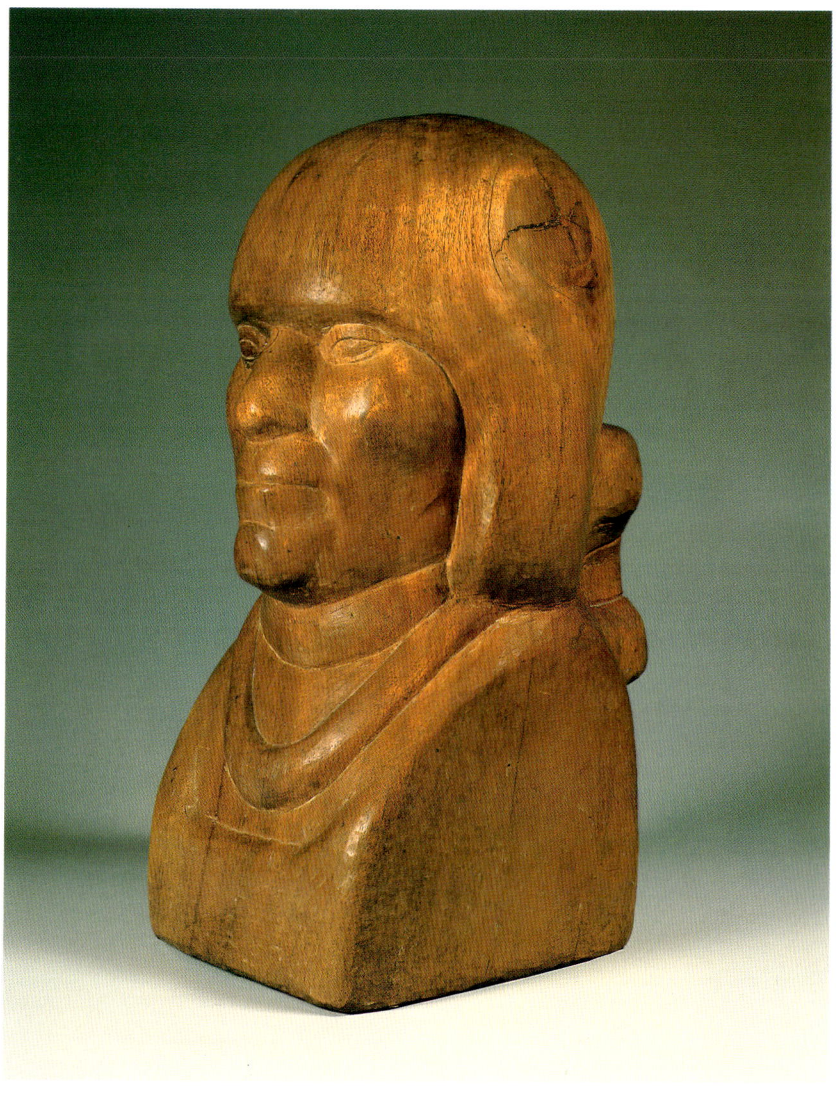

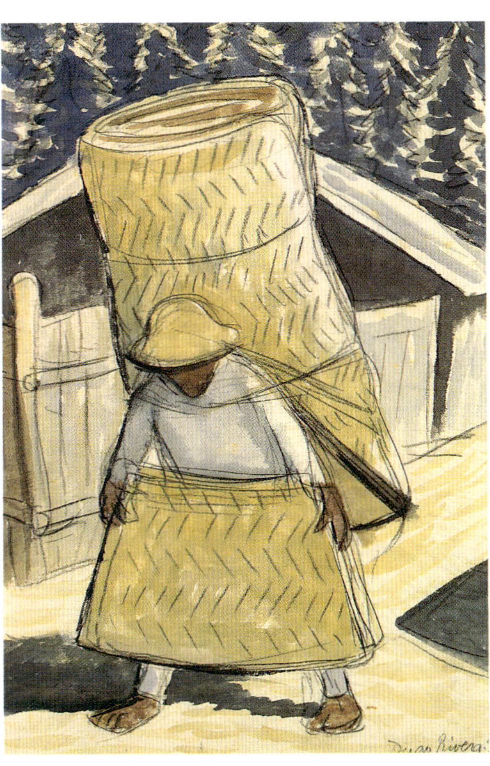

DIEGO RIVERA
Untitled (Man with Straw Mat and Rolls), 1934
Watercolor on paper
15 × 10½ in.
From the Estate of Joan Cady Sartorius, 1991

FEW TWENTIETH-CENTURY artists have been as influential as Mexican painter Diego Rivera. His leftist political views, concentrated upon issues of class struggle in Mexico, Russia, Europe, and the United States, as well as his many public commissions in these countries, made him a hero for the working class and an easy target for the new industrialists. Among his admirers, some favored his politically charged murals while others preferred his more decorative portraits of Mexican families and customs.

During the mid-1920s and 1930s, Rivera came to prominence for murals whose monumental, classical figures set a new international standard for large-scale public works. He simultaneously in this period completed a large body of work in both oils and watercolors that focused on Mexican peasants, children, and marketplaces, among which this piece is characteristic. His easel and paper work provided Rivera with a measure of financial stability and doubtless a degree of emotional relief from the more technically demanding and controversial murals.

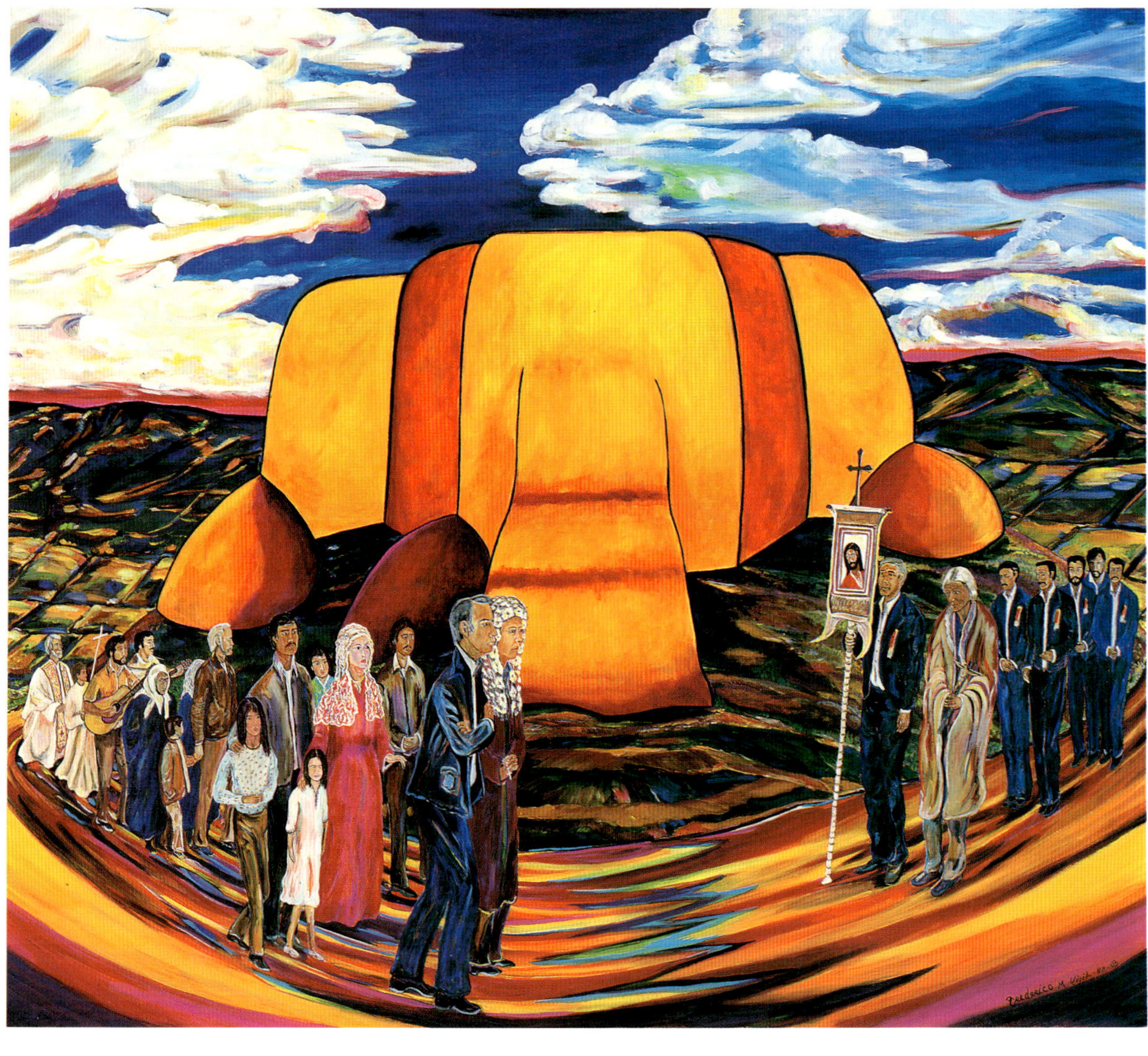

THE TRADITIONAL HISPANIC folk art of the *santero*, one who renders images of saints in two-dimensional paintings (*retablos*) and three-dimensional carvings (*bultos*), is influencing a growing number of contemporary artists who are attempting to bridge the span between past and present. Vigil's first paintings in the early 1960s, executed on wood and tin, were copies of the *retablos* in the churches of New Mexico's Mora County. His art has continued to reflect his Hispanic heritage. In his only formal training, Vigil has most recently studied fresco painting with Stephen Dmitroff and Lucienne Bloch, former assistants of Diego Rivera.

During the 1980s, Vigil embarked on an ambitious ongoing series of large canvases, "Funciones: Communal Ceremonies of Hispanic Life," in which he depicts baptisms, processions, burials, and *bailes* from rural New Mexico life. *Encuentro en Ranchos* portrays a procession in front of Ranchos de Taos Church, where the *hermanos*, members of the Penitente Brotherhood, carrying their banner of the suffering Christ, meet the families of the Orthodox Catholic church. The painting expresses a solemn joining of two extremes within the Catholic church.

FREDERICO VIGIL
Encuentro en Ranchos, 1982
Oil on canvas
36 × 42 in.
Anonymous gift, 1986

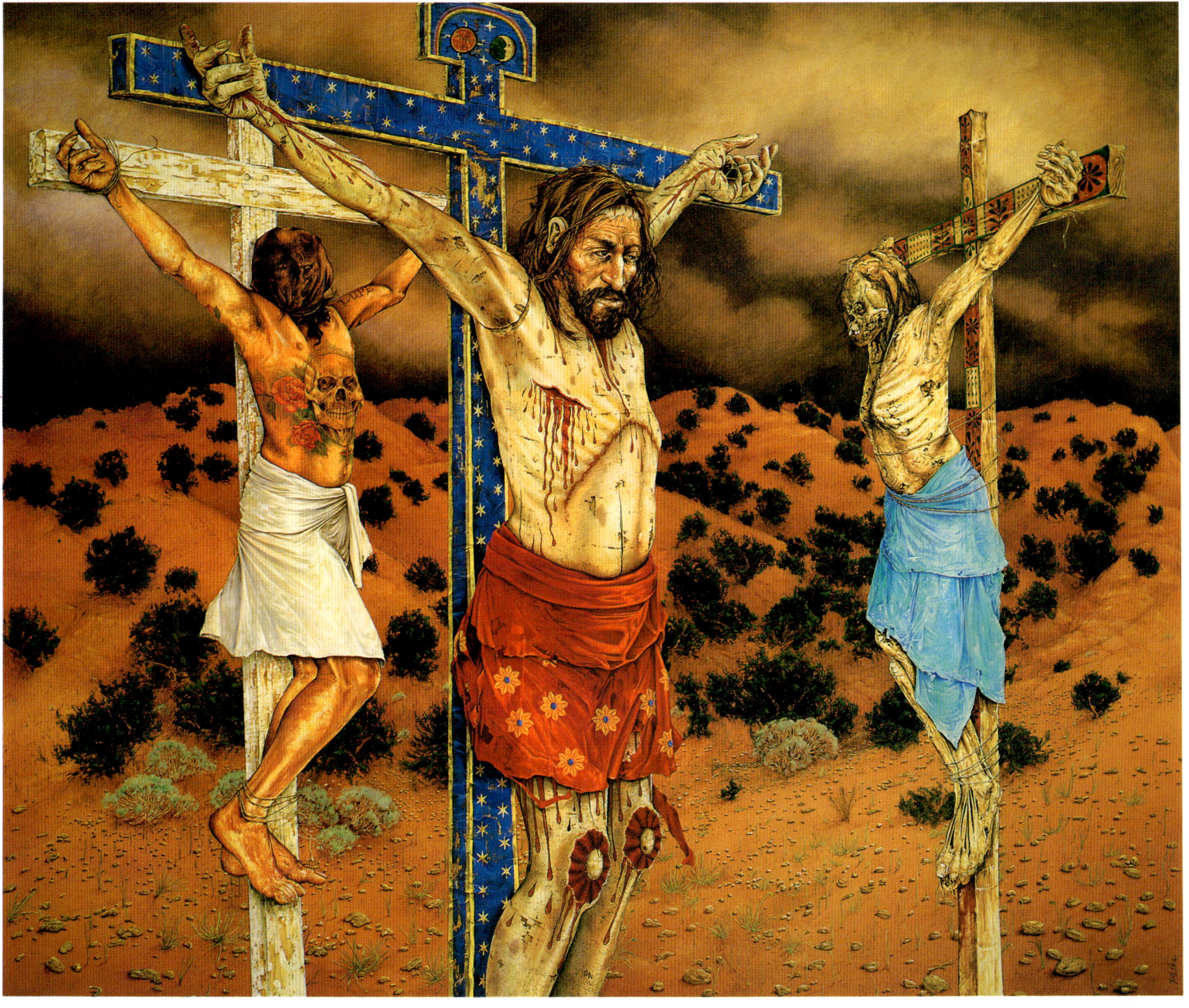

PAUL PLETKA
Los Hermanos at Sangre de Cristo,
1987
Acrylic on canvas
78 × 95 3/4 in.
Promised gift of Dr. Luther W. Brady

PLETKA PAINTS in the tradition of inspired realism. Fascinated with cultural artifacts, especially those of the Native American and Hispanic cultures of the Southwest, he utilizes these objects as the basis of meticulous personal narratives that allude to history. Pletka's perception of cultural and historical truth, embellished with his unique interpretive slant, produces paintings of shocking realism.

In *Los Hermanos at Sangre de Cristo,* Pletka depicts a traditionally composed crucifixion scene with commanding attention to the pain and suffering of Christ and the two thieves. He adds to this a curious reference to traditional Hispanic folk art by portraying the body of Christ as part flesh, part wood, as if it has been transformed from a carved wooden *bulto.*

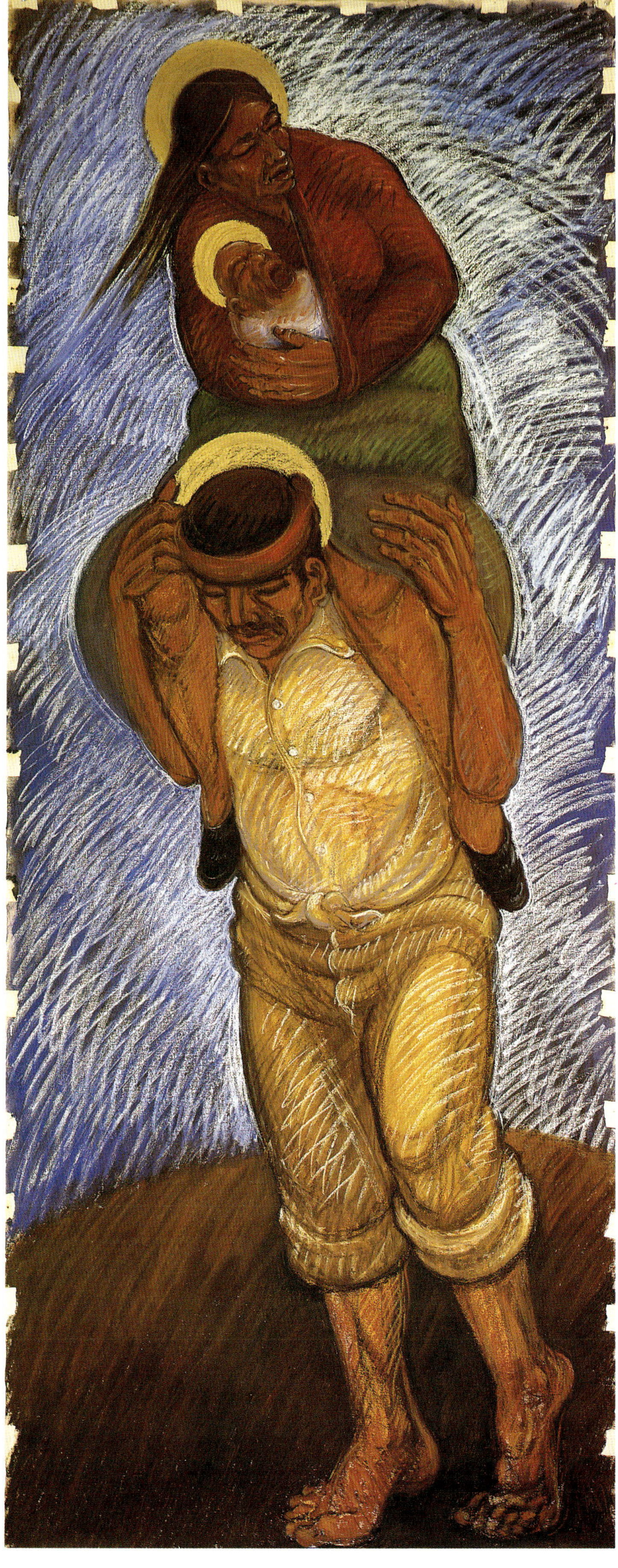

LUÍS JIMÉNEZ
Border Crossing, 1990
Oilstick on canvas
120 × 48 in.
Museum purchase, Fine Arts Acquisition Fund, 1990

LUÍS JIMÉNEZ is internationally recognized for monumental public sculptures that depict the American experience from many cultural perspectives, especially that of his own southwestern Mexican-American heritage. At the same time, his works contain references to the history of art from the Renaissance to pop art. Frederic Remington's bronze cowboys, the powerful imagery of Diego Rivera, and Rodin's *Balzac* are some of the works whose influence is evident in the popular dramas that Jiménez produces for sites throughout the United States.

The sculpture *Border Crossing* is sited in Los Angeles's MacArthur Park, the theme of which was continued in this two-dimensional work that communicates much of the intensity of the fiberglass piece. A Mexican variant on the story of Mary and Joseph, Jiménez's subject matter is enriched by the fact that the artist's Mexican-born father waded across the Rio Grande into Texas in 1922.

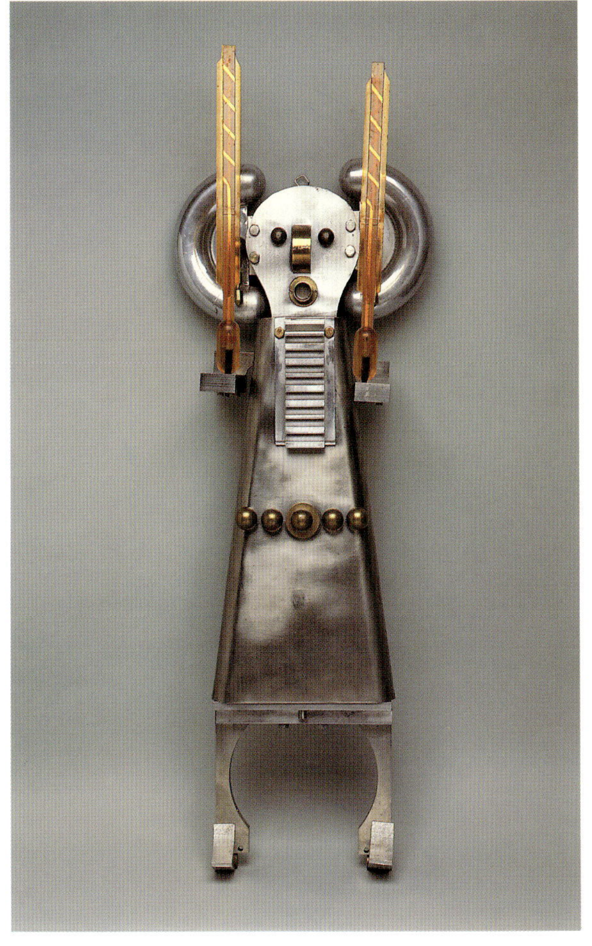

TONY PRICE
Hopi Nuclear Maiden, 1987
Metals, plastic
$34\frac{1}{4} \times 11\frac{1}{4} \times 6\frac{3}{4}$ in.
Gift of Ted and Barbara Flicker, 1988

IN THE LATE 1960s, Price discovered the Zia scrap metal yard at Los Alamos National Laboratory. He found there the metallic discards of the nation's nuclear weapons birthplace. The finely tooled metal fragments that are gathered in weekly sojourns to the facility are assembled by Price into constructions that range from masks to furniture to musical instruments to monumental totems.

Price's artistic transformation of nuclear industry waste is the outward result of a process he calls "sympathetic magic" by which the artist attempts alchemically to transmute the destructive materials into constructive art.

Hopi Nuclear Maiden, from his Native American "Kachina Mask" series, poignantly appropriates ancient images from the Hopi culture juxtaposed with materials from the nuclear weapons culture. The results have won Price a deserved place of respect in both the art and political arenas.

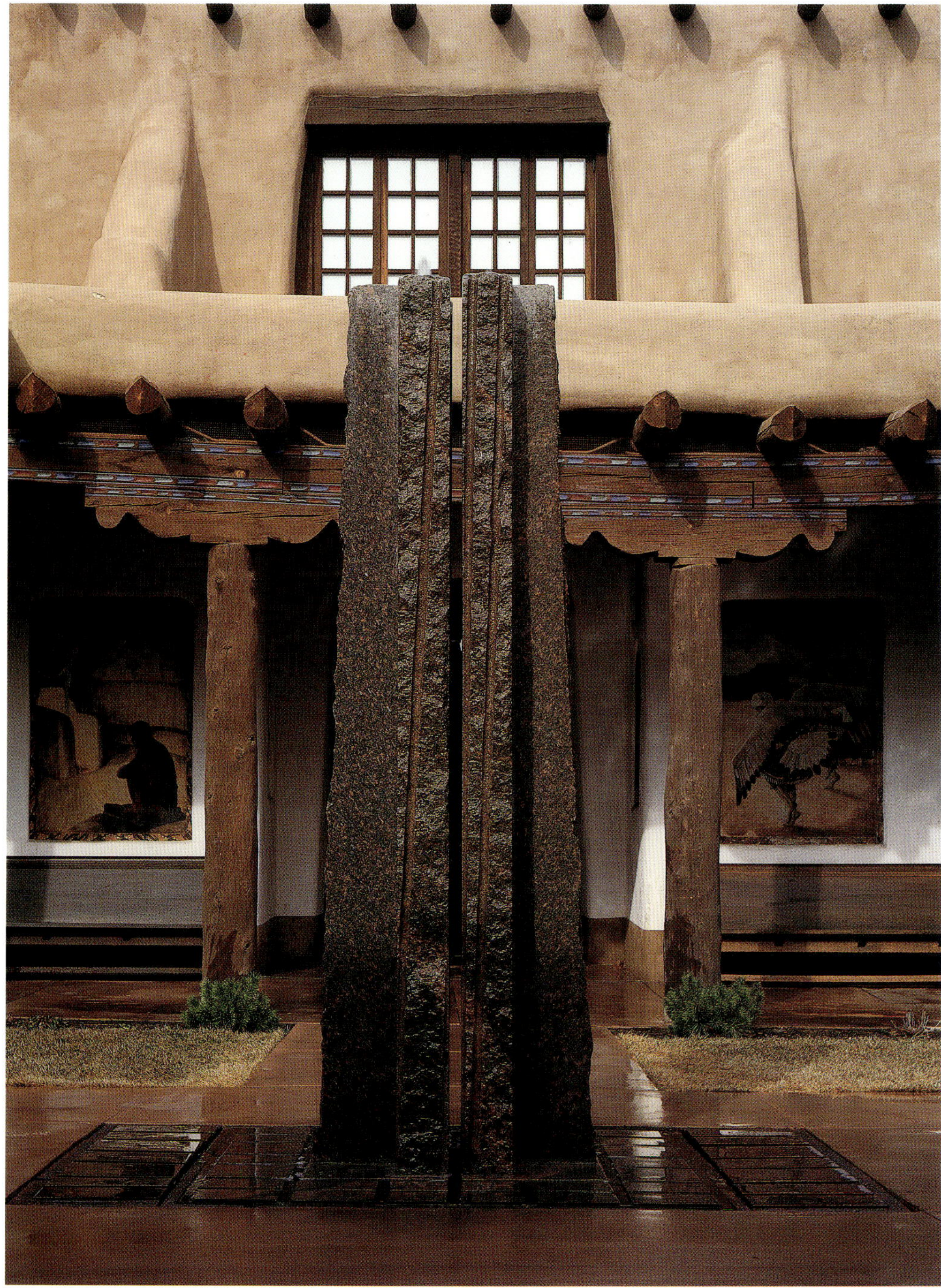

WORKING OUT OF his stonecutting shop in Rockport, Texas, equipped with many of the same tools as the expert craftsmen who carve architectural details on urban skyscrapers and personalized remembrances on family tombstones, Moroles creates sculpture for diverse sites, ranging from prime public locations in New York City to private home patios in the New Mexico hills.

Mountain Fountain is the central focus of the interior courtyard at the Museum of Fine Arts.

In this classically proportioned sculpture, the jagged edges contrast with the smooth, dark stone facades in a way that perfectly mirrors the relationship between the rough-hewn wooden columns and the smoothly curved stucco walls of the local architecture. The sculpture is simultaneously regional and universal, organic and formal, traditional and modern.

JESÚS BAUTISTA MOROLES
Mountain Fountain, 1984
Dakota granite
108 × 36 × 30 in.
Given in celebration of the marriage of Kathryn Boeckman and Peter Howd, October 12, 1985

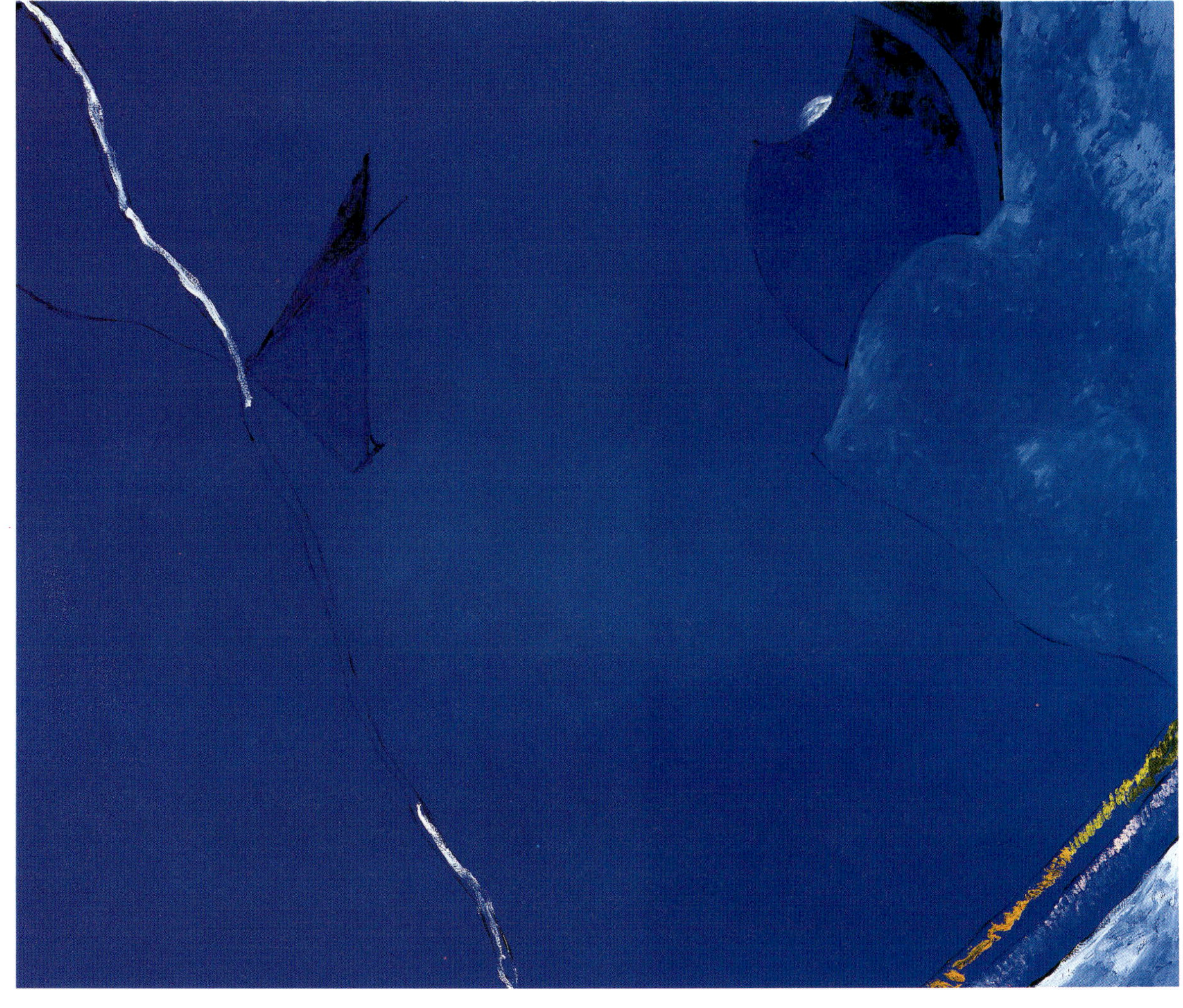

SAM SCOTT
Ax and Moon, 1977
Oil on canvas
66 × 80 in.
Gift of Dr. Thomas Jackson, 1988

THE MAN who lived with the Ogalala Sioux Indians in South Dakota and the Makiritare in the Amazon makes paintings that reveal the intense life-energy he experienced in both places. Scott's paintings reveal a restlessness and curiosity about physical and spiritual mysteries of the world. In *Ax and Moon*, energy is not created by line and form, as might be the case. Instead, energy is compressed into a space of chilling blue that threatens to overpower the viewer with its intense cosmic beauty.

About this series Scott said, "I had never faced, confronted the color blue before. I thought it would be difficult, especially living in the Southwest, to deal with a blue format and not have the paintings come out 'marine' paintings. After working awhile, the blue became a comfortable element for a space somewhere in between heaven and earth where things could happen and allusions to infinite space could be made.

"I like the idea of turning one's back on comfort," he said. "The particular thing that I'm after in these paintings is that objective, cold, ruthless beauty in the eye of a hawk–that completely uncompromising stare is the stare I want from the paintings" (from "Sam Scott" by Bill Peterson, *Artspace* 1, no. 3, Spring 1977).

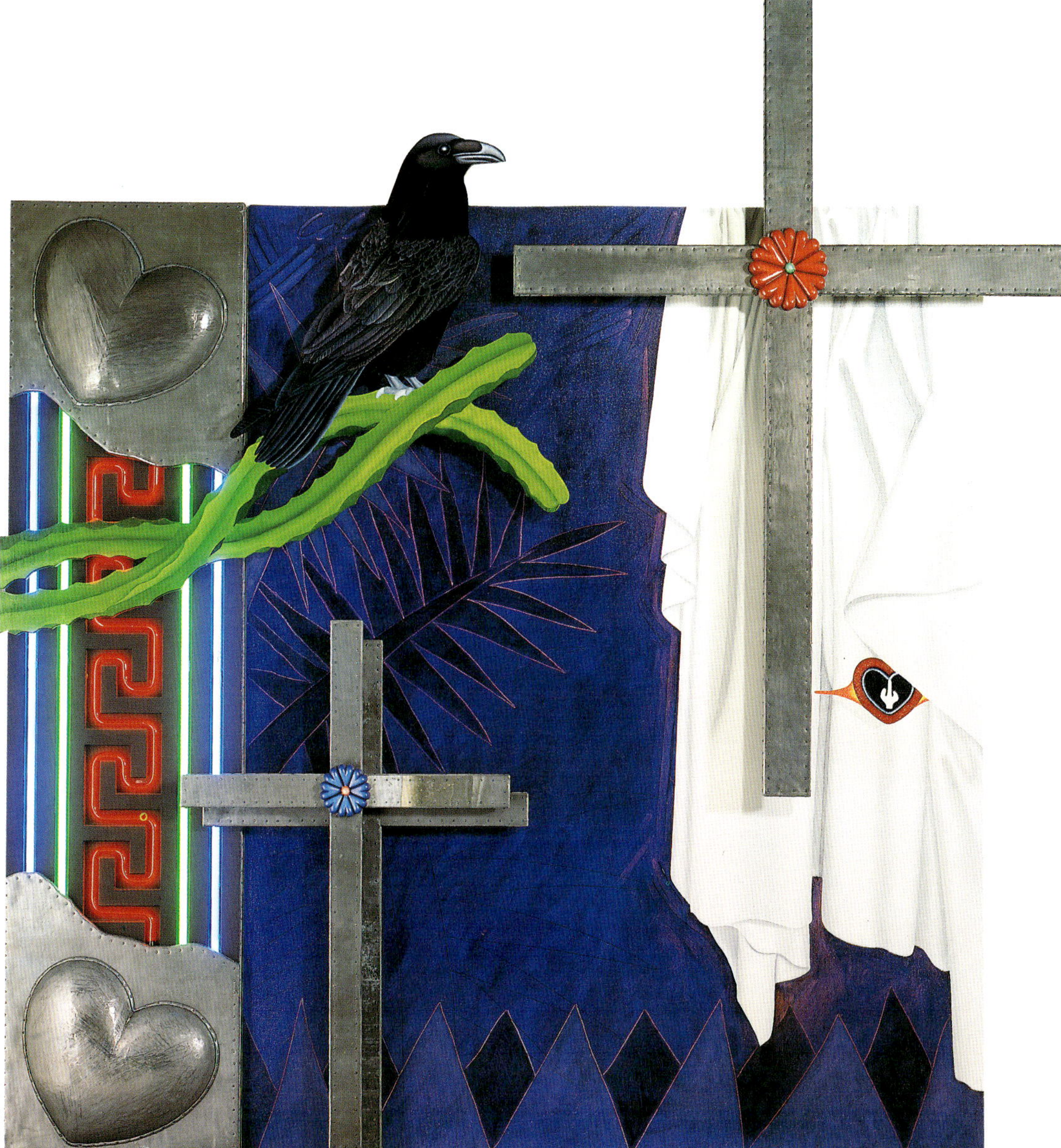

THIS PAINTING refers to the "discovery" of the Americas by Christopher Columbus. Fernandez, born in Colorado, was active in art and Chicano politics in Arizona and New Mexico in the 1970s and 1980s. During these decades, he created a large body of work that employs beauty and strong symbolism to express facets of his life as a Chicano and his love of art.

Extensive travel in Mexico inspired his imagery and educated him about the true history of the Western Hemisphere. Fernandez's work, influenced by Hispanic folk art, religious art, and his personal life, also reflects an active involvement with American culture–from abstract expressionism and pop art to realism and kitsch. It is dramatic and lush, sensual as well as symbolic.

In *1492*, Fernandez uses the symbolism of fifteenth-century Spain to reinterpret history in a nonsentimental way. The concepts of purity (the drape), loyalty (the blue), and ominous tidings (the raven) dominate. Three crosses covered with lead symbolize the Roman Catholic church and the three ships of Columbus. About the discovery of America, Fernandez said, "Nothing is all positive or negative, but so much history has been glossed over. The price paid [for European dominance of the United States] was much greater than we want to think."

RUDY FERNANDEZ
1492, 1991
Wood, lead, neon, oil on canvas
79 × 66 in.
Promised gift of Frank Ribelin, 1991

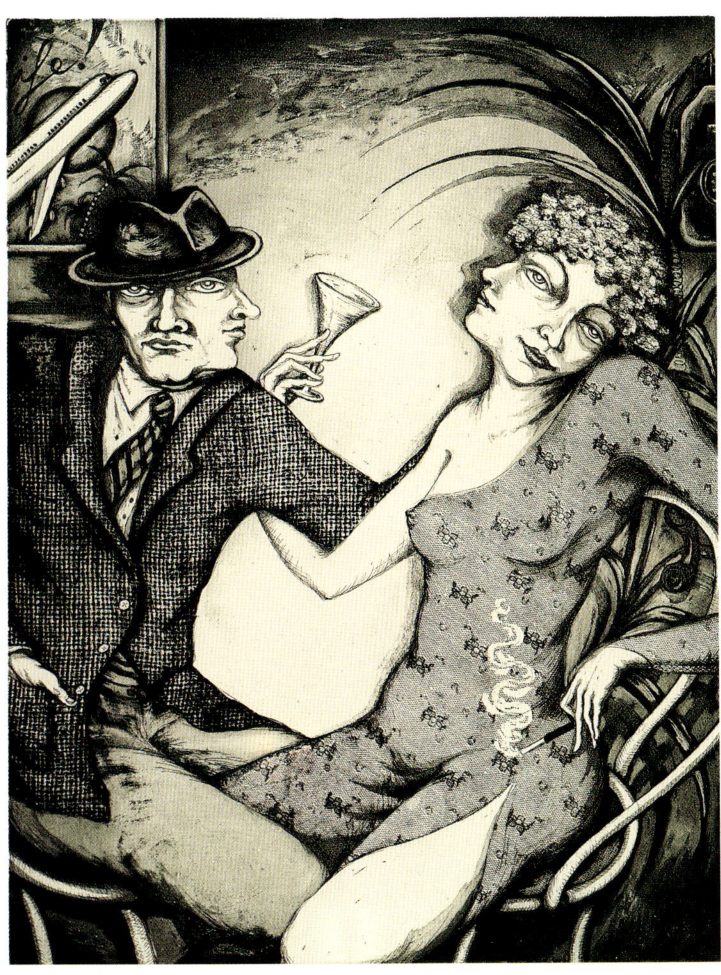

ZARA KRIEGSTEIN
Double Talk, 6/15, 1986
Hand-colored etching on paper
$17\frac{3}{4} \times 13\frac{3}{4}$ in.
Gift of Dr. Robert Bell, 1991

THE ATMOSPHERE of Berlin, Kriegstein's birthplace, is strongly suggested in all of her works, whether they be prints, paintings, or murals. The acidity and sense of evil that permeate her characters recall the work of German expressionists George Grosz and Otto Dix. Morality—or, more often, lack of morality—is Kriegstein's impassioned subject matter. To view her work is to enter the world of the cabaret, of the peasantry of Brueghel, and of Grosz's human zoo.

Kriegstein's interest in the Mexican muralists brought her to Santa Fe in the early 1980s, where she began to bring her subjects to life in mural form. Although successful as a muralist, she turned to painting and printmaking to support herself. The etching *Double Talk* expresses the artist's contempt for hypocrisy while alluding to her belief in inner transformation.

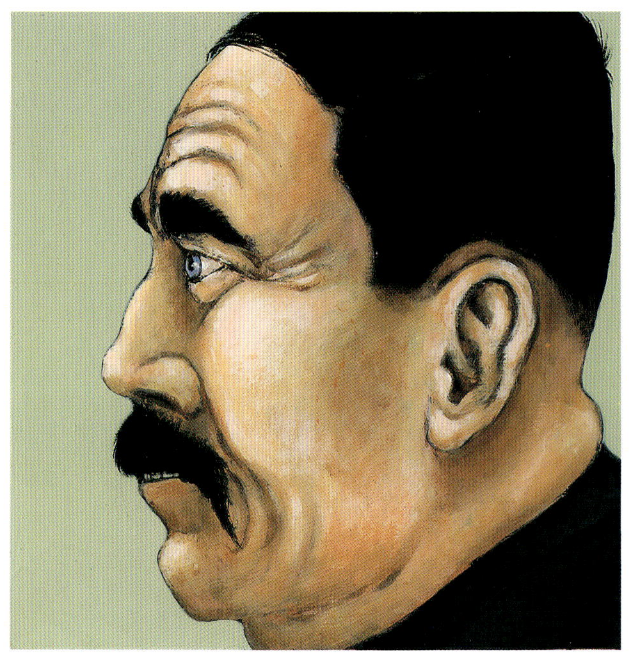

CATRON'S ROOTS lie deep in New Mexico history, beginning in 1860 when the first Catron, a lawyer, left Missouri for Santa Fe. This contemporary artist, a self-taught painter, has always lived in Santa Fe, a fact that may explain his lack of interest in depicting regional subjects that other artists have found exotic. Catron has instead turned his expressionist approach toward such "invented" portraits as is shown here.

Untitled is one of three such portraits in the museum's collection, each of which is characterized by mug-shot compositions amplified by tight cropping and a human intensity that recalls the Flemish and northern European treatments of the figure by such artists as Hans Holbein and Lucas Cranach. In the era of contemporary art, they resemble the psychological portraits of Lucien Freud and Alice Neel. As in their works, Catron's portraits have a palpable paint surface that adds physicality to image, and the images themselves are not straightforward portraits but penetrating psychological documents that reveal the inner while concealing the outer reality. Through distortion of form, Catron implies distortion of the psyche in a way that leaves us wondering whether all people possess a slightly monstrous dimension.

STEVE CATRON
Untitled, 1981
Oil on Masonite
$11^{13}/_{16} \times 11^{13}/_{16}$ in.
Gift of Lew and Lynn Pollock, 1990

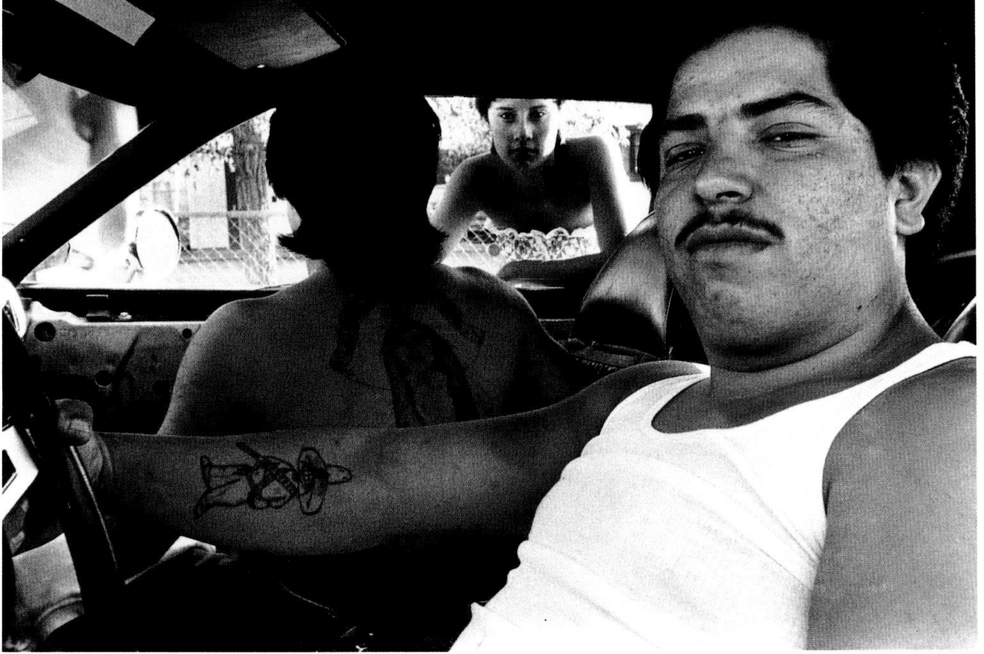

MIGUEL GANDERT
Melissa Armijo, Eloy Montoya, and Richard "El Wino" Madrid
Albuquerque, 1983
Selenium-toned gelatin silver photograph
$12\frac{5}{8} \times 17\frac{7}{8}$ in.
New Mexico Photographic Survey Collection, funded by a grant from the National Endowment for the Arts, 1985

MIGUEL GANDERT'S cinematic portraits of Albuquerque's South Valley depict people through likeness to their environment. In his work, surroundings are an important means of revealing character. As a significant element in the social landscape, the automobile is a place for human interaction outside of stationary establishments. The movable environment provides the means to search, as cultural geographer John Jackson writes, for "identity in other ways."

To the three youths in this photograph, the automobile is an interior culture of independent values and substitutes for the external society of family and home. As a symbol of mobility, the vehicle is the means to explore those values. The relationship of these youths to the vehicle helps to define their identity as individuals. The participation of the photographer acts as catalyst to personal revelation. "The process of self-definition cannot go on by itself," continues Jackson. "It is a dialogue, not a monologue."

The identities of these youths are expressed through their gestures toward the camera. Status is suggested by their tattoos, as well as by the car. The importance of the automobile in defining identity has become a fundamental fact of modern culture.

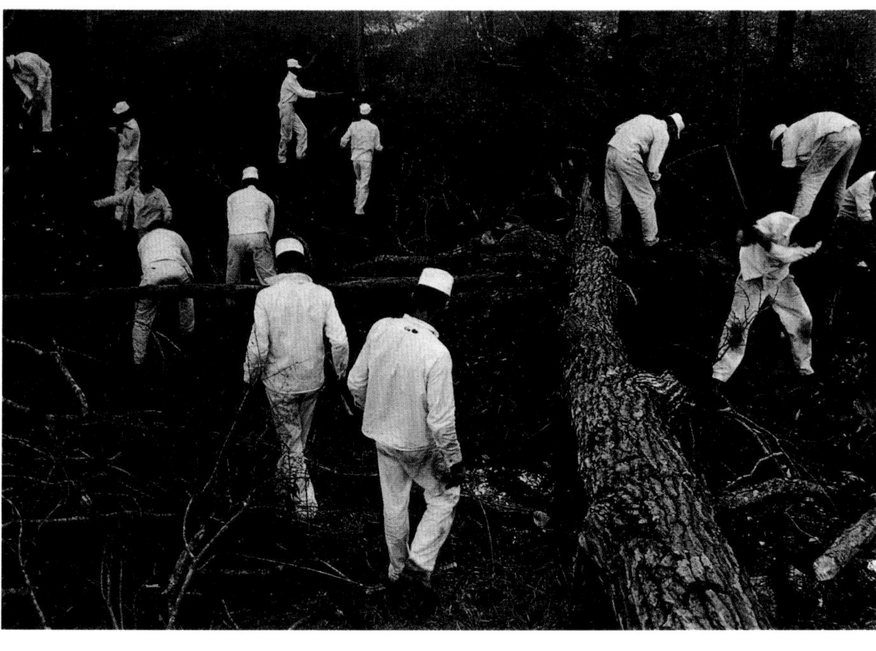

DOCUMENTARY PHOTOGRAPHY reveals, without fabrication, the human condition. As well, the artist's direct participation transcends language and allows a deeper message to be conveyed in visual terms; imagination imbues the human situation with poignancy.

In 1967, Danny Lyon was given permission to photograph freely within the prisons of Texas. For more than a year, he photographed life in six individual prison units within the system. The project, including letters and drawings by inmate Bill McCune, was published two years later as the book *Conversations with the Dead*.

The Ellis Unit, near Huntsville, was one of the toughest prison farms within the system and the place where the most dangerous convicts were sent. These convicts were assigned to farm labor teams that worked daily in the fields.

In the image of *Ellis Unit*, there is irony in the pure white clothing of the figures who work without remorse in an abyss. Light filtered from trees above offers little comfort, and the gigantic fallen tree with broken branches seems to parallel the plight of the inmate workers.

In the overall arrangement of independent gestures of these human forms, there remains a rigorous order. Are we being reminded that individual freedom exists only within the regulations of a system? This image does not make a statement about harsh punishment; it addresses the human condition and the society that enforces prison reform.

DANNY LYON
Ellis Unit, 1968
Gelatin silver photograph
11 × 14 in.
Gift of Andrew Smith, 1990

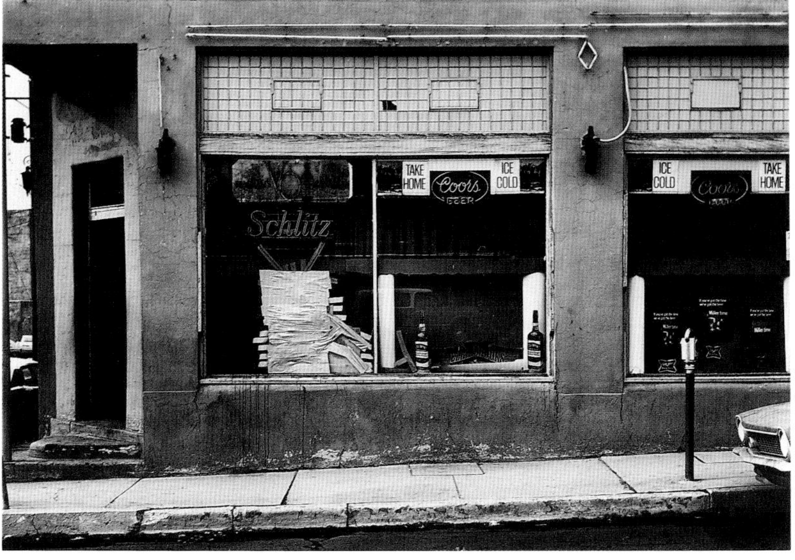

LEWIS BALTZ
Santa Fe, New Mexico, 1972
Gelatin silver photograph
$6\frac{1}{16} \times 9\frac{1}{8}$ in.
Gift of the artist, 1985

PERHAPS Lewis Baltz made only one photograph while traveling through New Mexico in 1972 because conditions in the region did not correspond to the major focus of his work: the transformation of the western United States by large developments and commercial investments. Similar changes would not encroach on the "land of enchantment" for another decade. What makes an artist select a related but unintegrated part of a body of work is always open to interpretation. Such tangential subject matter may foster ideas pertinent to the artist's principal focus and can be developed by pursuing them.

In *Santa Fe, New Mexico*, Baltz depicts Angelo's Bar in Santa Fe, which remains one of the few reminders that Santa Fe was once a small town without anticipation of imminent change or growth. The surgical bandage repair of the large broken windowpane has a metaphorical association with what Baltz saw happening to the western landscape. This photograph expresses a balance of formal and historical concerns that suggests the ironies of past and present.

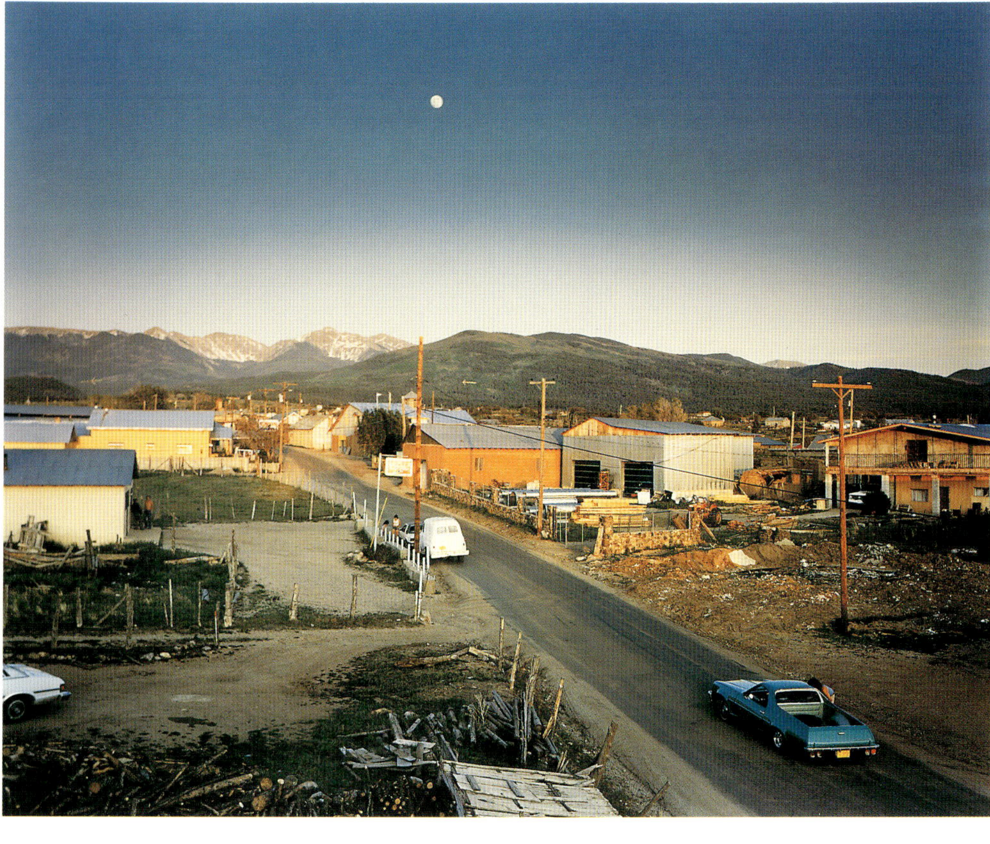

TRUCHAS, a portrait of a village in northern New Mexico, expresses a collective identity focusing on the cultural landscape. The cultural landscape conveys human values and meaning through individuals as well as through the interactions of people. It allows for discovery of our past and present identity. In the village of Truchas, tradition is tied to contemporary currents; life exists here as a vital form of self-sufficiency, much as it did at the time the first Hispanic travelers settled in the seventeenth century. The photograph evokes a sense of constancy perhaps amplified by the full moon in the center of the sky. Yet the cars and other trappings of contemporary life, as well as the photographer's use of color to depict the scene, give the image a modern feeling.

ALEX HARRIS
Truchas, June 1982
Ektacolor photograph
$14\frac{13}{16} \times 18\frac{3}{4}$ in.
New Mexico Photographic Survey Collection, funded by a grant from the National Endowment for the Arts, 1985

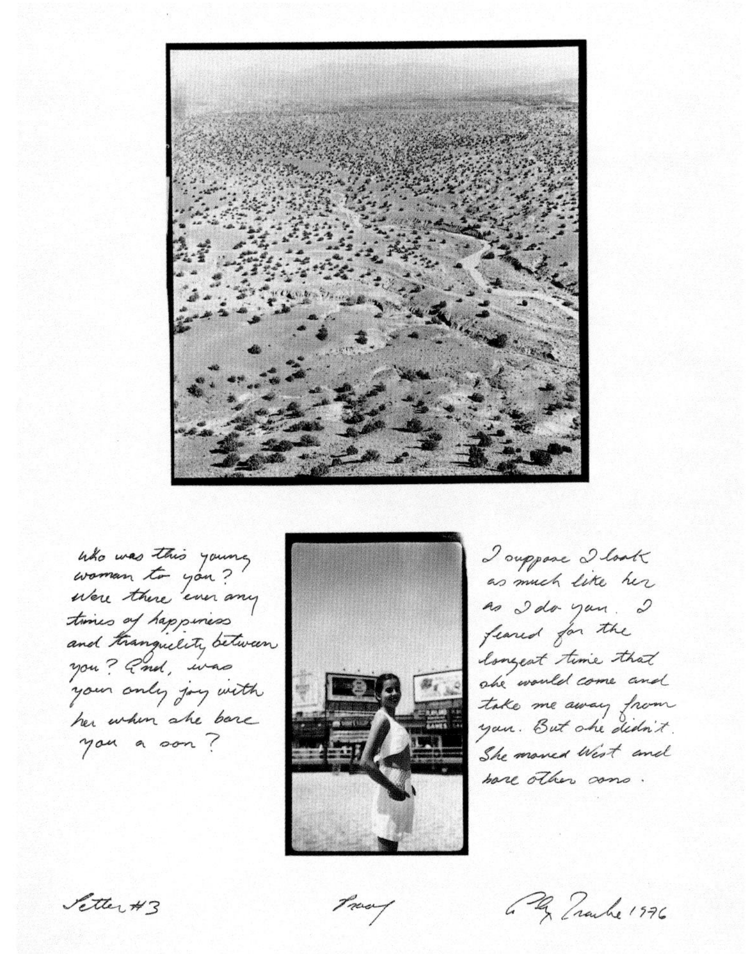

ALEX TRAUBE
Letters to My Father, Letter No. 3,
1976
Gelatin silver photograph montage
$13\frac{15}{16} \times 10\frac{7}{8}$ in.
Gift of Celia Rumsey, 1982

ALEX TRAUBE combines the snapshots of his family's childhood with his own photographs to express ideas that create a poetic bridge of history. This picture of his mother in her early years coupled with the landscape in which he now lives are joined with his own writing to his father. The artist's alliance of words and pictures is a personal revelation.

Present and past, child and parents, sandy boardwalk, beach, and arid New Mexico landscape offer new dimensions relating personal histories. The viewer becomes an active element with the sentiments that evoke intimate combinations of materials on personal and formal levels.

Traube's extended word portraits are a provocative hybrid. They sustain a mixture of reality and fiction that prompts the mind to rekindle experience while activating the imagination. Language and camera create life and present a universal theater for both audience and actors.

THE MASTERS of contemporary photography fully recognize the potential use of photographic imagery not originated by the artist. Early in the twentieth century, photographs made by anonymous sources were instrumental in key art movements. From the German dadaist use of photomontage by such figures as John Heartfield to the Russian avant-garde experiments with photocollage by artists such as El Lissitzky, there is a rich history of the use of photographic imagery by complex artistic means. More recently, American artists such as Robert Rauschenberg and Robert Heinecken have rekindled such explorations, incorporating photographs from magazines and electronic media into their works.

The associations within the pages of Paula Hocks's handmade books are even more divergent. The combination of fragments of sentences and photographs gleaned from a variety of sources creates enigmatic images. She unites materials in collages, then melds them by making single color reproductions (Xerox) on selected papers that are then bound in sequence. The subject of *Etruscan Lunches* is process, the relation of the photographic image and the printed word to reality, especially when they are combined in new ways that separate them from their original sources. Hocks has said: "How can this new thing, while it willfully cuts itself off from its origin in nature . . . establish its authenticity? What is the nature of its relation to the world . . . and not the imagined world from which it originally came?" The reader is motivated through the visual experience of turning such pages to discover more than one answer.

PAULA HOCKS
Etruscan Lunches, 1/25, 1979
Handmade book, collage, and color xerography, limited edition
$9\frac{1}{8} \times 10$ in.
Gift of the artist, 1990

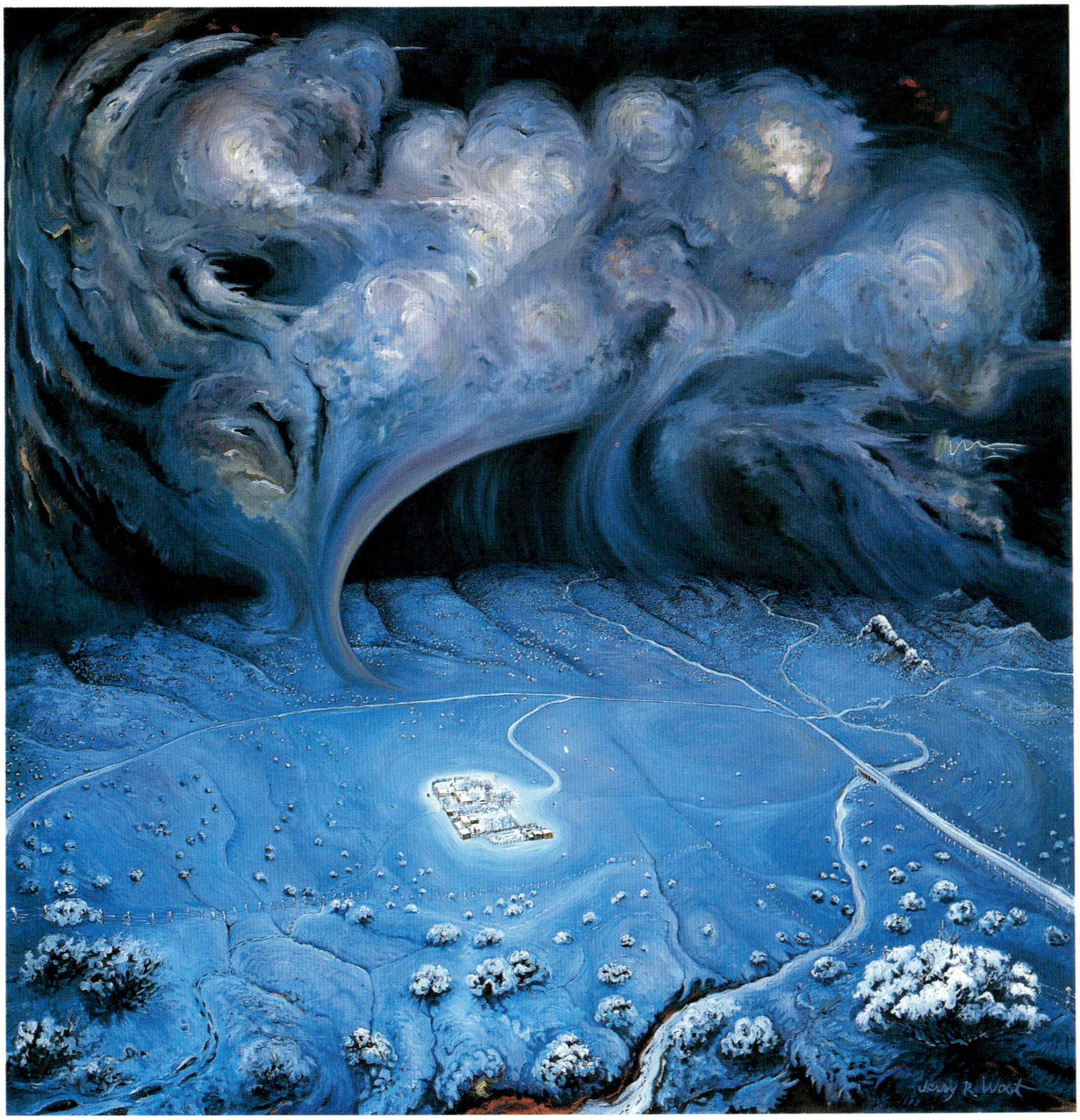

JERRY WEST
Prairie Winter with Approaching Cosmic Storm, 1989
Oil on canvas
71 × 75 in.
Gift of Ray Graham, 1991

JERRY WEST has said, "To be born on the prairie means to wander all your life, always being pulled back. It means accident, incident, drama, movement. It always means dream." West, born in Ohio and raised outside Santa Fe, is the son of a subsistence farmer and painter. He was educated in New Mexico and Colorado and became a visionary chronicler of the unfolding human drama of the area. His [Santa Fe] City Hall mural, *Recuerdos y Sueños de Santa Fe*, 1989, reveals a commitment to community and a natural love of storytelling.

At mid-career, West began to explore the dark and light sides of his personal history in "Prairie Night," a series that focuses on human vulnerability as a central theme. Specific scenes bring to mind influences as diverse as Albrecht Dürer, Grant Wood, Francisco Goya, and even American animation classics. West's works also present an urgent ecological commentary. They tell of the vulnerability of the entire planet and its people. In *Prairie Winter*, it is quite evident that the approaching storm is not simply a threatening rainstorm but indeed has cosmic dimensions. The painting, in fact, was executed in the land where the Los Alamos National Scientific Laboratory underground nuclear storage facilities and the White Sands test site make the notion of a cosmic storm something more than a fairy tale.

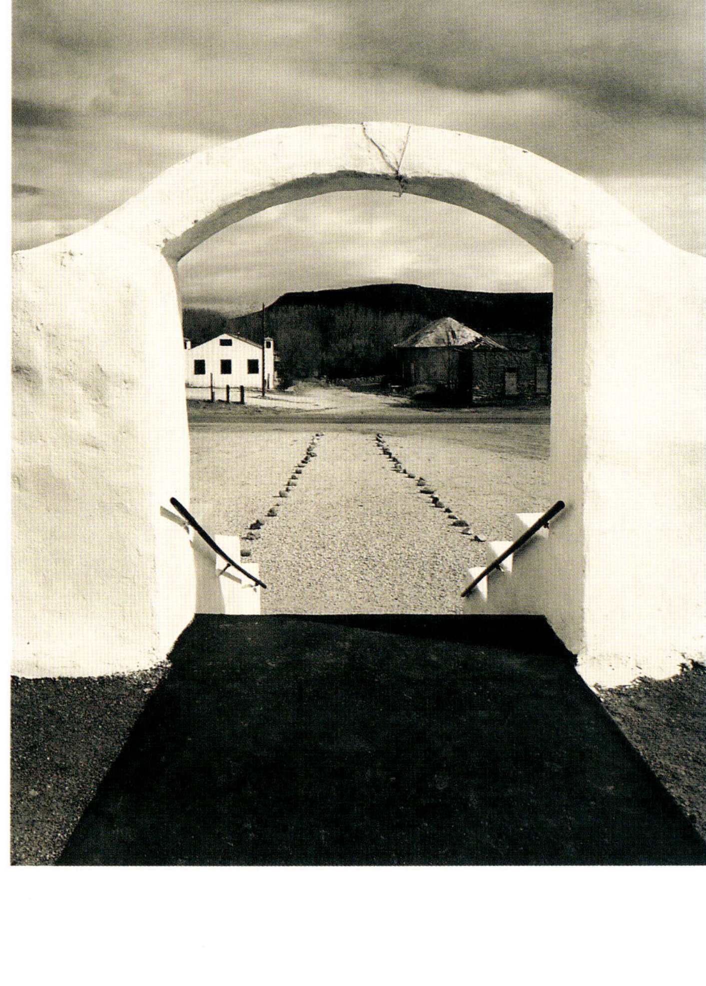

IN HER QUEST to reconstruct a vision of the Santa Fe Trail of the previous century from its present remnants, Joan Myers combines a modern eye with a historical sensibility. Before the railroad displaced this famous trade route in 1880, monuments of pioneer life existed from Franklin, Missouri, to Santa Fe. Today, only vestiges of villages and structures remain to recall the lives of the generations of earlier travelers who shaped the evolution of the Southwest.

How does a photographer convey a sense of the past through what remains in the present? To address this problem, Myers studied history by reading journals of the times, guidebooks, early maps, and other accounts before she began the photographic project. Over a period of years, she followed what was left of the trail, capturing existing images and writing notes. In *San Miguel, New Mexico*, it is the traveler who sees through the mission gates the rock-lined path that points through the village into the landscape. By depicting a path toward the unfamiliar, and a journey to the unknown, the photographer successfully conveys a heightened sense of history and exploration.

JOAN MYERS
San Miguel, New Mexico, 1982
Platinum-palladium photograph with hand-coloring
13 × 10 5/16 in.
New Mexico Photographic Survey Collection, funded by a grant from the National Endowment for the Arts, 1985

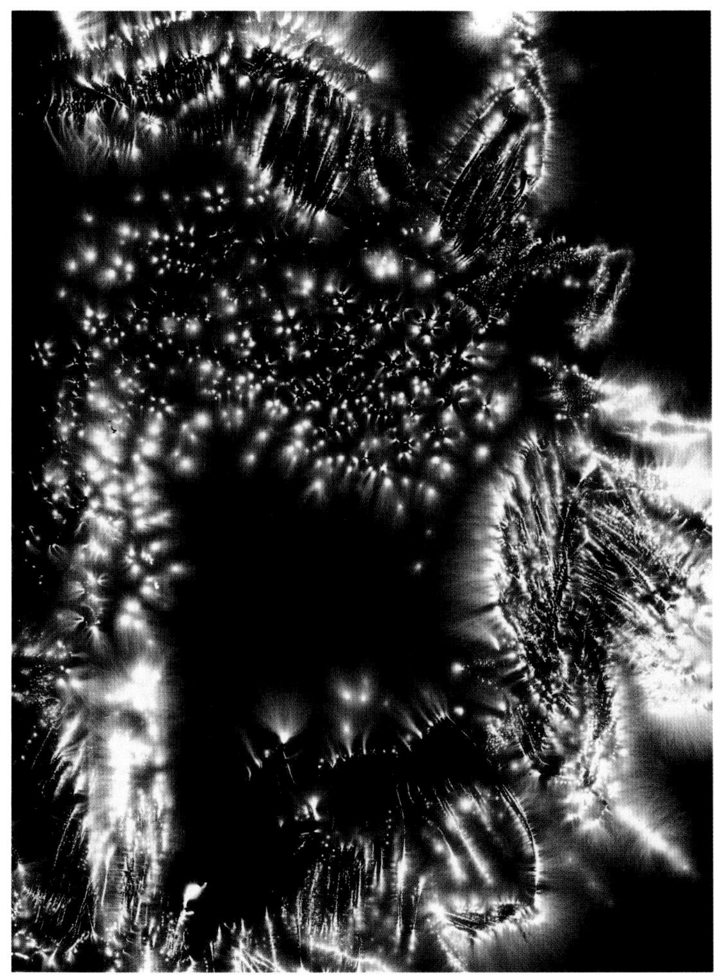

WALTER CHAPPELL
Metaflora, 1976
Gelatin silver photograph
19 × 13¼ in.
Gil Hitchcock Collection, 1988

SINCE ITS INVENTION, photography has engendered many innovations. Henry Fox Talbot, the English inventor, wrote about the scientific implications in the February 2, 1939, issue of the *Literary Gazette*: "The art of photogenic drawing," as he described it, was the "forming of pictures and images of material objects by means of solar light." By the time of this announcement, scientists had begun applying the new process to other physical means of transformation such as "thermometric, barometric and magnetic variations."

While the visible world was the most immediate subject for the camera, experimentation created other kinds of photographic imagery. In the twentieth century, Alfred Stieglitz offered expressive alternatives that metaphorically extended the meaning of photographs. Pictures of trees or clouds conveyed inner truths and realities that went beyond their surface textures.

In 1974, Walter Chappell began using parts of the natural garden, an endearing subject of his childhood, to make camera-less photographs. By exposing the electromagnetic currents of nature onto photographic negatives, imagery invisible to the eye was turned into tangible abstract forms. Fields of energy within living things have their own light-bearing architecture. Chappell transformed these photographically into metaphysical statements of mysterious luminescence.

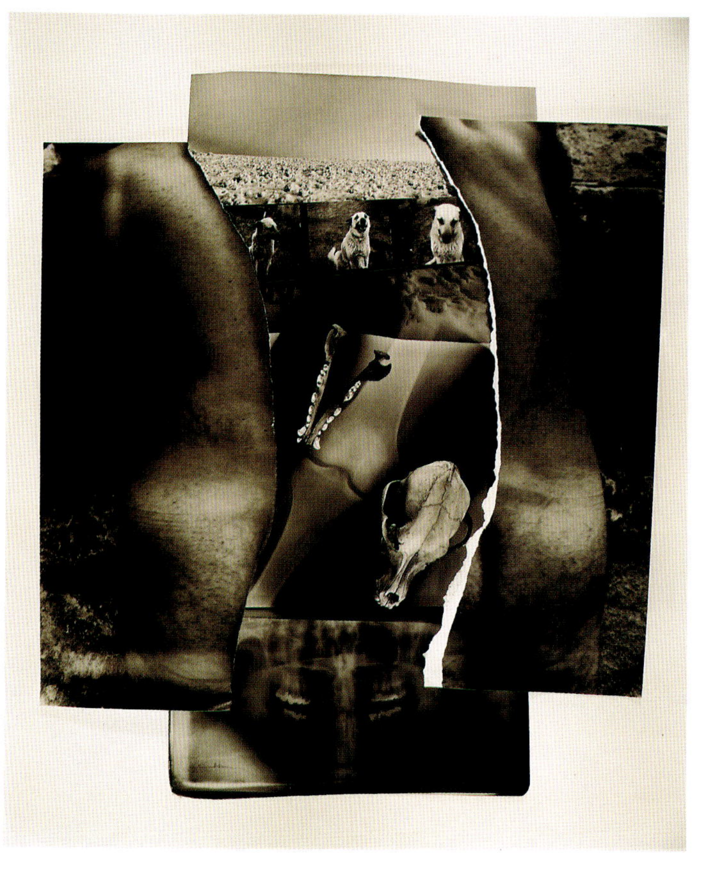

MERIDEL RUBENSTEIN's investigation of truth takes on the dimensions of southwestern mythology. Metaphor emerges through photographic composites. Familiar images from past and present activate our individual remembrance, and we know these fragments of reality; new combinations of imagery, therefore, act on our subconscious.

In *Call of the Wild*, pictures of torn pictures rephotographed suggest the reality of the mind, where imagination dissolves limitations. This landscape holds a power that transforms rigid perceptions into a modern, poetic world. Historic structure and meaning occur through juxtaposition. This photographic montage stresses relations, forms of content, and the content of forms.

MERIDEL RUBENSTEIN
Call of the Wild, 1984–85
Platinum photograph montage
$16\frac{1}{8} \times 13\frac{3}{4}$ in.
Gil Hitchcock Collection

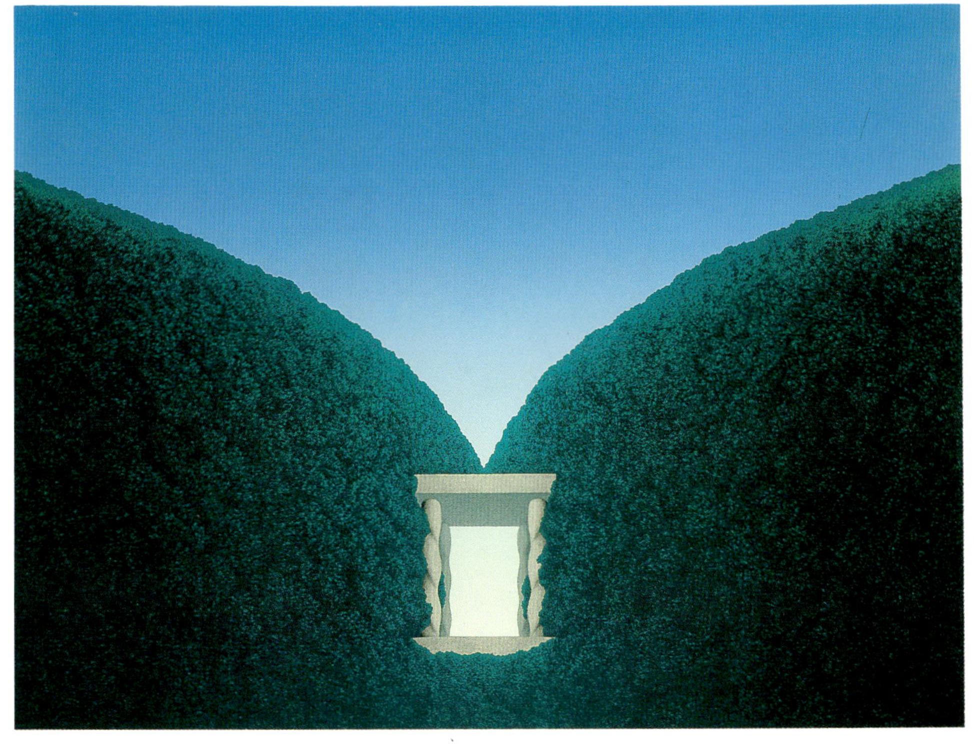

BRUCE LOWNEY
Gateway, 1975
Color lithograph
19 × 26 in.
Gift of John B. Metzenberg, 1976

AFTER ARRIVING IN New Mexico from his native California, Bruce Lowney studied lithography at the University of New Mexico under Garo Antreasian, influential lithographer and teacher. Exceptionally skilled in the lifelike precision of lithographic technique, Lowney is equally at ease with the use of oils in painting, creating magical, mystical landscapes such as *Gateway* that are simultaneously realistic and surrealistic in vision.

A solitary man, Lowney works in a boxcar studio on the 160-acre ranch in El Moro, New Mexico, called the "Peace and Quiet," which provides the open space and tranquility necessary for his work. Concerned with modern mythologies, Lowney's works reveal both tragic and comic aspects of experience. The titles of his work often provide clues to the enigmatic messages that his works convey.

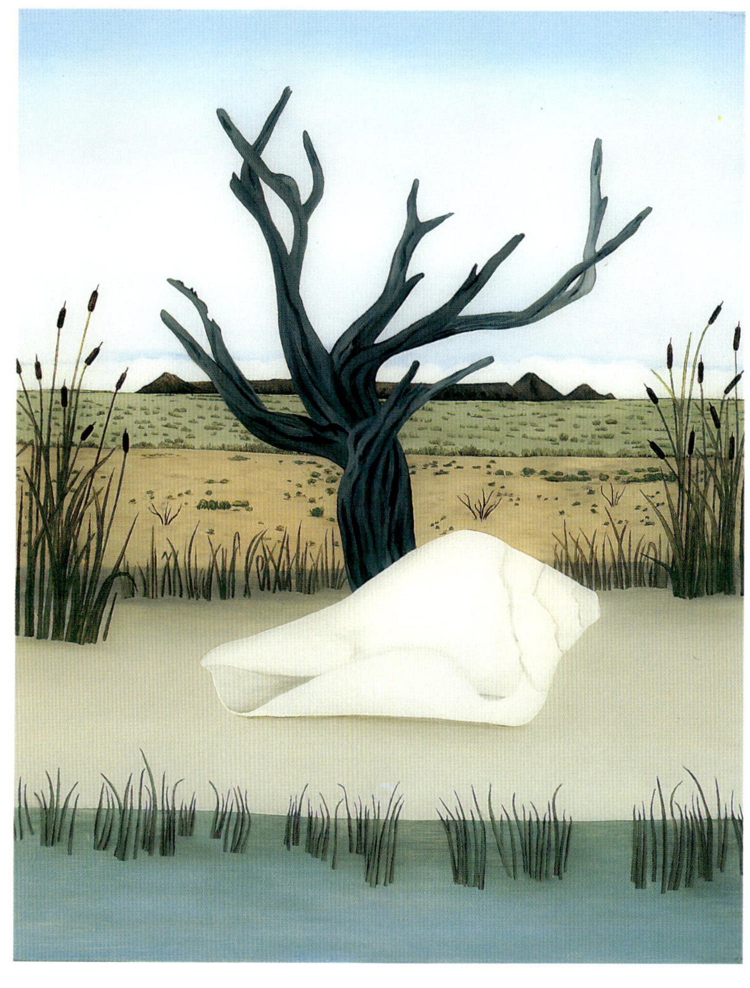

BORN IN LONDON to American parents, Rebecca James, her twin sister Rachel, and their brothers grew up associated with the Buffalo Bill Wild West Show, which their father managed until his death in 1902. In 1922, James married photographer Paul Strand and became an intimate of the famed Stieglitz circle in New York. In 1929, James and Georgia O'Keeffe spent the summer as guests of Mabel Dodge at her Taos compound, where O'Keeffe gave James artistic encouragement and criticism. Inspired by this support and by her own growing mastery over the difficult mediums of pastel and reverse oil on glass, she began in earnest her career as an artist.

A self-taught artist, James worked with many materials during the 1920s but found her principal medium when she began painting with oils on glass, a medium she valued because of its sharp-edged quality, lack of surface texture, and luminous effect.

The exacting process of this medium requires the artist to first apply the foreground details of the image to the reverse side of the glass and work backward to the background. However, James quickly mastered the technique of this colonial American folk art medium, infusing it with her own personal, modern style. *Earth and Water* reflects symbolism and her personal iconography, both important aspects of her work.

REBECCA SALSBURY JAMES
Earth and Water, 1950
Oil on glass
$19\frac{3}{4} \times 16$ in.
Bequest of Helen Miller Jones, 1986

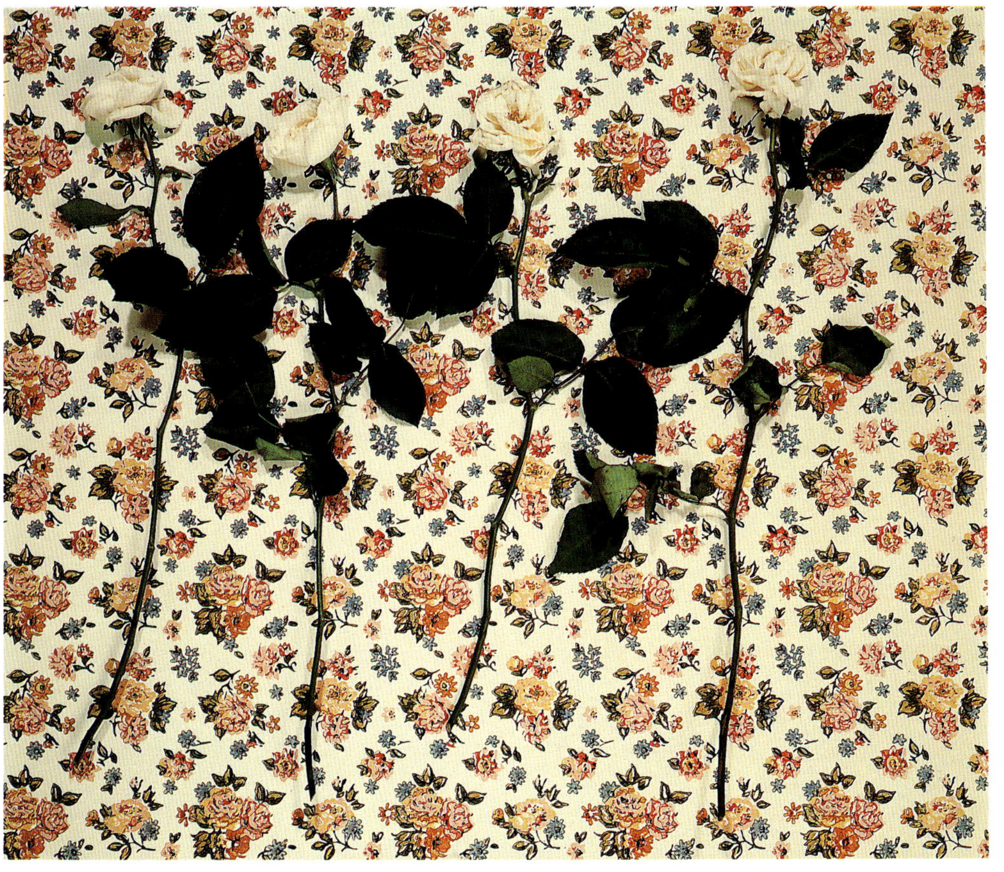

BETTY HAHN
Cut Flowers: Roses, 1/3, 1979
Polacolor II photograph
20 × 23⅝ in.
Museum purchase through a grant by the Museum of New Mexico Foundation, 1980

THE CAMERA enables its user to homogenize—to create an image blending reality and imitation. The result—the photograph—creates a visual pun that encourages the question: What is reality in a postmodern world of repetition, imitation, and separation from original forms?

In 1979, Betty Hahn addressed the question when she was invited to create her own personal work with a modern large Polaroid view camera, which produces one-of-a-kind 20 × 24-inch prints that render a subject with remarkable clarity.

Hahn was knowledgeable about science's fascination with exhibition. This knowledge, in combination with her understanding of this camera's potential, provided the impetus for the image *Cut Flowers: Roses*.

By moving the camera close to her subject, Hahn magnified and intensified the roses on the wallpaper so that they appear more dominant than they did in reality; at the same time, the four long-stemmed white roses, placed flat on the paper's surface, appear to be reduced in significance, blending into the background. In the photograph, they have been transformed to a design motif like the printed roses on the wallpaper.

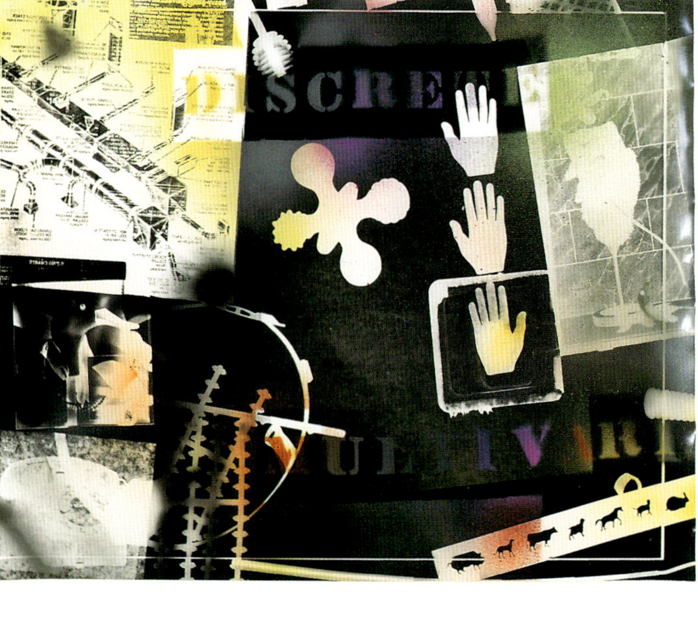

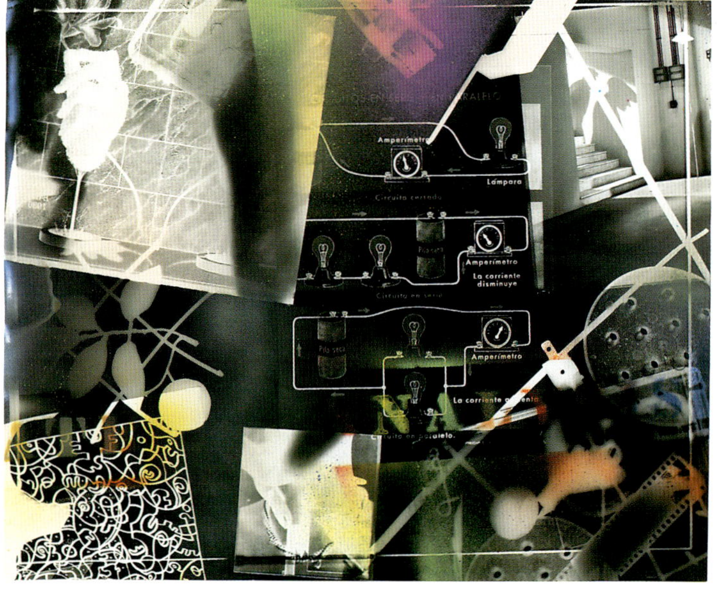

PHOTOGRAPHIC INVENTIONS in the 1830s provided expressive possibilities with or without the use of a camera. Placing objects on light-sensitive paper and exposing them directly to light was one process that permitted a literal transcription of the artistic world. "Photogenic drawing," as English inventor William Henry Fox called it, became the genesis of the modern photogenic medium.

European avant-garde artists Laszlo Moholy-Nagy and Man Ray independently *reinvented* the cameraless photograph in the first decades of this century as a means of visual exploration outside other major art forms. The photogram, as it became known, was another method of creating form with the medium and light. Everyday objects placed on photographic paper were transformed into reversals of their contours. The artist could amplify the characteristics of objects or further abstract their qualities with these photographic materials.

The image *Discrete Multivariate Analysis* utilizes both idioms. The objects of American material culture, from remnants of plastic toys to pages of scientific diagrams and a film noir still from the 1940s, present an encyclopedic anthology of our time. Words, spray painted through letter stencils, extend the notion of the coexisting positive and negative forms of the photogram, add color and texture, and reaffirm the modern qualities of photography. The myriad contrasts in this image reflect photography's expansive vocabulary and the complexity of our modern existence.

THOMAS BARROW
Discrete Multivariate Analysis, 1981
Two gelatin silver photograms with lacquer spray paint and epoxy enamel
15⅞ × 19¹³⁄₁₆ in. each
Gift of Patti and Frank Kolodny, 1990

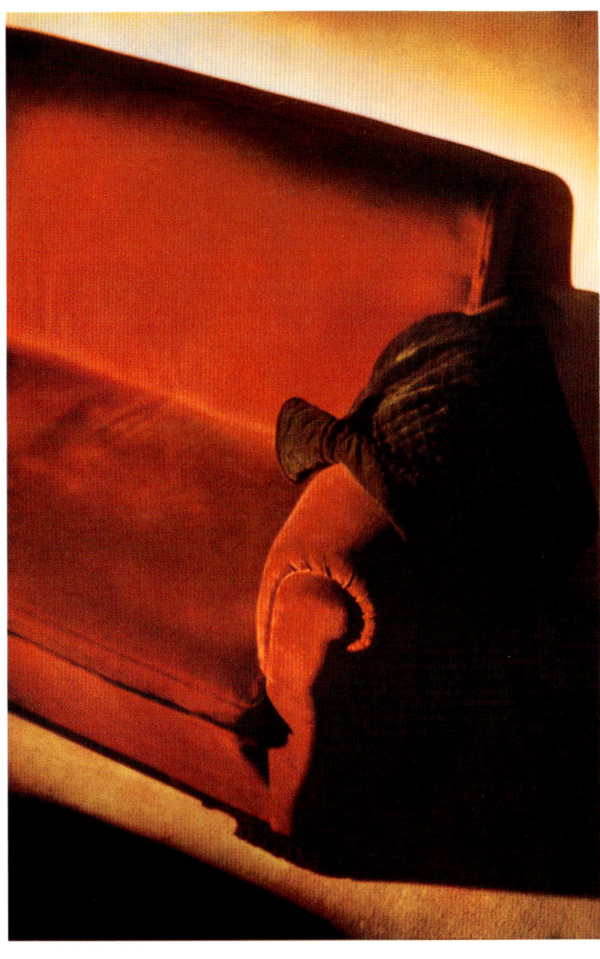

BERNARD PLOSSU
Madrid, Spain, 1975
Fresson color print
24 × 16½ in.
Anonymous gift, 1985

THE QUALITIES of color in photography are by-products of the specific color process with which the artist chooses to work. A "palette" is created in part by the base of materials, such as dyes or pigments, used to make the final print. How the artist decides to utilize color apart from the normal camera rendering of reality by the camera is a challenge all color photographers have to face.

In *Madrid, Spain*, Plossu utilizes the Fresson technique, a unique process created by one family in France. Pigmented color combined with the camera images offer qualities associated with painting. Oil color permeates the paper surface and diffuses the hard optical delineation of the camera's lens. Interpretation from the color transparency into the final print allows for an expressive dimension. In this process, the quality and intensity of hues can transcend those of reality and can transform mundane objects, such as the section of the couch in *Madrid, Spain*, into metaphoric subject.

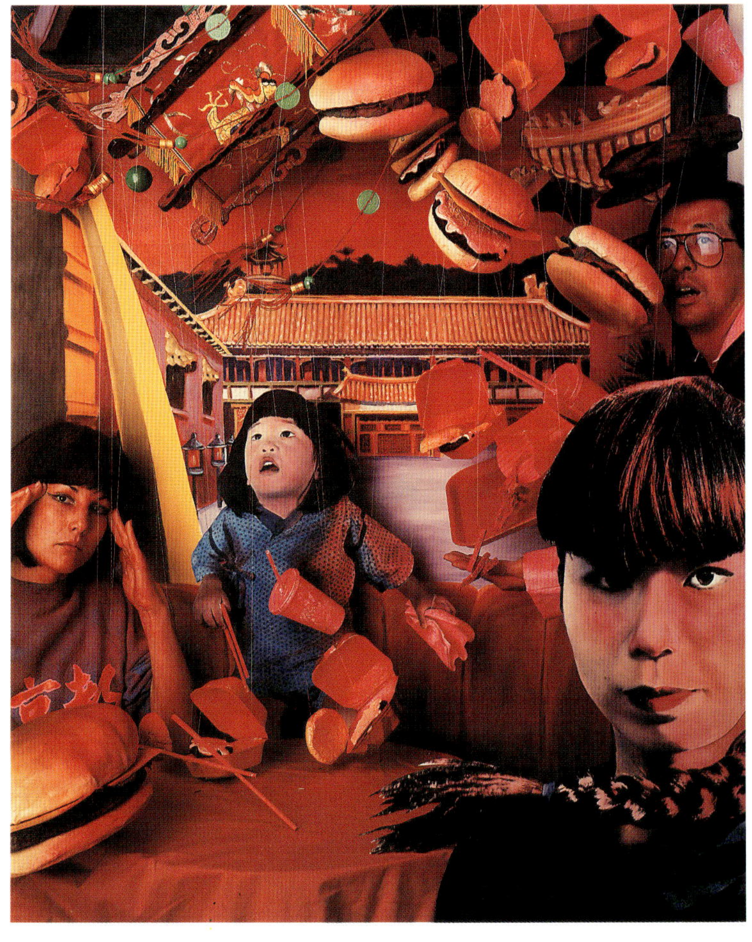

THE MAMMOTH Polaroid camera that produces this instant 20×24-inch photograph weds uncompromising detail in the subject with the bright metallic-like color of the Polacolor process. It is this combination that lends extra conviction to the worlds created by Patrick Nagatani and Andree Tracey. Their statements rely on our instincts that truth and the photograph are somehow synonymous.

Yet, on closer inspection, we realize that the images have been fabricated. These artists collaborate over hundreds of hours to create realistic sets that gain power from the transformation produced by this camera and process. Nagatani and Tracey invent photographic images from the tangible world that comment on our American culture and its relation to the nuclear threat. In *Radio Active Red*, symbols of popular culture are suspended by or incorporated as collage elements. This reflects the barrage of visual information we are confronted with on a daily basis.

Irony and subtle contradictions are essential elements of the meaning in this work. Here we may encounter ominous forebodings and truths that we cannot or may not want to fully understand, such as the threatening aspects of the red glow, suggesting the instantaneous flash of a nuclear explosion. Such testimonials are reminiscent of John Heartfield's photomontages that exposed the inhumanity of Adolf Hitler's Germany.

PATRICK NAGATANI and
ANDREE TRACEY
Radio Active Red, 1986
Diffusion transfer/Polaroid ER Land photograph
24×20 in.
Gift of Ray Graham, 1991

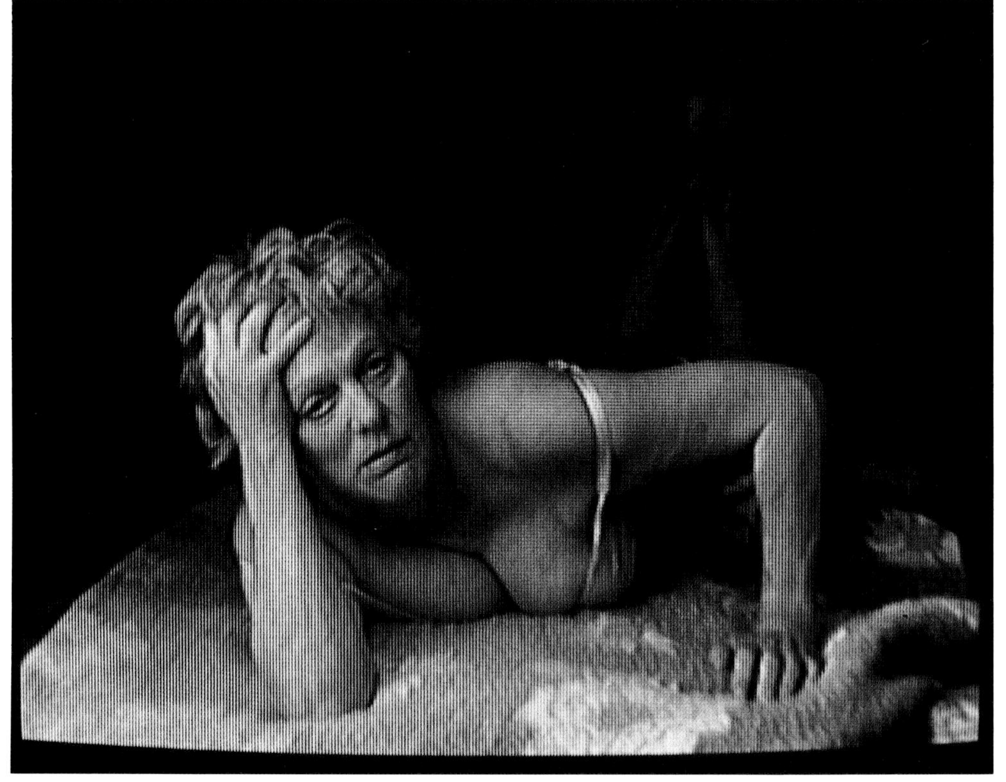

ANNE NOGGLE
One of Us, from a series "Recent Follies," 1985
Gelatin silver photograph
$14 \times 18\frac{1}{2}$ in.
Gift of Mary Pease, 1988

ONE COMPONENT OF the photographic medium that artists have cultivated in recent years is the use of repetition. Classically, this capacity for manipulation has had limited application often relating only to graphic concerns, but the need to expand upon photography's expressive potential has led to the use of repetition to create new meanings.

Anne Noggle's continuing self-portrait over many decades has taken on many dimensions, from her role as a pilot in World War II to the painful process of a face-lift. This is a cinematic, narrative approach without dialogue. In Noggle's photographs, the focus is life in all its improprieties as well as special moments. In *One of Us*, the pretension of a self-portrait is reinterpreted in a picture made from a video monitor set up in her studio. The idea of autobiographical revelation contrasts, ironically, with the broadcasted image. The effect is that of distancing the viewer from any intimate knowledge of reality.

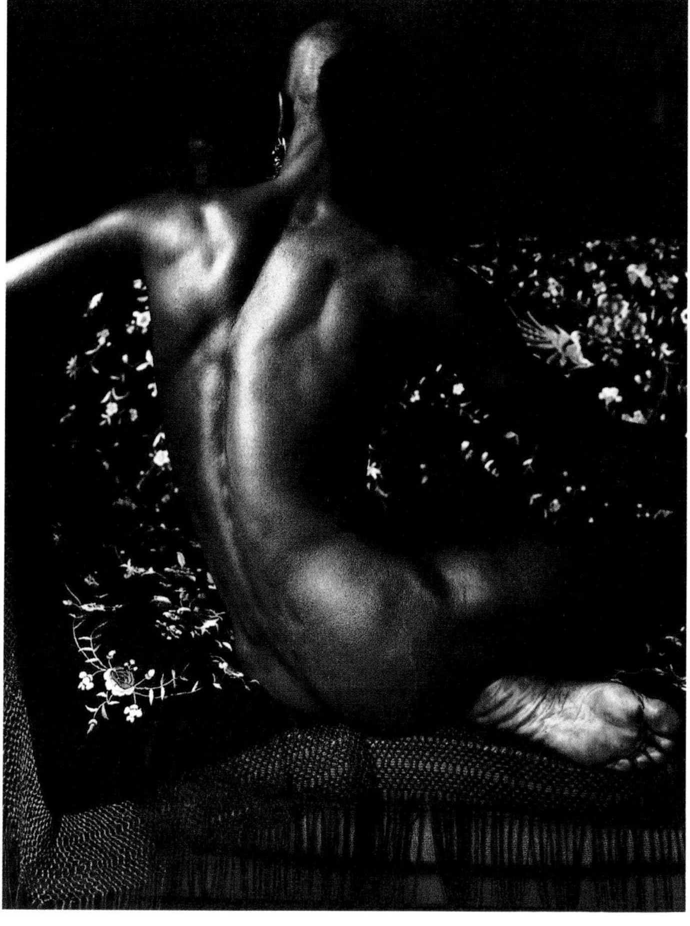

PERHAPS ONE OF the most difficult challenges for a photographer is portraiture. When the invention of photography was announced to the world in 1839, the camera offered an immediate clarity in rendering subjects, and thus new possibilities, for portraiture. Photographs of nude models, known as "academies," were popular for use by the artists of the day.

Early in the history of photography, the simplicity of portraits was often the consequence of long exposures. The sitter would pose still for at least half a minute before the image was complete; movement would ruin the result. While the technical demands are different for the modern photographer, the creative problems remain. The challenge of deliberately positioning a model in order to make a self-sustaining work of art requires special capabilities.

While the bold simplicity of Judy Dater's straightforward photograph of a model's back recalls the spirit of the academie, it transcends these nineteenth-century studies for artists. In *Nehemiah*, the smooth texture of the figure's skin is revealed in a way only photography can convey. Intimate in arrangement and imaginative in its formality, the model's posture borders on the theatrical. This image demonstrates that elegance and beauty in sculptural terms can be the subject of the photographer as well as the painter.

JUDY DATER
Nehemiah, 1975
Gelatin silver photograph
$13\frac{1}{4} \times 10\frac{1}{4}$ in.
Jane Reese Williams Collection

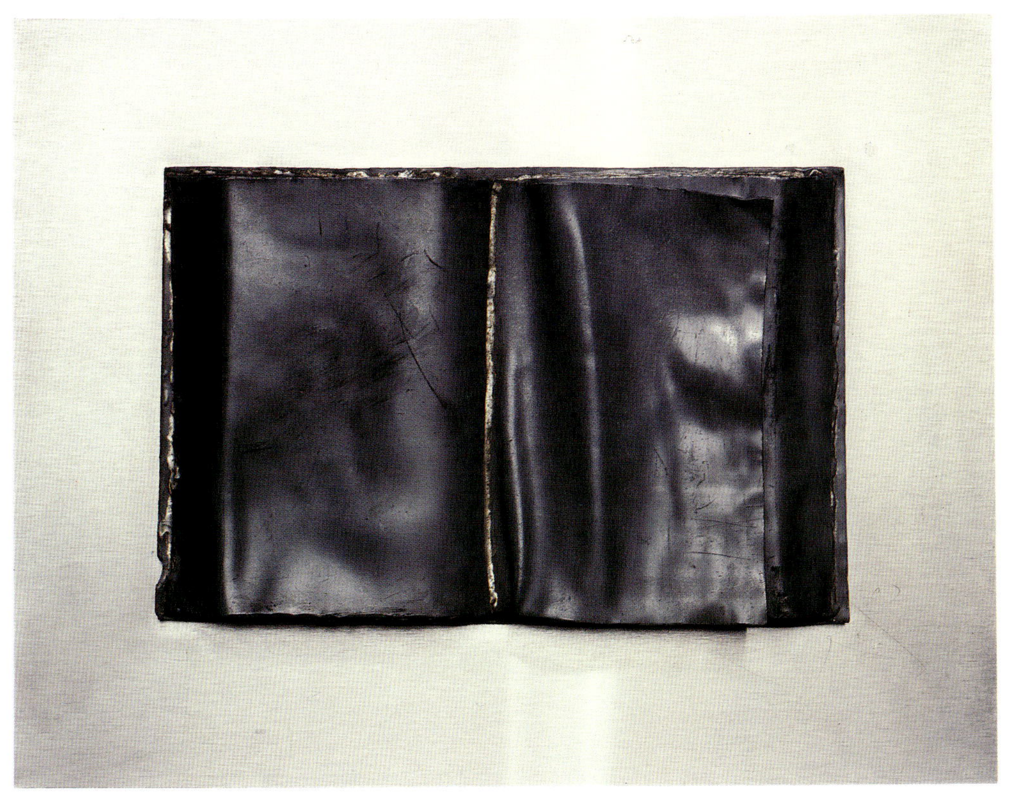

DORIS CROSS
The Lead Book, 1982–83
Lead on stainless steel
15 3/8 × 20 3/16 × 5 1/8 in.
Museum purchase, Fine Arts Acquisition Fund at the Museum of New Mexico Foundation, 1986

IN THE ART WORLD, Doris Cross is one link between New Mexico and New York. She studied at the Art Students League, the Pratt Institute, and the Hans Hofmann School, as well as with Josef Albers. Following her studies, she pursued a career on the East Coast. When Cross first came to New Mexico in the 1970s, she was uncertain if she could live in the area permanently and returned to New York often. In the 1990s, she remains a resident of New Mexico and a prolific artist. Her media includes painting, filmmaking, sculpture, printmaking, and writing.

The Lead Book expresses in a weighty physical form Cross's intense and complex relationship with books, a theme that has been the basis for her art for the past ten years. This work complements her images on paper, exhibited regularly, which manipulate the printed page. In these strong abstract compositions, she obliterates parts, draws on, and collages over sections. This process creates cryptic personal messages from discovered text and invented imagery. In *The Lead Book*, she shifts from a conceptual to a physical point of view, making the book into a sacred object, cast in an impenetrable material.

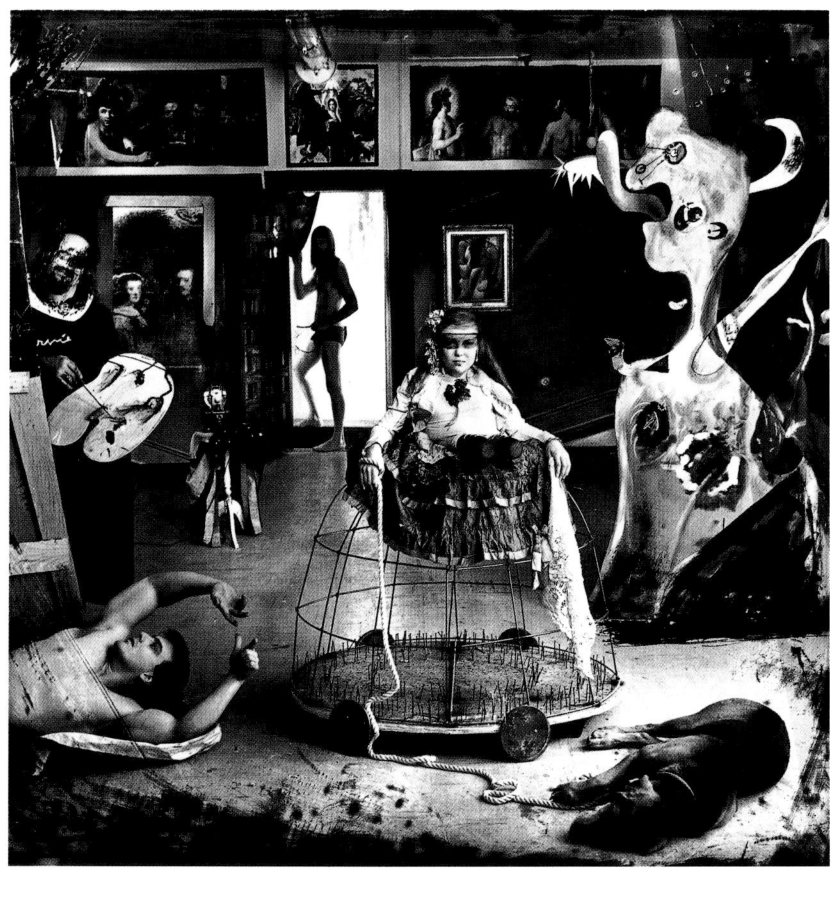

THE INVENTORS of photography often describe the first photographs as the "mirror of nature" because of the facility of the medium for rendering detail in a scientific manner. However, in the hands of the artist, the camera has proved that it can express the world of the imagination equally well.

Las Meninas, New Mexico is a mirror of both reality and fantasy based on Velázquez's seminal painting (1656). While it pays homage to the three greatest Spanish painters over the centuries–Velázquez, Picasso, and Miró–incorporating direct references to their paintings, the photograph also celebrates the independence of the critical mind. The expression of personal vision through Witkin's staging, people (including himself), and handmade props in his studio offers a *tableau vivant* that juxtaposes various historical eras. This assemblage is filled with historical references and metaphorical associations. The doorway from the photographer's studio to the darkroom is illuminated. The viewer wonders: What lies outside the open door in the world beyond the artist's inner reality?

As well, the illumination reinforces the notion that this is a theater of the mind. Here the photographer, portrayed as both the painter next to the canvas (as is Velázquez in the original painting) and as a Christ figure in the opened doorway, sees the evanescence of life and mortality. As Montaigne wrote in the sixteenth century: "My sole purpose here is to disclose myself." The photograph transcends the immediate world for more impalpable territory.

JOEL-PETER WITKIN
Las Meninas, New Mexico, 8/15, 1987
Gelatin silver photograph
15 × 15 in.
Gift of Barbara Erdman, 1988

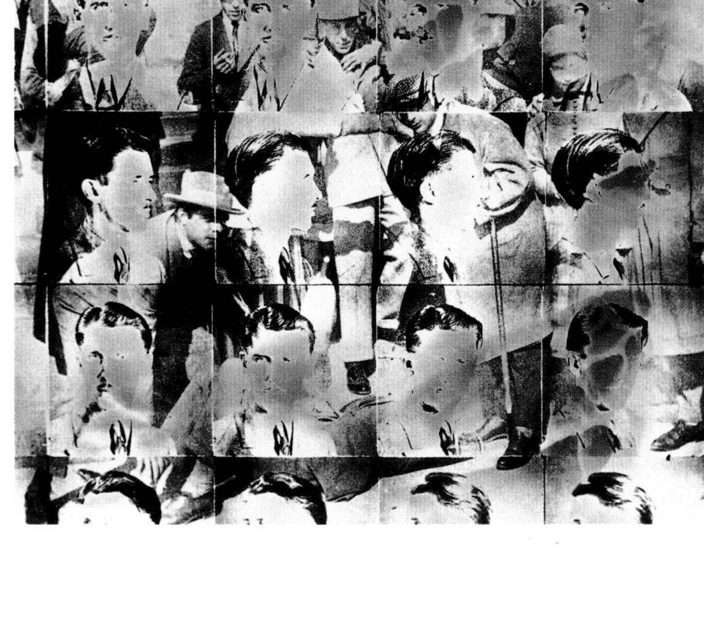

VAN DEREN COKE
Homage to the Dada Constructivists,
from the "New Mexico" portfolio,
1974
Gelatin silver photograph
$8\frac{7}{16} \times 9\frac{3}{4}$ in.
Museum purchase, Public
Contributions Fund, 1978

IN 1922, several artists met in Weimar, Germany, to bid farewell to their brief but tumultuous period of "anti-art" activities under the name of dadaism. What they had helped start, an antibourgeois European art movement that upset all categorizations and reason, became the seed for another movement—surrealism.

An unknown photographer took a group portrait at this artists' reunion. The photograph symbolized the crossroads of two artistic movements, dadaism and constructivism, and became the catalyst to Van Deren Coke's *Homage to the Dada Constructivists*. Coke, a photographer and educator of art history, copied this picture from a book to reuse as a collage in the experimental spirit of the period. However, his appropriation was further modified to generate a third, and more didactic, counterpoint.

Attributes of the art movements of dadaism, constructivism, and surrealism are combined in this photograph. Two states of mind are represented in this collage of negative and positive images: the inventive disposition of avant-garde photographers such as Man Ray and Laszlo Moholy-Nagy and the realm of dream, a domain that was to become a prominent motif of the surrealists.

The influence of dadaism, constructivism, and surrealism remains significant, particularly in innovative American photography over recent decades.

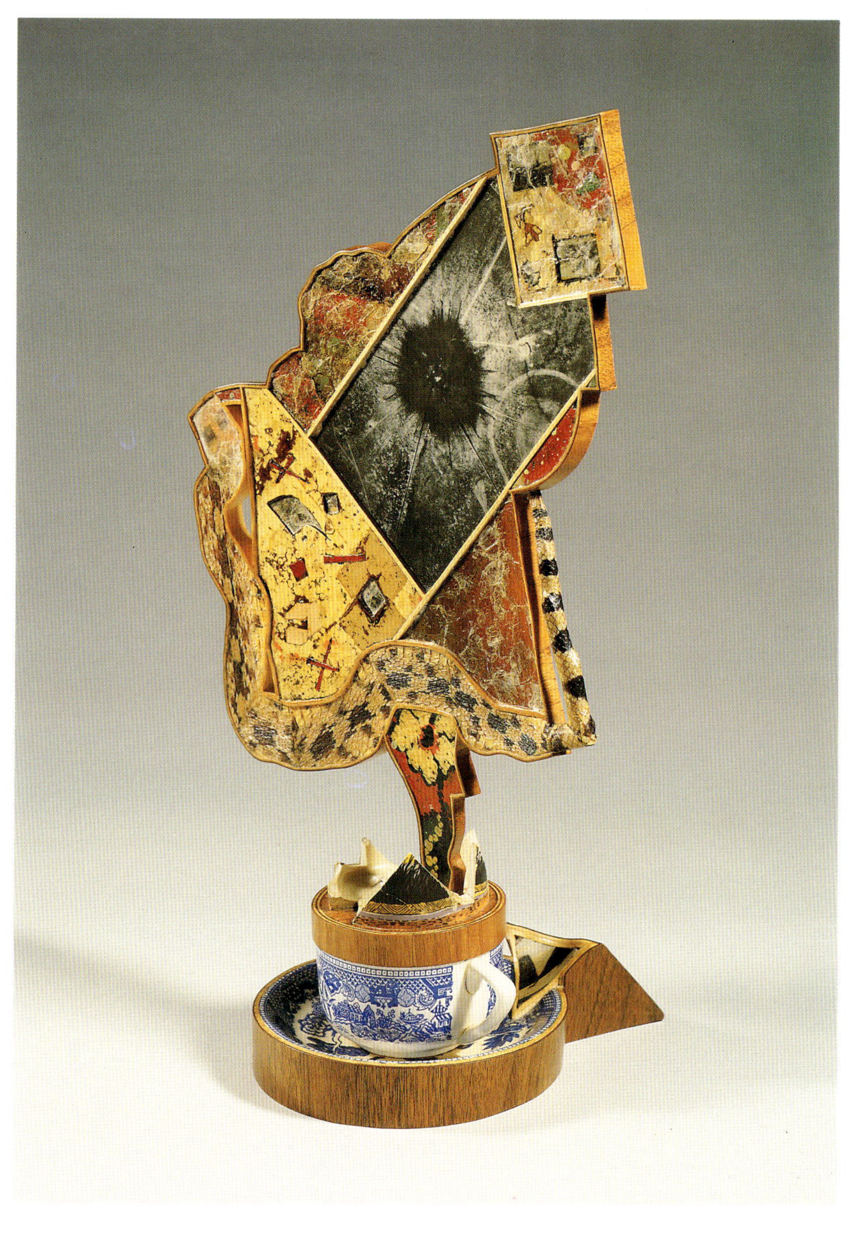

ROGER SWEET
World Cup, 1982
Ceramic and mixed media
$18 \times 11 \times 8\frac{1}{2}$ in.
Gift of the artist, 1986

ROGER SWEET came to New Mexico in the mid-1970s when his first wife, an anthropologist, was studying the dances of the Pueblo Indians. After a collaborative book project, Sweet began teaching at the University of New Mexico. During this period, he used a variety of media, including video and installations, often working in concert with Rick Dingus. In 1980, Sweet left Albuquerque and the University of New Mexico art department to build a home and studio in a small village in the Jemez Mountains. The materials in Sweet's work are all found or given to him by friends, neighbors, or acquaintances. Currently, he draws inspiration for his work from his dreams and his quiet, rural life. Earlier in his career, he had also worked on the theme of the atomic bomb.

In *World Cup*, an ordinary vessel unleashes a bouquet of ominous images—or is it a mushroom cloud?—that include a roadkill snake, flakes of mica, the 1950s "duck and cover" symbol reminding schoolchildren what to do during a nuclear attack, and an aerial image of the earth's scars resulting from the detonation of a bomb. Since 1985, Sweet's work has been concerned with metamorphoses of the commonplace into the profound: *World Cup* transforms the idea of the mundane activity of drinking a warm beverage into concepts that reflect serious challenges to the planet.

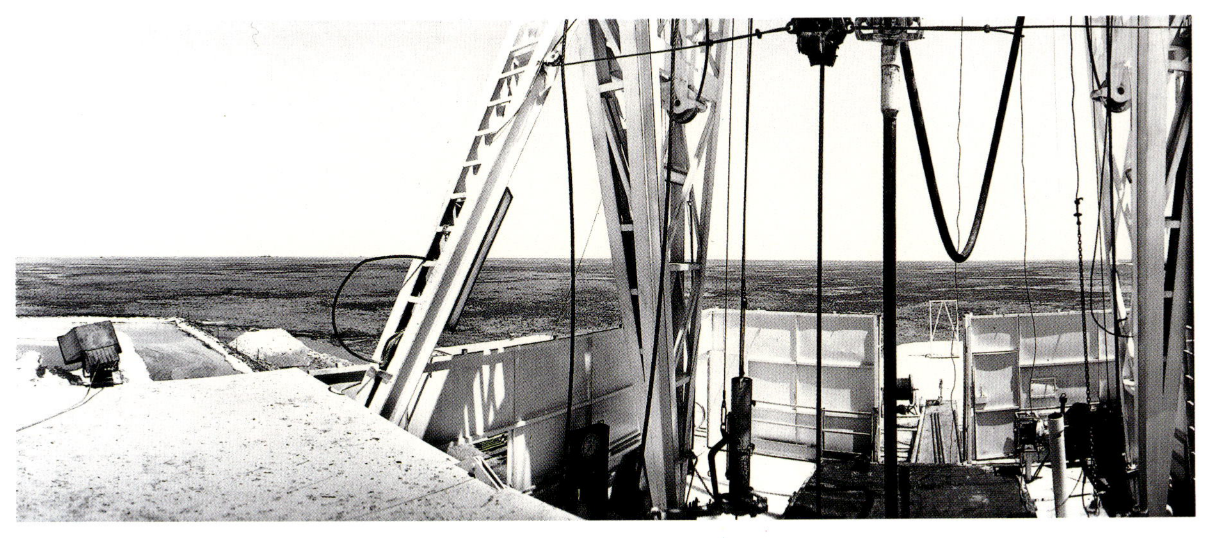

MARY PECK
Yates Petroleum Company, Exploratory Well, West of Lovington, New Mexico, 1983
Toned gelatin silver photograph
6×15 in.
New Mexico Photographic Survey Collection, funded by a grant from the National Endowment for the Arts, 1985

MARY PECK has photographed the most uncompromising and uninhabitable landscapes. In 1982, she worked in eastern New Mexico and western Texas, where there was, as she put it, "no place for the eye to rest, no seeming point of interest." The horizon became the only tangible reference rather than the region's scarce details of human existence. However, for Peck, such attributes opposed the tradition of the grand landscape and offered new challenges. Realizing that conventional approaches to photographing these unending flatlands would produce banal results, Peck chose to work with a panoramic camera.

Instead of diminishing the nature of the land's ceaseless repetitious features, the photographer, with this camera, was able to expand on these aspects of the region; the wide perspective emphasized a point of view that reinterpreted, metaphorically, the unyielding sense of perpetual terrain. The enduring qualities of these desolate surroundings touch upon such human personal values as solitude and undying convictions. Perhaps these panoramic landscapes also hint at what is unchanging, timeless, and immortal.

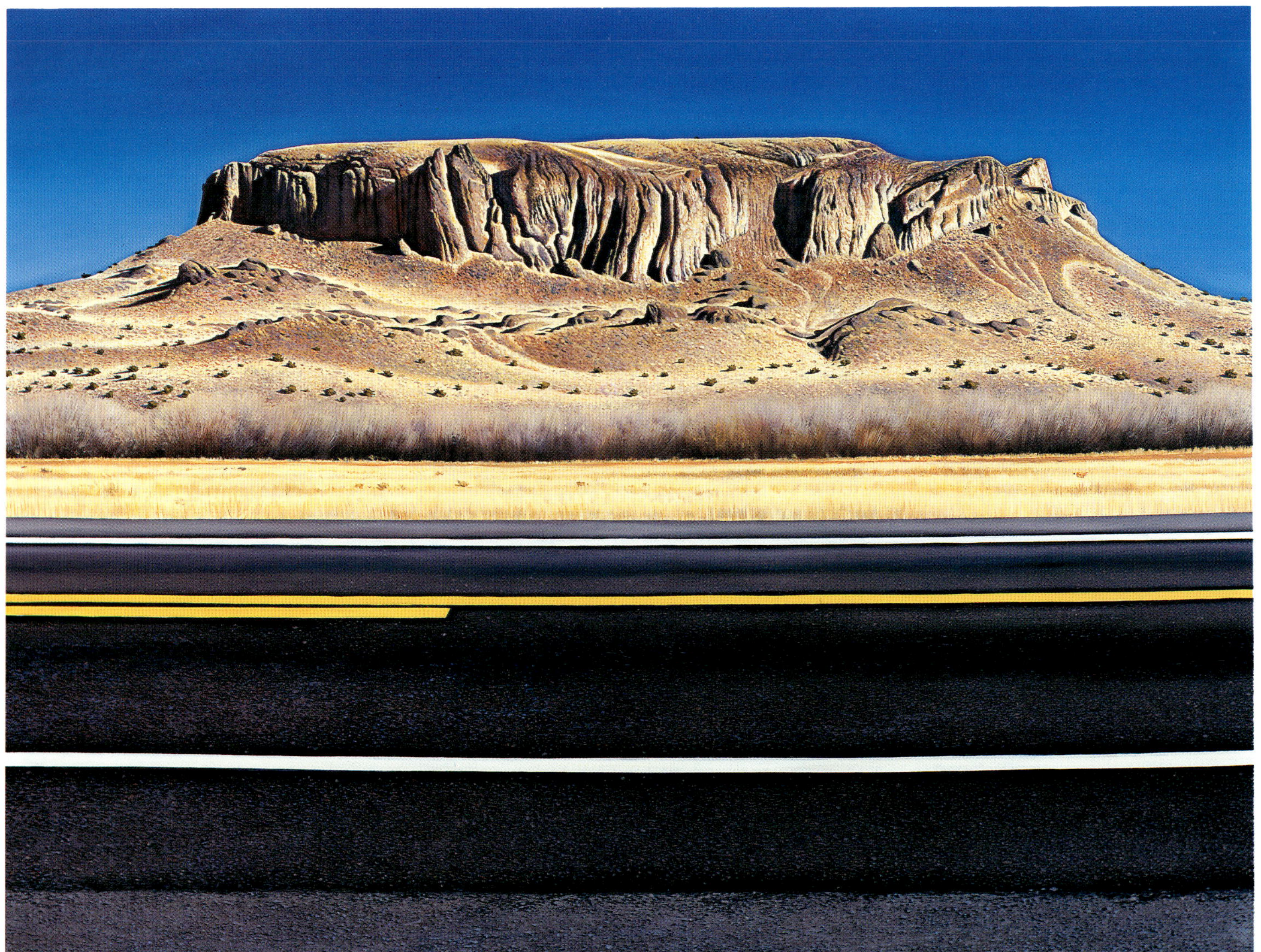

THE TRADITION of romantic landscape painting in America is rooted in Rousseau's nineteenth-century concepts of natural primitivism that evolved from Thomas Cole's Arcadian compositions into the Hudson River School of painting, all of which emphasized the moral beauty in nature. Careful contemplation of the landscape or its depiction in art could be an elevating experience inspired by the ideal.

Gwyn represents the new romantic landscape painter. His stark views of the desert Southwest, intersected by impersonal but omnipresent highways and bridges, are modern images of an ideal beauty that brings the viewer closer to the reality of nature. These paintings reflect his direct responses to life, where truth and beauty come from common, everyday scenes. The large-scale size of the newest oil paintings is effective in physically placing the viewer within the intense vast spaces that Gwyn selects for us to experience.

WOODY GWYN
Highway and Mesa, 1982
Oil with alkyd resins on linen
60 × 78 in.
Museum purchase, Museum Is a Wonder Fund, 1982

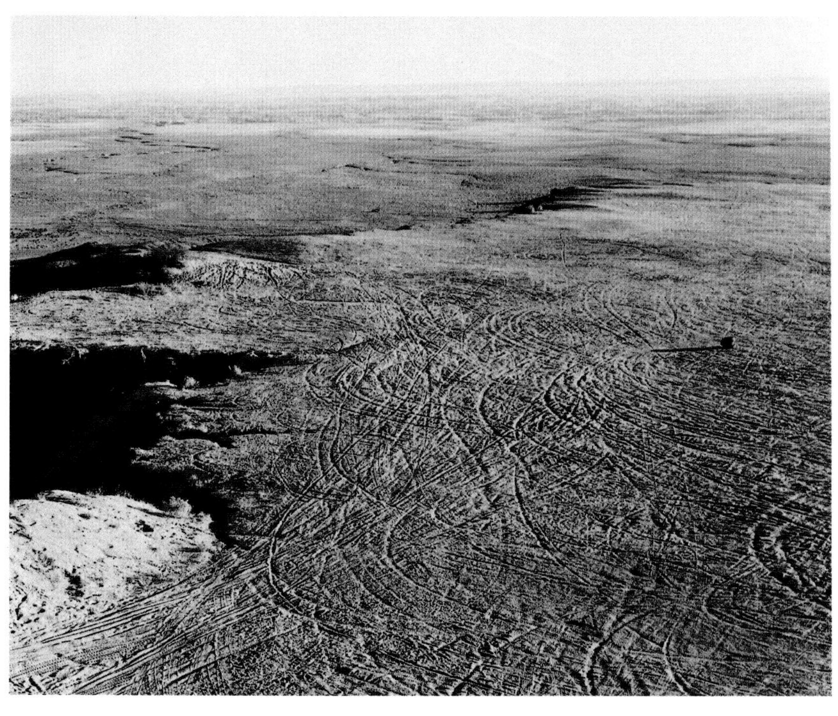

ROBERT ADAMS
Quarried Mesa Top, Pueblo County, Colorado, 1978
Gelatin silver photograph
$9 \times 11\frac{1}{4}$ in.
Museum purchase with funds from the New Mexico Council on Photography, Diane Jergins Award, 1985

HUMAN PRESENCE in the landscape has motivated artists in many disciplines to search for historic truth. In this century, we have come to see the landscape as a canvas of human values that expresses more than geologic time.

The delicate grace of *Quarried Mesa Top, Pueblo County, Colorado* reflects what Adams hopes the photographer can discover: "a tension so exact that it is peace." The unremitting tire tracks etched into the top of the mesa, seen with accompanying panoramic splendor, depict the infinite complexity of nature juxtaposed with the intricate, entangled fabric of modern life. There is a tension here between beauty and intrusion. The inscriptions of man on the natural landscape create a paradox, for they simultaneously allude to enduring human aspirations and human folly. Adams combines a discerning faculty for understanding the past with an ability to confront and integrate realities of the present in his work.

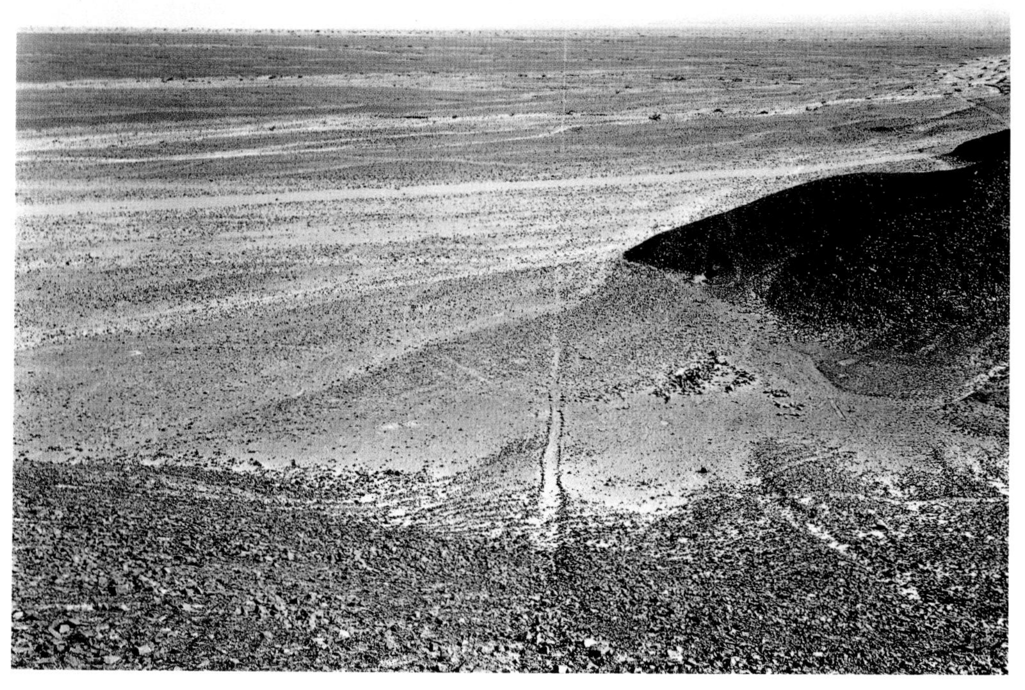

ON THE COASTAL PLAINS of Peru, there are large-scale drawings in the landscape where the desert meets the ocean. These immense markings date back to the Nazca culture (ca. 370 B.C.–A.D. 450). Why these individuals turned their creative energies toward the uncertainties of topography remains a mystery, although the drawing of numerous straight lines for miles in the dry terrain indicates a functional purpose. Archaeological evidence suggests that this was a civilization of discernment, whose concepts of space and time bridged a gap between ancient and modern worlds.

Such questions about ancient civilizations are critical aspects of Edward Ranney's photographic explorations. A tenacious investigator, he examines the place and cultural record for clues to a civilization's perception. The placement of the camera and the artist's perspective on the subject become as essential as what might be expressed through the process of printing. The Nazca line in *Nazca, Peru,* like a wire stretching to the horizon, makes space comprehensive on another level; humanization of space transcends geologic time. We view through the eyes of an artist the undercurrents of the Nazca sensibility.

EDWARD RANNEY
Nazca, Peru, 1985
Selenium-toned gelatin silver photograph
12½ × 18½ in.
Gil Hitchcock Collection, 1989

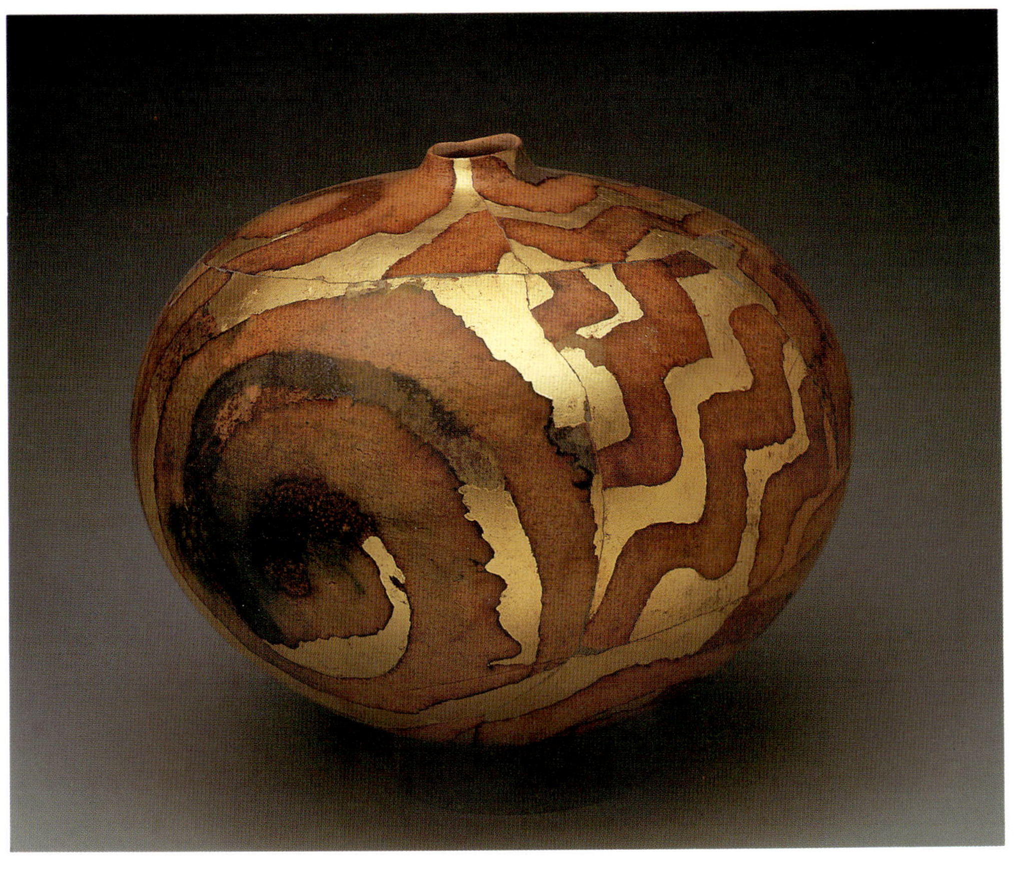

RICK DILLINGHAM
Untitled, 1985
Ceramic with gold leaf, enamel, and glazes
11 × 14 × 14 in.
Gift of John Metzenberg, Mel Pfaelzer, and Jack Satin, 1987

RICK DILLINGHAM'S background in anthropology, especially his work in the reconstruction of shattered pots at the University of New Mexico, informs his art. He studied at the Claremont Graduate School in California, where he earned an M.F.A., but his love of ceramics dates to the time of his youth. When he was in the sixth grade, he bought two small pots in Tucson for $4 and later, when he was at the University of New Mexico, researched the identity of the potters. He discovered that one was Hopi and the other was from Acoma Pueblo. This early research, even in childhood, helped to influence him to become both a dealer in Pueblo pottery and Navajo textiles and an artist.

Well known and avidly collected, Dillingham's exquisite vessels possess qualities of raw beauty and authenticity. The process of breaking fired pots, firing the pieces, and then reassembling them began in Los Angeles and continues in Santa Fe. Such reassembly is often random, bringing new ideas and energies to the original composition. A sense of timelessness makes Dillingham's ceramics idiosyncratic in the American ceramics movement, one that has thrived and has produced work of increasingly higher quality over the past twenty years.

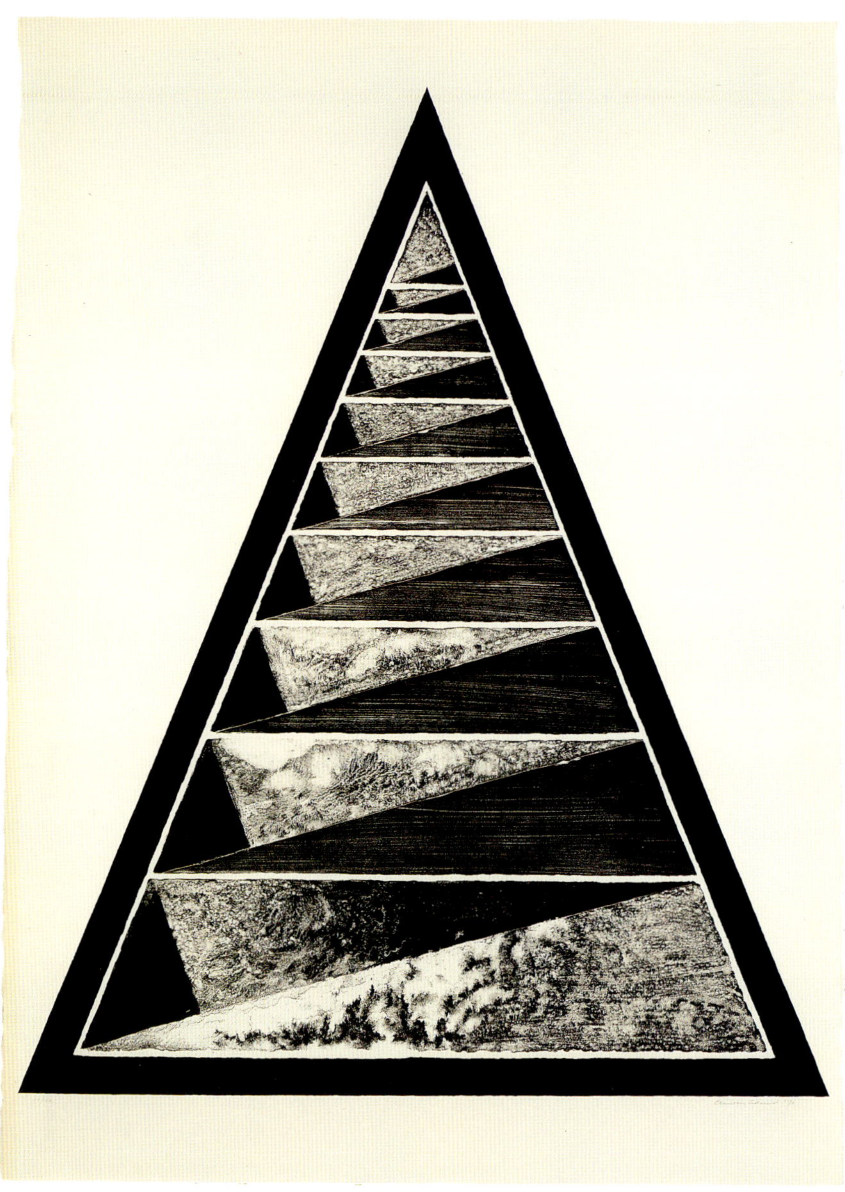

CLINTON ADAMS was born into a talented family of musicians and motion picture technicians, who encouraged his artistic leanings. In 1942 he received a master of arts degree from UCLA and after military discharge in 1946 drove from New York to Los Angeles with a stopover in Albuquerque. There he met Raymond Jonson. First and foremost a painter, Adams has distinguished himself in lithography, a technique that was nearly lost to artists of his generation. During his tenure as Dean of the College of Fine Arts at the University of New Mexico between 1961 and 1985, he became a major figure in the revival of the lithographic art. He continues to serve as editor of the *Tamarind Papers: A Journal of the Fine Print.*

Strata is one of three Adams lithographs published by Tamarind Institute in 1970, the year the workshop relocated from Los Angeles to the University of New Mexico in Albuquerque. A sophisticated and restrained colorist, Adams's use of classical order and precision, overall dramatic shape, a reliance on white, and nuanced texture are highlighted in this work.

CLINTON ADAMS
Strata, 10/10, 1970
Lithograph
30 × 22¼ in.
Museum purchase, Fine Arts Acquisition Fund, 1988

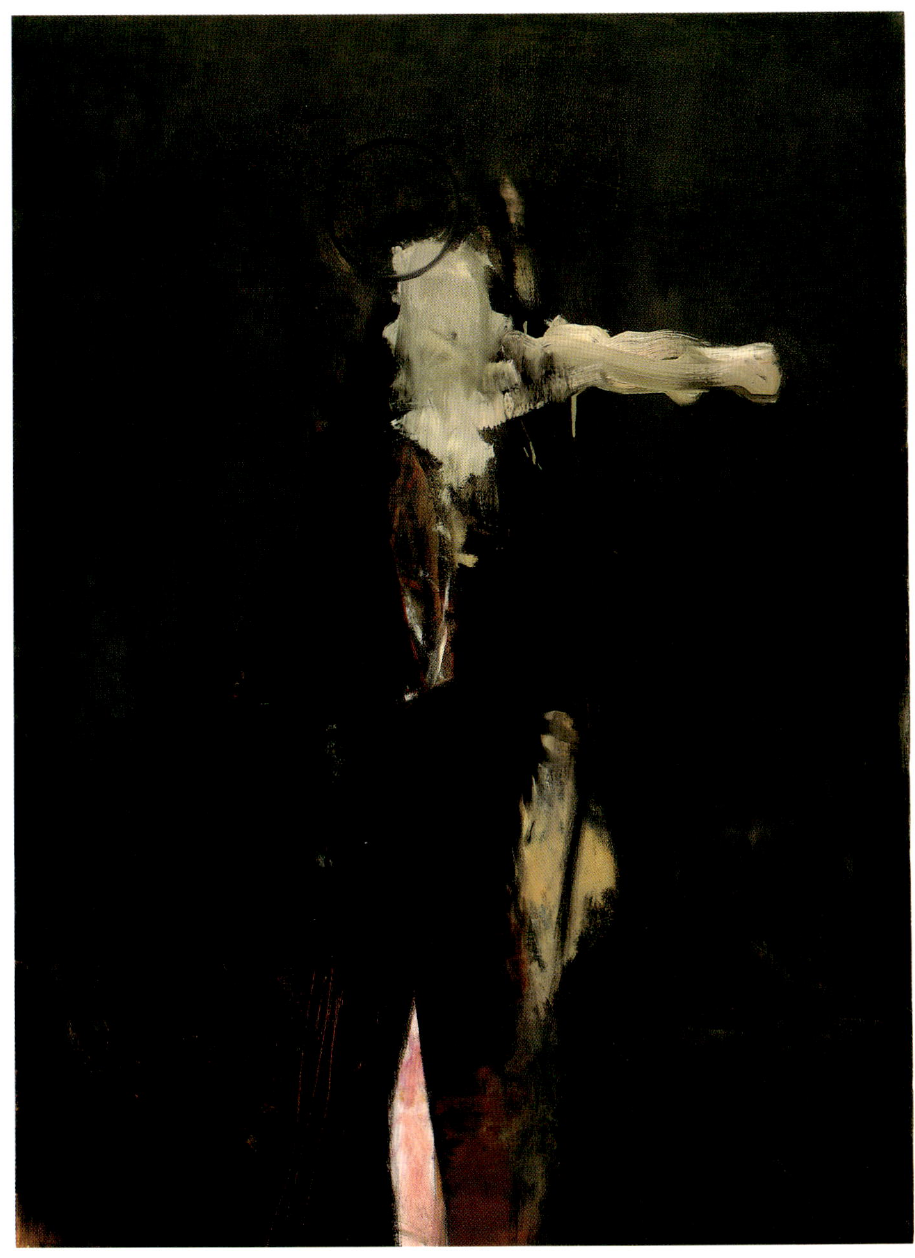

EUGENE NEWMANN
Black Figure, 1977
Oil on canvas
$48 \times 35\frac{3}{4}$ in.
Museum purchase in memory of Rebecca Blackburn, 1978

EUGENE NEWMANN's Czechoslovakian heritage, his life in Colombia, where Spanish was his first language, his traditional Jewish upbringing in New York after age ten, and his education in mathematics and physics at the University of Chicago make him a painter of unusual breadth of knowledge and life experience. His paintings, such as *Black Figure*, express the indelibility of human presence in universal terms. Here the figure hovers between a concrete physical realm and an amorphous emotional or spiritual realm.

"A lot of people of my generation, who had families wiped out in the Holocaust–followed by the Cold War, the Berlin crisis, the Cuban missile crisis–felt the whole world was about to be destroyed. The question for us was what thread we were going to live on if the logic of our ancestors, the confidence in the rationality and justice of the West, was shot. And that led eventually to my definition of myself as an artist, at the age of 40" (from "The Cover-Up Makes the Artist" by Bill Clark, *Albuquerque Journal*, 16 October 1988).

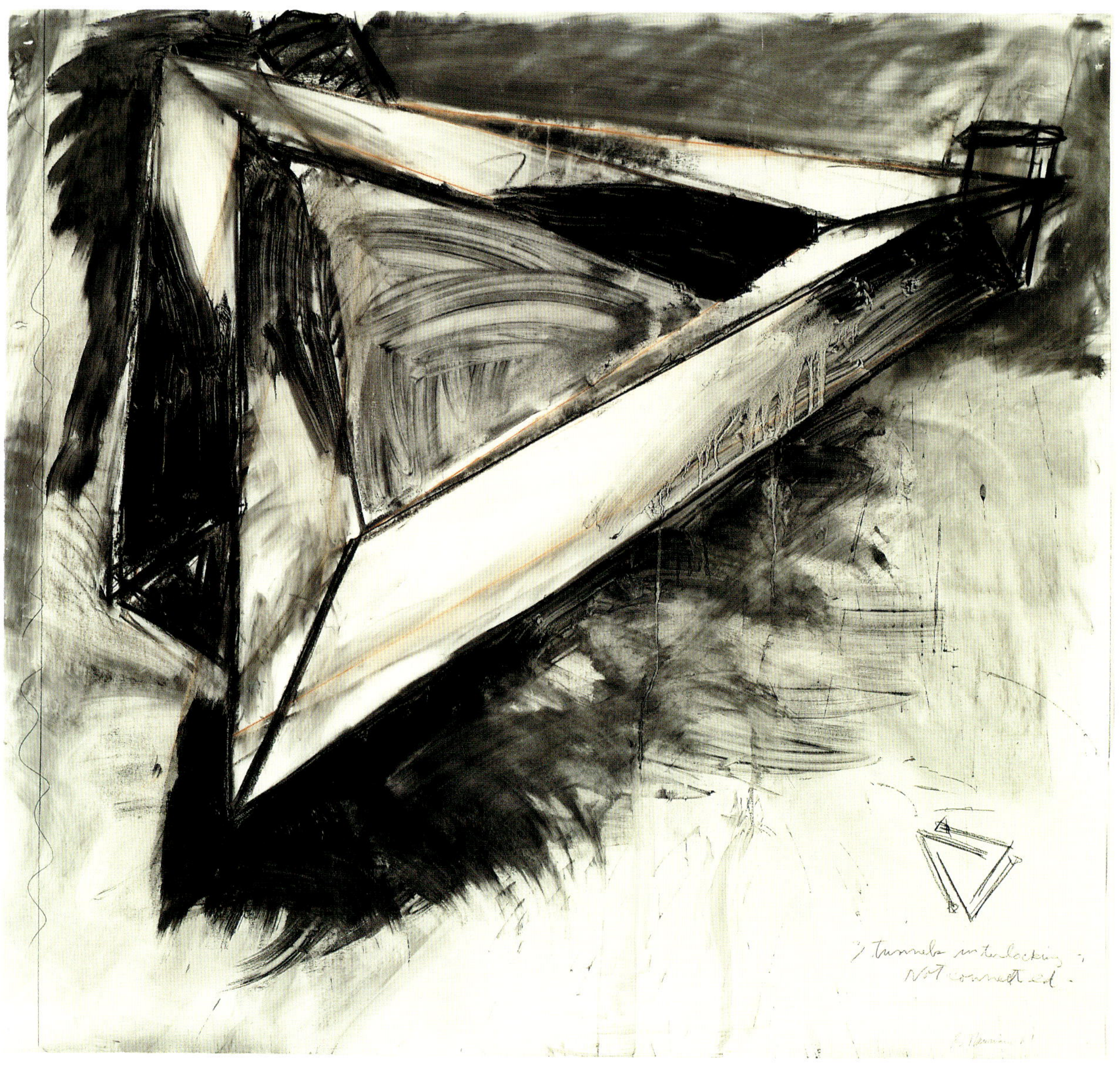

BRUCE NAUMAN's drawings are often intellectual pursuits later made manifest in other media, either traditional granite, plaster, and concrete, or modern technological media, such as neon and video. *Three Tunnels Interlocking, Not Connected* is one of a group of large drawings that presents structural puzzles for planned sculptures. Drawn just two years after the creation of his important *South American Triangle*, which features an upside-down chair suspended over a "floating" concrete circle, *Three Tunnels Interlocking, Not Connected* visually presents the classic form of a three-dimensional triangle; yet the "legend" in the lower right tells us that it is actually a series of three overlapping right angles that appears to form a whole piece. This sculpture has not yet been built; however, a sculpture was built from a related drawing for a special exhibition in Houston in 1982.

BRUCE NAUMAN
Three Tunnels Interlocking, Not Connected, 1981
Charcoal, powdered charcoal, and chalk
59½ × 65 in.
Museum purchase with funds donated by Robert L. B. Tobin, 1989

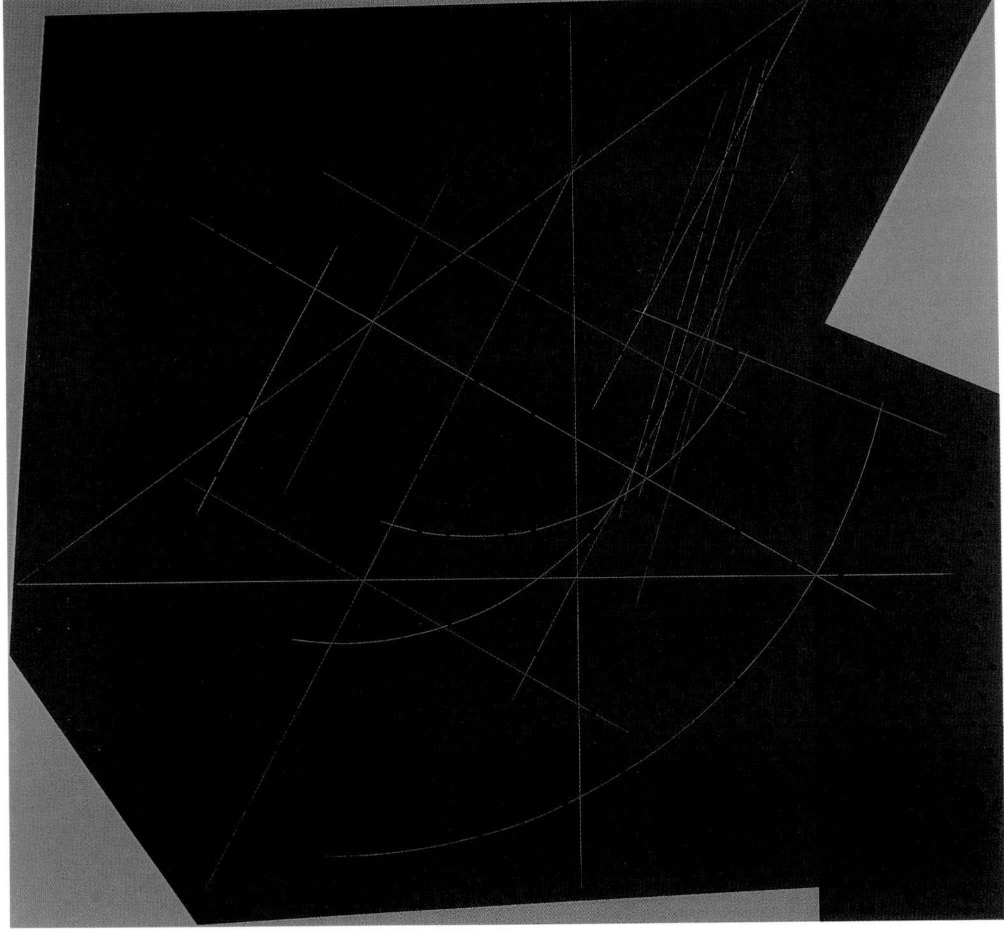

GARO ANTREASIAN
Ramagir, 1983
Embossed color serigraph
$30\frac{7}{8} \times 34\frac{1}{2}$ in.
Museum purchase, Fine Arts Acquisition Fund at the Museum of New Mexico Foundation, 1988

BEST KNOWN for his contribution to the art of lithography, Antreasian has also experimented with other forms of graphics, as well as with painting, examples of which are in the museum's collection. For many years, Antreasian directed the Tamarind Institute Workshops of Lithography after it moved from Los Angeles to Albuquerque. He also served as chairman of the University of New Mexico's Department of Art, where he taught for twenty-three years.

Ramagir belongs to a series primarily of lithographs that pays homage to cities in Asia Minor and to Antreasian's Armenian heritage. His forms frequently evoke both Islamic geometric designs, endemic to the region, and the area's cultural mélange. In this work, the subtleties of the dark background colors are contrasted with highlights of embossed ink that create a surface of active tension.

AGNES MARTIN is a major figure in the history of modern art. Her reductivist paintings and drawings have gained worldwide respect and are included in major museum collections. Her writings on life, aesthetics, and personal philosophy augment the meaning of her canvases, which are extremely purist and seem to express sensation rather than material substance.

Living in the New York art world during the 1950s and making abstract expressionist paintings set her on the modernist track. Although she began to travel to New Mexico in the late 1940s and has been a permanent resident since 1969, her vision remained modern and unaffected by local subject matter and trends. Though considered by some an isolationist, Martin is a thoughtful painter who takes no interest in the cult of personality so popular in America.

Her compositions are best described in her own words: "One time I was coming out of the mountains," she said, "and having painted the mountains, I came out on this plain, and I thought: Ah, what a relief! I thought: This is for me! The expansiveness of it. I sort of surrendered. This plain . . . it was just like a straight line. It was a horizontal line. And I thought there wasn't a line that affected me like a horizontal line. Then the more I drew that line, the happier I got" (from "Agnes Martin, Paintings and Drawings," exhibition catalog, Stedelijk Museum, Amsterdam, 1991).

AGNES MARTIN
Untitled No. 6, 1980
Acrylic and graphite on canvas
72 × 72 in.
Gift of the American Art Foundation, 1982

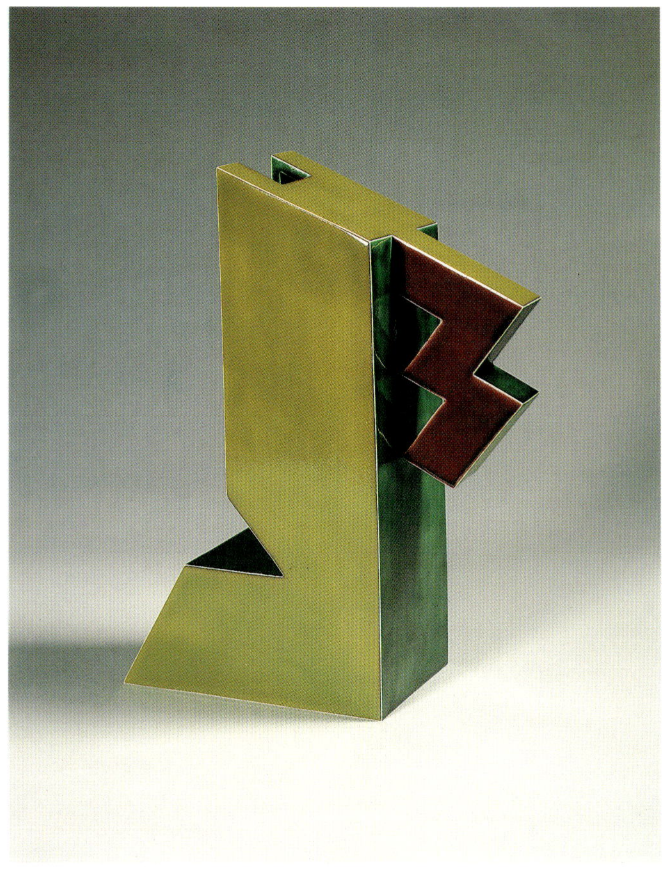

KENNETH PRICE
Untitled, 1980
Ceramic
$11\frac{1}{2} \times 10 \times 4$ in.
Gift of Mr. and Mrs. Wally Sargent, 1982

PRICE HAS long been associated with the Southern California art scene of the 1960s—variously called the "LA Cool School" or the "LA Space and Light" movement, described as art made with a "finish fetish." After receiving a B.F.A. from the University of Southern California in 1956, he studied with Peter Voulkos at the Otis Art Institute and then completed an M.F.A. at Alfred University in New York State, the oldest school of ceramics in the country. Returning to Los Angeles, his work was immediately exhibited at the now infamous Ferus Gallery. After moving to Taos in 1971, Price created hundreds of Mexican-style plates and cups that were shown as installations entitled *Happy's Curios* five years later.

Untitled, a ceramic pitcher that is small in size yet monumental in concept, harkens back to Price's hard-edged, geometric cups of the early 1970s. First prominent for his dense, organic "eggs" made in the 1960s, he has consistently expanded on the vocabulary of the medium of ceramics, especially in his use of color and surface textures. In this cup/building hybrid, the odd colors and lush surfaces challenge the high art traditions of both painting and sculpture. All of Price's work transmits unsettling aftershocks. Formal rigor is mixed with dark humor; wit and commentary on artistic objects are given physical form, expressed through the types of materials used and the manner in which they are combined.

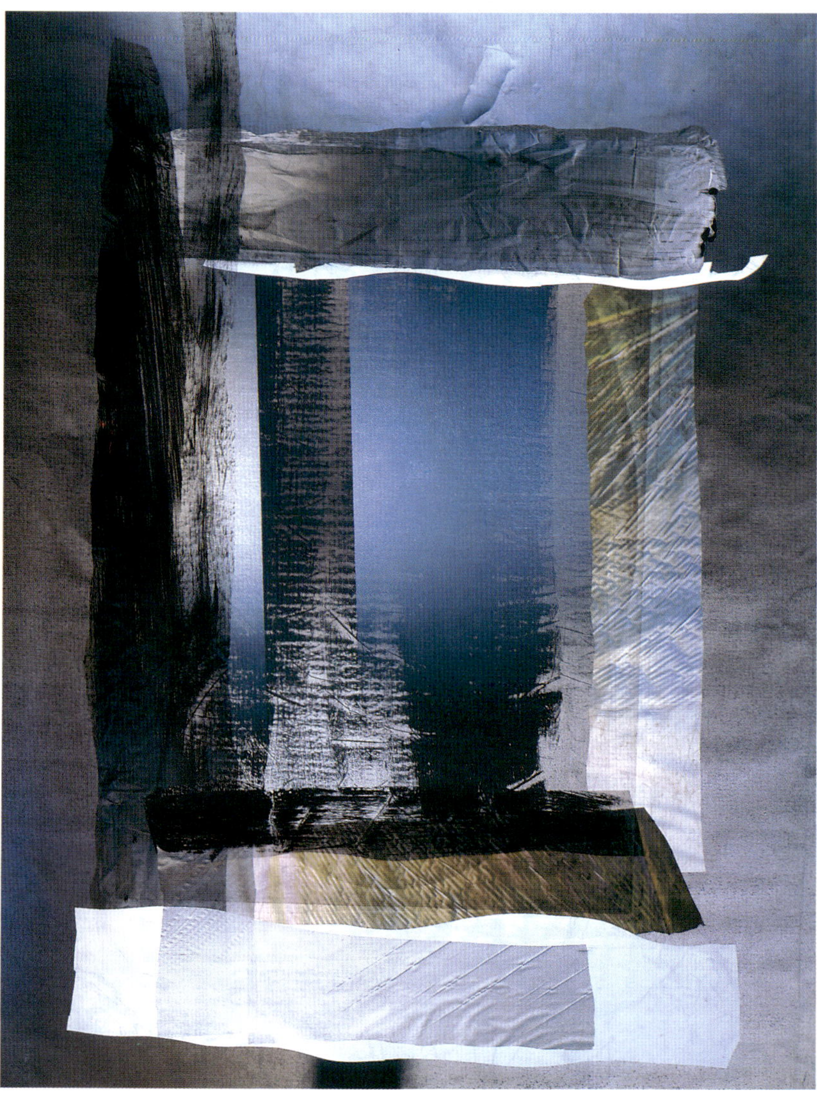

LARRY BELL is a true twentieth-century explorer. His inquiry into the physics of reflective materials and light is fueled by an innate curiosity that leads him to innovative discoveries equal to those of research scientists. In his workspace in Taos, vacuum chambers, hot tables, and the absence of paint tubes, brushes, and pens suggest a scientific laboratory rather than an artist's studio. However, while his tools and methods may be those of modern industry, his finished paintings are products of a thoroughly contemporary artist who infuses nonfigurative imagery with invigorating new life.

One of Bell's most successful images, *The View* is part of a series of "mirage paintings" he has created by fusing reflective materials, such as thin sheets of plastic and aluminum, into the canvas with heat. His intuitive sense of design enables him to arrange colors and shapes that take on forms from incidental light that falls on them. The luminous qualities in the paintings are the result of light reflected from the canvas surface, creating a kind of contemporary "impressionism." Although Bell's approach is dependent on various aspects of technology and science, the element of chance also plays an important role in determining the final composition and effect of each work.

LARRY BELL
The View, 1988
Mixed media on canvas
56 × 44 in.
Museum purchase, Fine Arts Acquisition Fund of the Museum of New Mexico Foundation, matched with a grant from the National Endowment for the Arts, 1989

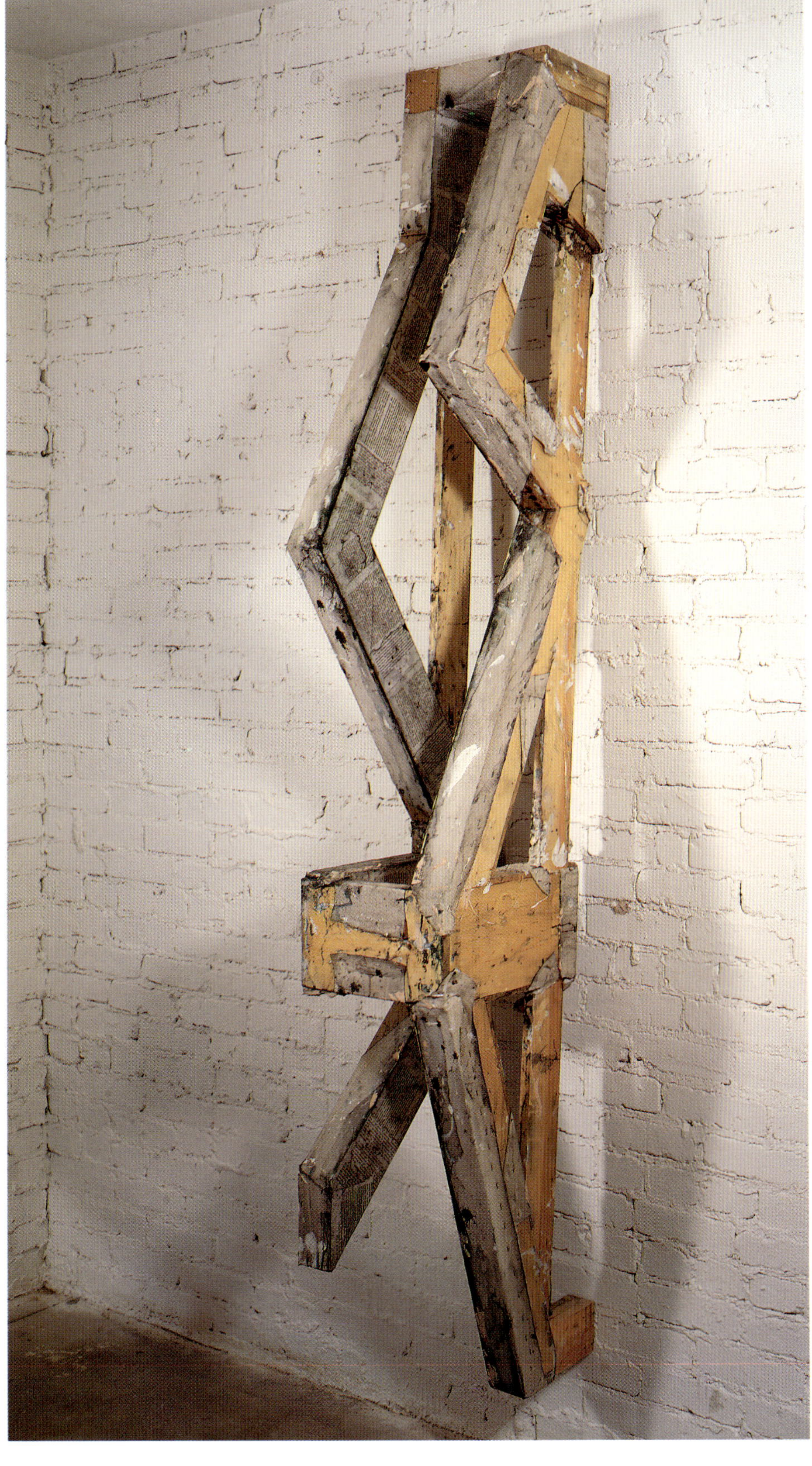

ALLAN GRAHAM
Chartres, 1984
Wood, canvas, oil, water-base pigment, pages from New Testament in Navajo
87 × 13 × 19 in.
Gift of Joann and Gifford Phillips, 1987

PROTRUDING cathedral buttresses, a primitivist ideal of construction, and the Navajo Bible were some of the diverse objects and ideas that influenced the creation of *Chartres*. In this piece, a wood support bent like a genuflecting figure is partially layered with bits of canvas and pages from the Navajo Bible then covered with oil and water-based pigment. While three-dimensional, this is a work related to painting, especially to Graham's series of large herring-boned canvases, an example of which is also in the museum's collection.

Graham's career has explored the subtle boundaries between nonfigurative painting, sculpture, and collage. He has constructed angular canvas frames that protrude from the wall and in his most recent work has set up illusions of the planar surface in seemingly flat, even canvases whose slight curvature challenges the viewer's equilibrium. In all of this work, Graham presents a new, personal sense of order.

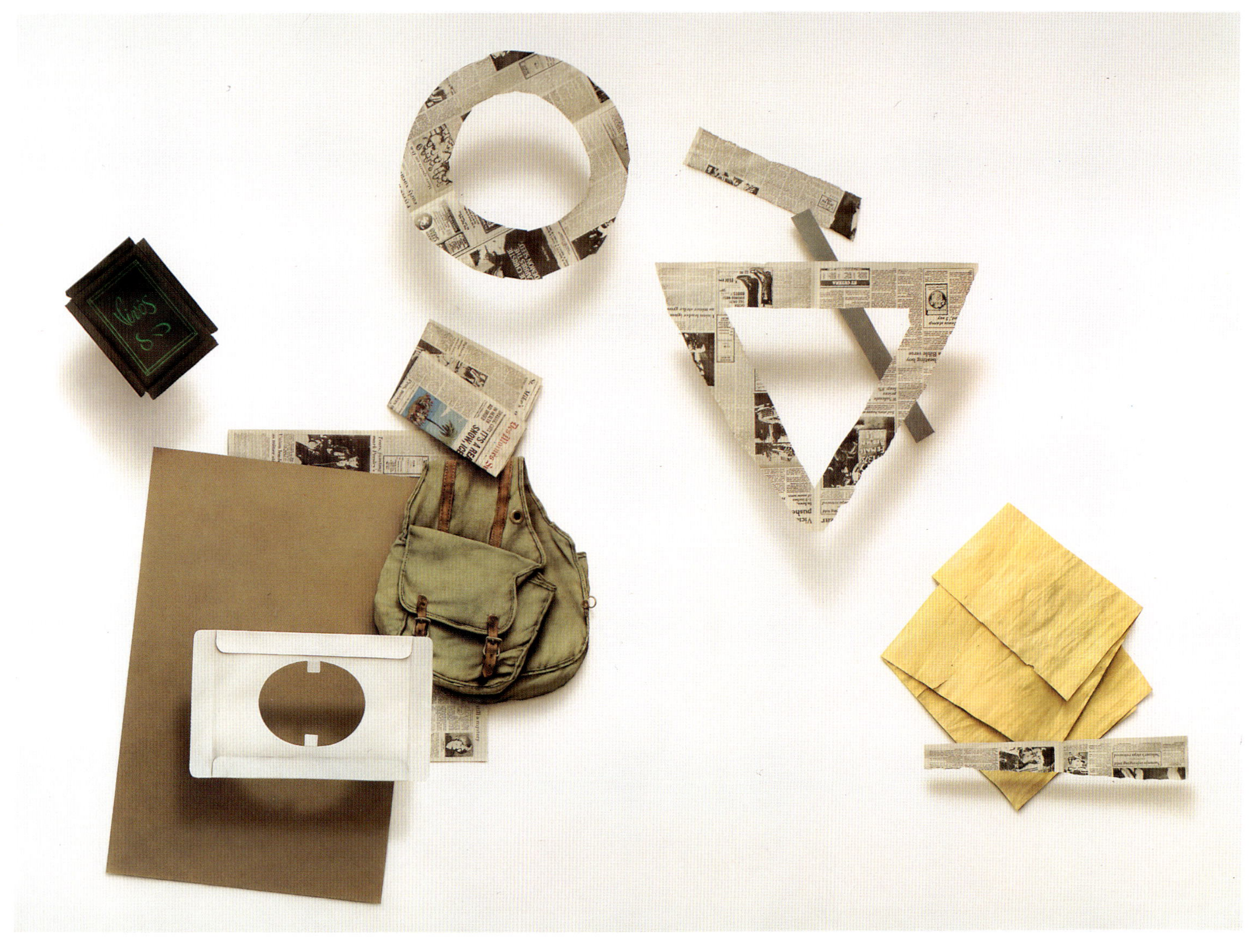

VIEWERS OF Paul Sarkisian's *trompe l'oeil* paintings invariably approach the works directly, then move to one side, examining them from various angles. Layers of artifacts and pieces of cardboard and newspaper at first create the impression of a collage, but the works are really paintings. So refined has the artist's technique become that even those who know his methods occasionally find themselves having a closer look for affirmation.

Sarkisian has long been associated with the art of illusion and for over twenty years has been on the leading edge of the style referred to as "superrealism." These modern paintings, although influenced by the realist tradition of William Hartnett and John F. Peto, have a new scale and contemporary subject matter. In recent years, Sarkisian has begun work on a series of "transfer paintings," combining the freedom of gestural painting with the discipline of printmaking.

Although Sarkisian has lived in New Mexico since the early 1970s, this internationally exhibited artist by his own choice has rarely exhibited in the state.

PAUL SARKISIAN
Untitled, 1977
Acrylic on linen
79 × 104 in.
Gift of Frank Ribelin, 1987

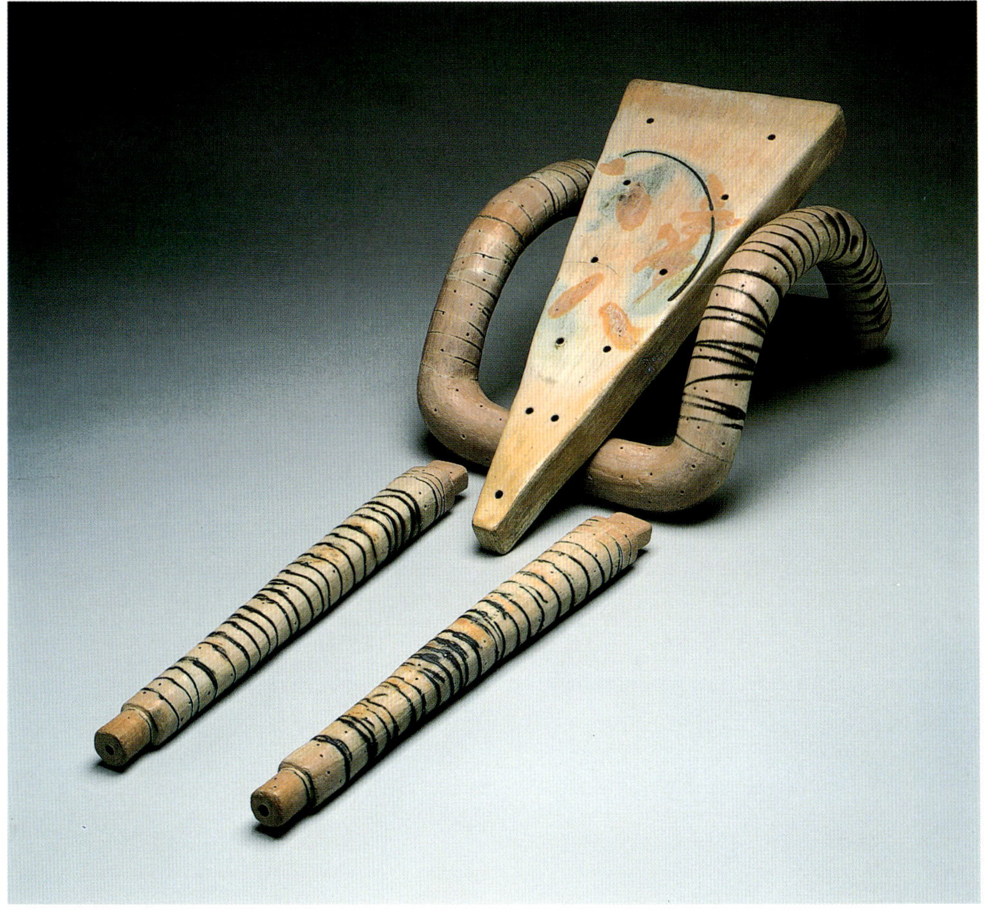

GLORIA GRAHAM
Laid Back, 1982
Burnished, seaweed-fired ceramic
12 × 38 × 13 in.
From the Rosalind Constable Collection, 1989

INSPIRED BY American Indian and Asian ceramics and African primitive sculpture, Gloria Graham's clay sculpture has taken many forms – from vessels, cylinders, and figures to minimalist floor sculpture and slip-surfaced wall works. She studied painting as well as ceramics at the University of California, Berkeley, at the University of Wisconsin, and with Jacques Mennassier in Paris, finishing at the University of New Mexico in Albuquerque.

Laid Back is an anthropomorphic work in four parts. Humor is expressed in the physical-conceptual wordplay and in the reclining posture of the piece. Graham says that she burnishes her sculpture, a technique that all ancient cultures used – Chinese, Aztec, Toltec, and American Indian. Then she fires it with seaweed, which leaves a natural residue of chemical markings – very likely composed of iodine and iron. Concerning her methods, she has said, "I work with each piece for a long time through each stage, with great consideration. I enjoy all the possibilities, [all the] chances of change in each stage."

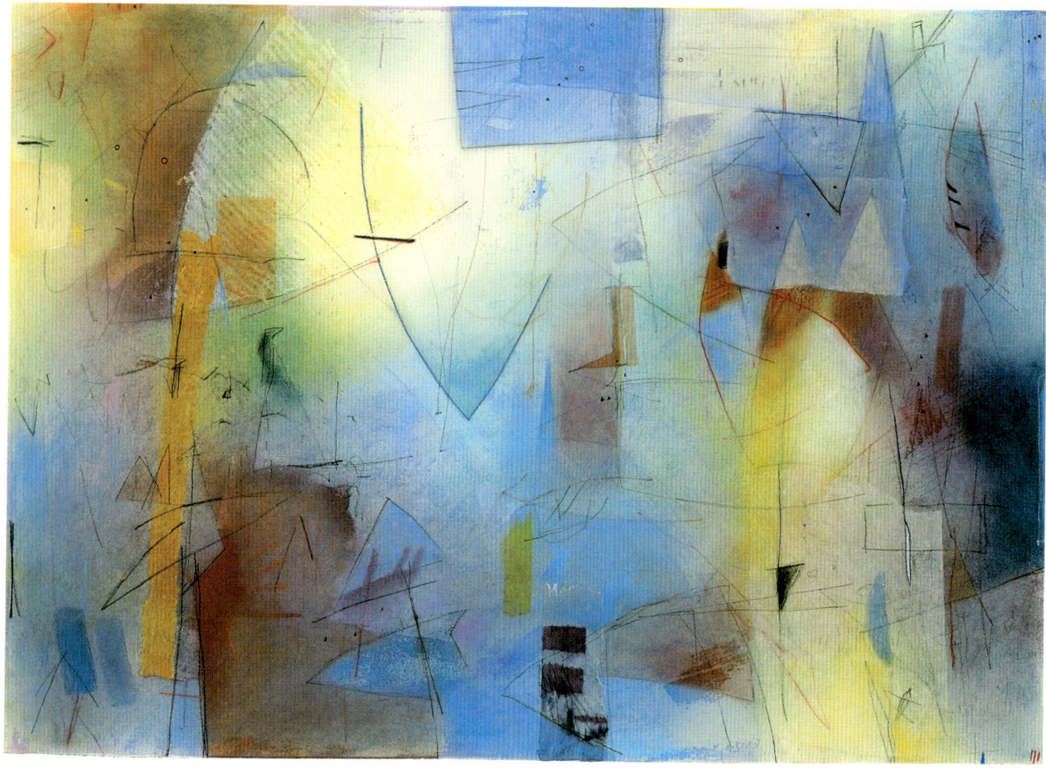

EMMI WHITEHORSE spent her childhood on the Navajo reservation northeast of Chaco Canyon and eventually studied in the Art Department at the University of New Mexico with prize money she won in an art competition and a tribal scholarship. Whitehorse is a person suspended between two cultures. She remains close to her traditional Navajo family while creating a body of nonfigurative drawings, prints, and paintings that speak in a universal language. She says she likes flipping back and forth between Navajo thinking and Western views and ideas while trying to remain in balance with self.

During the early 1980s, she began the *Kin-Nah'-zin'* ("Standing Ruins") series of drawings. In these, she has rubbed the pastel and chalk pigment deep into the porous paper to create the soft, luminous background on which she draws fragmented shapes. They often refer to personal items, such as her father's brands or her grandmother's weaving patterns. The placement of the shapes are intuitive as she makes the decisions moment by moment, depending on the rightness of the feeling. The three small red hash marks in the lower right corner of the paper indicate the final decision of the direction and format of the finished drawing.

EMMI WHITEHORSE
Kin-Nah'-zin' No. 223, 1983
Mixed media on paper
$27\frac{1}{2} \times 39\frac{1}{2}$ in.
Gift of Joann and Gifford Phillips, 1985

APPENDIX OF BIOGRAPHICAL INFORMATION OF ARTISTS REPRESENTED

BIOGRAPHICAL REFERENCES include only activity in New Mexico, except where noted.

Ansel Adams, *46*
Born 1902 San Francisco, California
1927 Santa Fe and Taos visitor
1928–1980 New Mexico regular visitor
Died 1984 Carmel, California

Clinton Adams, *151*
Born 1918 Glendale, California
1942, 1946 Albuquerque visitor
1961 to present Albuquerque resident

Robert Adams, *148*
Born 1937 Orange, New Jersey
1950 Hobbs visitor
1962–1971 Santa Fe and Taos visitor
1970–early 1980s Santa Fe and Taos visitor periodically

Ron Adams, *84*
Born 1934 Detroit, Michigan
ca. 1972 Albuquerque and Santa Fe visitor
1973 to present Santa Fe resident

Garo Antreasian, *154*
Born 1922 Indianapolis, Indiana
1964 to present Albuquerque resident

Timothy App, *107*
Born 1947 Akron, Ohio
1978 to 1990 Albuquerque resident

Jozef Bakos, *35*
Born 1891 Buffalo, New York
1920 Santa Fe visitor
1921–1977 Santa Fe resident
Died 1977 Santa Fe, New Mexico

Henry C. Balink, *39*
Born 1882 Amsterdam, Holland
1917–1919 Taos resident
1924–1963 Santa Fe resident
Died 1963 Santa Fe, New Mexico

Lewis Baltz, *126*
Born 1945 Newport Beach, California
1962, 1972 Santa Fe visitor

Patrocinio Barela, *91*
Born ca. 1900–1908 Bisbee, Arizona
ca. 1911–1914, 1930–1964 Taos resident
Died 1964 Taos, New Mexico

Thomas F. Barrow, *137*
Born 1938 Kansas City, Missouri
1972 to present Albuquerque resident

Gustave Baumann, *42*
Born 1881 Magdeburg, Germany
1918–1971 Santa Fe resident
Died 1971 Santa Fe, New Mexico

Larry Bell, *157*
Born 1939 Chicago, Illinois
1973 to present Taos resident

George Bellows, *31*
Born 1882 Columbus, Ohio
1917 Summer in Santa Fe
Died 1925 New York, New York

Thomas Benrimo, *87*
Born 1887 San Francisco, California
1939–1958 Taos resident
Died 1958 Taos, New Mexico

Ruth Bernhard, *55*
Born 1905 Berlin, Germany
1935 Santa Fe visitor
1947 Santa Fe and Santa Clara visitor

Oscar E. Berninghaus, *27*
Born 1874 St. Louis, Missouri
1899–1924 Summers in Taos
1925–1952 Taos resident
Died 1952 Taos, New Mexico

Emil Bisttram, *82*
Born 1895 Hungary
1930, 1931 Taos visitor
1932–1976 Taos resident
Died 1976 Taos, New Mexico

Ernest L. Blumenschein, *40*
Born 1874 Pittsburgh, Pennsylvania
1898 Taos visitor
1910–1918 Summers in Taos
1919–1960 Taos resident
Died 1960 Albuquerque, New Mexico

Manuel Alvarez Bravo, *56*
Born 1902 Mexico City, Mexico
Works primarily in Mexico

Paul Burlin, *30*
Born 1886 New York, New York
1913–1920 Santa Fe resident part-time
1918 Summer in Taos
Died 1969 New York, New York

Larry Calcagno, *100*
Born 1913 San Francisco, California
1958 Taos visitor
1972 to 1990 Taos resident

John Candelario, *65*
Born 1916 Santa Fe, New Mexico
1916–1934, 1936–1974, ca. 1953, 1957 Santa Fe resident
1947 Albuquerque resident
1958 to present Albuquerque resident

Paul Caponigro, *98*
Born 1932 Boston, Massachusetts
1969 Albuquerque visitor
1973 Pojoaque resident
1974 to present Santa Fe resident

Gerald Cassidy, *23*
Born 1869 Covington, Kentucky
1890 Albuquerque resident
1912–1934 Santa Fe resident
Died 1934 Santa Fe, New Mexico

Steve Catron, *123*
Born 1945 Hollywood, California
1945 to present Santa Fe resident

Walter Chappell, *132*
Born 1925 Portland, Oregon
1954 El Rito visitor
1966–1967, 1984 Santa Fe resident
1968–1971 Velarde resident
1979–1981 Truchas resident
1983 Pilar resident
1987 to present El Rito resident

William Clift, *57*
Born 1944 Boston, Massachusetts
1964, 1968, 1969 Santa Fe visitor
1971 to present Santa Fe resident

Van Deren Coke, *144*
Born 1921 Lexington, Kentucky
1962–1979 Albuquerque resident
1987 to present Santa Fe resident

John C. Collier, Jr., *60*
Born 1913 Sparkhill, New York
1920 to present Santa Fe frequent visitor
1942 New Mexico periodic fieldwork with Farm Security Administration (FSA), which was transferred to the Office of War Information in 1943
December 1942 Villages of Taos County
January–February 1943 Truchas, Trampas, Questa, Peñasco, and other northern New Mexico towns
1947–1958 Taos resident
1959 to present Taos resident part-time

Howard Cook, *79*
Born 1901 Springfield, Massachusetts
1925–1928, 1935, 1938–1967 Taos resident
1967–1975 Roswell resident
1976–1980 Santa Fe resident
Died 1980 Santa Fe, New Mexico

Doris Cross, *142*
Born New York, New York
1970 to present Santa Fe resident

Andrew Dasburg, *45*
Born 1887 Paris, France
ca. 1918–1932 Taos annual visitor
1921–1932 Santa Fe resident
ca. 1933–1979 Taos resident
Died 1979 Taos, New Mexico

Judy Dater, *141*
Born 1941 Hollywood, California
1974, 1978, 1979 New Mexico visitor
1980–1982 Santa Fe resident
ca. 1988 Santa Fe visitor

Randall Davey, *77*
Born 1887 East Orange, New Jersey
1919 Santa Fe visitor
1920–1964 Santa Fe resident
Died 1964 Baker, California

Warren Davis, *101*
Born 1932 Amarillo, Texas
ca. 1947–1950 Taos, Santa Fe, and Red River visitor
1960s Santa Fe visitor intermittently
1970 Santa Fe visitor
1971–1974 Tesuque resident
Died 1974 Tesuque, New Mexico

Jack Delano, *62*
Born 1914 Kiev, Russia
1943 New Mexico FSA Office of War Informatioı assignment

Richard Diebenkorn, *95*
Born 1922 Portland, Oregon
1950–1952 Albuquerque resident
1985, 1986 Santa Fe visitor

Rick Dillingham, *150*
Born 1952 Lake Forest, Illinois
1970–1974 Albuquerque resident
1974–1976 Santa Fe frequent visitor
1976 to present Santa Fe resident

W. Herbert Dunton, *41*
Born 1878 Augusta, Maine
1912 Summer in Taos
1914–1936 Taos resident
Died 1936 Taos, New Mexico

Fremont F. Ellis, *70*
Born 1897 Virginia City, Montana
1919 Santa Fe visitor
1921–1985 Santa Fe resident
Died 1985 Santa Fe, New Mexico

Nicolai Fechin, *38*
Born 1881 Kazan, Russia
1926 Taos visitor
1927–1933 Taos resident
Died 1955 Santa Monica, California

Rudy Fernandez, *121*
Born 1948 Trinidad, Colorado
1952–1954 Resident of various New Mexico communities
1968–1974 Northern New Mexico visitor
1975 Spring researcher throughout New Mexico
1980–1987 Santa Fe frequent visitor
1987 to present Santa Fe resident

Lee Friedlander, *97*
Born 1934 Aberdeen, Washington
1972 Albuquerque and Santa Fe visitor
1975 Santa Fe visitor
1990 Santa Fe and northern New Mexico visitor

Miguel Gandert, *124*
Born 1956 Española, New Mexico
1956–1959 Española resident
1959–1970 Santa Fe resident
1973 Santa Fe temporary resident
1974 to present Albuquerque resident

Laura Gilpin, *54*
Born 1891 Colorado Springs, Colorado
1919–1925 Santa Fe, Taos, and Navajo country visitor
1924–1940s Photographed in New Mexico
1946–1979 Santa Fe resident
Died 1979 Santa Fe, New Mexico

Allan Graham, *158*
Born 1943 San Francisco, California
ca. 1960 Albuquerque visitor
1964–1966 Albuquerque resident
1968–1969 Albuquerque resident
1972 to present Albuquerque resident

Gloria Graham, *160*
Born 1940 Beaumont, Texas
1953 Summer in Mora County
1965–1966, 1968–1969 Albuquerque resident
1972 to present Albuquerque resident

Woody Gwyn, *147*
Born 1944 San Antonio, Texas
Late 1960s Velarde and northern New Mexico visitor
1973–1974 Cerrillos resident
1974–1987 Galisteo resident
1987 to present Santa Fe resident

Betty Hahn, *136*
Born 1940 Chicago, Illinois
1976 to present Albuquerque resident

Frederick Hammersley, *106*
Born 1919 Salt Lake City, Utah
1968 to present Albuquerque resident

Alex Harris, *127*
Born 1949 Atlanta, Georgia
1972–1974 Peñasco resident
1974 Rodarte resident
1975–1977, 1980–1984 El Valle of Chamisal resident part-time
1978–1979, 1985 El Valle of Chamisal resident
1986 to present El Valle of Chamisal resident par time

Marsden Hartley, *49*
Born 1877 Lewiston, Maine
1918, 1919 Santa Fe and Taos visitor
Died 1943 Ellsworth, Maine

William Penhallow Henderson, *32*
Born 1877 Medford, Maine
ca. 1880 Santa Fe visitor
1916–1917, 1919–1943 Santa Fe resident
Died 1943 Tesuque, New Mexico

E. Martin Hennings, *25*
Born 1886 Penns Grove, New Jersey
1917 Taos visitor
1921–1956 Taos resident
Died 1956 Taos, New Mexico

Robert Henri, *36*
Born 1865 Cincinnati, Ohio
1916, 1917, 1918, 1922 Summers in Santa Fe
Died 1929 New York, New York

Victor Higgins, *43*
Born 1884 Shelbyville, Indiana
1913 Santa Fe and Taos visitor
1914–1949 Taos resident
Died 1949 Taos, New Mexico

Hilaire Hiler, *108*
Born 1898 St. Paul, Minnesota
ca. 1940, 1943–1944 Santa Fe visitor
1945–1953 Santa Fe resident
Died 1966 Paris, France

Paula Hocks, *129*
Born Muskogee, Oklahoma
ca. 1959 Santa Fe visitor
ca. 1967 Santa Fe visitor
1973 to present Santa Fe resident

Allan Houser, *112*
Born 1914 Apache, Oklahoma
1934–1938 Santa Fe resident part-time
1940 Dulce resident
1962 to present Santa Fe resident

Russell Vernon Hunter, *67*
Born 1900 Hallsville, Illinois
1907 Las Vegas resident
1907–1921 Texico resident
1917 Summer in Las Vegas
1922–1923 Los Cerrillos and Santa Fe resident
1923 Summer in Silver City
1928 Clovis resident
1932–1934 Texico resident
1934–1935 Puerto de Luna resident
1935–1944 Santa Fe resident
1952–1955 Roswell resident
Died 1955 Roswell, New Mexico

Peter Hurd, *68*
Born 1904 Roswell, New Mexico
1904–1921 Roswell resident
1928–1929 Roswell resident
1930–1939 Roswell and San Patricio resident part-time
1939–1984 San Patricio resident
Died 1984 Roswell, New Mexico

Rebecca Salsbury James, *135*
Born 1891 London, England
1926, 1929–1933 Taos visitor
1934–1968 Taos resident
Died 1968 Taos, New Mexico

Luís Jiménez, *117*
Born 1940 El Paso, Texas
ca. 1955–1960 Black Range visitor periodically
1957–1960 Cloudcroft visitor
1971–1976 Roswell resident
ca. 1975 to present Hondo resident

Raymond Jonson, *81*
Born 1891 Chariton, Iowa
1922 Santa Fe visitor
1924–1949 Santa Fe resident
1949–1982 Albuquerque resident
Died 1982 Albuquerque, New Mexico

Gene Kloss, *33*
Born 1903 Oakland, California
1925 Taos visitor
1926–1928 Summers in Taos
1929–1964 Taos resident
1965–1970 Taos visitor
1971 to present Taos resident

Ernest Knee, *64*
Born 1907 Montreal, Quebec, Canada
1931 Santa Fe visitor
1933–1943 Santa Fe resident
1947–1982 Santa Fe resident
Died 1982 Santa Fe, New Mexico

Zara Kriegstein, *122*
Born 1952 West Berlin, Germany
1972, 1978, 1979 Summers in Santa Fe
1980 to present Santa Fe resident

Leon Kroll, *29*
Born 1884 New York, New York
1917 Santa Fe visitor
Died 1974 New York, New York

Dorothea Lange, *61*
Born 1895 Hoboken, New Jersey
1918 New Mexico visitor
1931 Taos visitor
1932 Taos resident part-time
1935 New Mexico periodic fieldwork with the Resettlement Administration (RA), which became the FSA, 1937
Died 1965 Berkeley, California

Paul Lantz, *72*
Born 1908 Stromburg, Nebraska
1929–1939, ca. 1972–1974 Santa Fe resident
ca. 1974–1980 Springer resident
1980–1990 Miami, New Mexico, resident
1990–1991 Springer resident

Barbara Latham, *66*
Born 1896 Walpole, Massachusetts
1924 Taos visitor
1925–1928, 1935, 1937, 1938–1967 Taos resident
1967–1975 Roswell resident
1976–1989 Santa Fe resident
Died 1989 Santa Fe, New Mexico

Tom Lea, *44*
Born 1907 El Paso, Texas
1919–1924 Summers in Santa Fe
1926, 1928 Santa Fe visitor
1933–1935 Santa Fe resident
1985 Santa Fe visitor

Russell Lee, *63*
Born 1903 Ottawa, Illinois
1939 Mora, Wagon Mound, Taos, and Holman visitor
1940 Pie Town, Mogollon, Chamisal, Peñasco, Taos, Hobbs, Datil, Quemado, Llano de San Juan, and Isleta visitor; FSA photographer
1946–1980s New Mexico summer visitor
Died 1986 Austin, Texas

Janet Lippincott, *103*
Born 1918 New York, New York
1949 Summer in Taos
1949 to present Santa Fe resident

Robert Lougheed, *69*
Born 1910 Massie, Ontario, Canada
1952, 1953 Taos visitor
1952–1969 Autumns in Santa Fe
1960s Autumns at Bell Ranch and Conchas Dam
1970–1982 Santa Fe resident
Died 1982 Santa Fe, New Mexico

Reg Loving, *102*
Born 1943 Madisonville, Kentucky
1972 Spring in Santa Fe
1974–1975 Santa Fe resident
1975 El Rito resident
1976–1984 Albuquerque resident
1984 to present Santa Fe resident

Bruce Lowney, *134*
Born 1937 Los Angeles, California
1962–1964 White Sands resident
1966–1967 Albuquerque resident
1970, 1974 Roswell artist-in-residence
1972–1974 Placitas resident
1976 to present El Morro resident
1988 to present Albuquerque resident part-time

William Lumpkins, *92*
Born 1909 Clayton, New Mexico
1922–1928, 1933–1935 Capitan resident
1929–1931, 1934 Albuquerque resident
1932 Peñasco resident
1932 Summer in Cañoncito
1933 Summer in Albuquerque
1935–1952, 1967 to present Santa Fe resident

Danny Lyon, *125*
Born 1942 Brooklyn, New York
1967 Bernalillo visitor
1969–1982 Bernalillo resident
1983 to present Bernalillo resident

John Marin, *47*
Born 1870 Rutherford, New Jersey
1929, 1930 Summers in Taos
Died 1953 Cape Split, Maine

Agnes Martin, *155*
Born 1912 Maklin, Saskatchewan, Canada
1947 Summer in Taos
1948–1949 Albuquerque resident
1952–1957 Taos resident
1969–1977 Cuba resident
1977 to present Galisteo resident

Alfred Morang, *75*
Born 1901 Ellsworth, Maine
1937–1958 Santa Fe resident
Died 1958 Santa Fe, New Mexico

Jesús Bautista Moroles, *119*
Born 1950 Corpus Christi, Texas
1978, 1980 Santa Fe visitor
1985 to present Cerrillos resident part-time

Lee Mullican, *104*
Born 1919 Chickasha, Oklahoma
1938, ca. 1946 Santa Fe visitor
1962 Santa Fe and Taos visitor
1970 Summer in Santa Fe
1971–1972 Summers in Taos
1973 to present Taos resident part-time

Joan Myers, *131*
Born 1944 Des Moines, Iowa
1979 to present Santa Fe resident

Patrick Nagatani, *139*
Born 1945 Chicago, Illinois
1980, 1984 Albuquerque visitor
1987 to present Albuquerque resident

Willard Nash, *73*
Born 1898 Philadelphia, Pennsylvania
1920 Santa Fe visitor
1921–1936 Santa Fe resident
1942 Albuquerque resident
Died 1942 Albuquerque, New Mexico

Bruce Nauman, *153*
Born 1941 Ft. Wayne, Indiana
ca. 1975 Taos visitor
1978 Santa Fe visitor
1979–1990 Pecos resident
1990 to present Galisteo resident

Beaumont Newhall, *58*
Born 1908 Lynn, Massachusetts
1951 Santa Fe and Albuquerque visitor
1971–1974 Albuquerque resident
1975 to present Santa Fe resident

Eugene Newmann, *152*
Born 1936 Bratislava, Czechoslovakia
ca. 1957 Taos visitor
ca. 1965 New Mexico periodic visitor
1972 to present Santa Fe resident

Anne Noggle, *140*
Born 1922 Evanston, Illinois
ca. 1947–1948 Clovis and Hobbs; worked as pilot periodically
1949–1953 Santa Fe resident
1959 to present Albuquerque resident

B.J.O. Nordfeldt, *34*
Born 1878 Tulstorg Scania, Sweden
1918 Santa Fe visitor
1919–1937 Santa Fe resident
Died 1955 Henderson, Texas

Frederick O'Hara, *89*
Born 1904 Ottawa, Ontario, Canada
1937 New Mexico visitor
1941–1961 Albuquerque resident
Died 1980 La Jolla, California

Georgia O'Keeffe, *51*
Born 1887 Sun Prairie, Wisconsin
1917 New Mexico visitor
1929–1930 Summers in Taos
1931 Summer in Alcalde
1934–1938, 1941–1945 May–October at Ghost Ranch extensively
1940 Bought Ghost Ranch House
1945 Bought Abiquiu residence
1946–1984 Ghost Ranch and Abiquiu resident
1984–1986 Santa Fe resident
Died 1986 Santa Fe, New Mexico

Sheldon Parsons, *26*
Born 1866 Rochester, New York
1913–1943 Santa Fe resident
Died 1943 Albuquerque, New Mexico

Mary Peck, *146*
Born 1952 Minneapolis, Minnesota
1970 Taos visitor
1974 to present Santa Fe resident

Bert G. Phillips, *28*
Born 1868 Hudson, New York
1898–1956 Taos resident
Died 1956 San Diego, California

Paul Pletka, *116*
Born 1946 San Diego, California
1960s Taos visitor
1977–1987 Tesuque resident
1988 to present Santa Fe resident

Bernard Plossu, *138*
Born 1945 Dalat, South Vietnam
1973–1977 Albuquerque and Santa Fe summer visitor
1978–1980 Taos resident
1980–1985 Santa Fe resident

Eliot Porter, *53*
Born 1901 Winnetka, Illinois
1939–1941 New Mexico; worked periodically
1946–1989 Tesuque resident
Died 1990 Tesuque, New Mexico

Kenneth Price, *156*
Born 1935 Los Angeles, California
1969–1970 Taos visitor
1971–1982 Taos resident

Tony Price, *118*
Born 1937 Brooklyn, New York
1964 Taos and San Cristobal resident
1965–1970 El Rancho resident
1970–1971 Truchas resident
1972–1979 Nambe resident
1973–1974 Lamy resident
1975 Leyba resident
1978–1979 Española resident
1976, 1980, 1982 to present Santa Fe resident

Edward Ranney, *149*
Born 1942 Chicago, Illinois
1957, 1959, 1963 Santa Fe visitor
1970 to present Santa Fe resident

Robert Rauschenberg, *96*
Born 1925 Port Arthur, Texas
ca. 1963 Albuquerque visitor

Doel Reed, *78*
Born 1894 Logansport, Indiana
1940s Taos visitor
1959–1985 Taos resident
Died 1985 Taos, New Mexico

Louis Ribak, *93*
Born 1903 Lithuania
1944–1979 Taos resident
Died 1979 Albuquerque, New Mexico

Diego Rivera, *114*
Born 1886 Guanajuato, Mexico
Died 1957 Mexico City, Mexico

Elias Rivera, *111*
Born 1937 Bronx, New York
1982 to present Santa Fe resident

Meridel Rubenstein, *133*
Born 1948 Detroit, Michigan
1972 Santa Fe and Taos visitor
1973–1975 Albuquerque resident
1975 to present Santa Fe resident

Ramona Sakiestewa, *105*
Born 1948 Albuquerque, New Mexico
1952–1962 Albuquerque resident
1966, 1968, 1971 to present Santa Fe resident

Paul Sarkisian, *159*
Born 1928 Chicago, Illinois
1958–1972 Summers in Santa Fe
1971 Albuquerque resident
1972–1986 Cerrillos resident
1986 to present Santa Fe resident

Howard B. Schleeter, *90*
Born 1903 Buffalo, New York
1929 New Mexico visitor
1930–1935, 1939–1958, 1968–1970 Albuquerque resident
1936–1937, 1958–1968 Santa Fe resident
1937–1938 Las Vegas resident
1938 Conchas Dam resident
1970–1976 Placitas resident
Died 1976 Placitas, New Mexico

Fritz Scholder, *109*
Born 1937 Breckenridge, Minnesota
1964–1972 Santa Fe resident
1976–ca. 1981 Summers in Taos
1972 to present Galisteo resident part-time

Elmer Schooley, *74*
Born 1916 Lawrence, Kansas
1941 Taos visitor
1946–1947 Silver City resident
1947–1977 Montezuma resident
1977 to present Roswell resident

Sam Scott, *120*
Born 1940 Chicago, Illinois
1969–1978 Santa Fe resident
1983 to present Santa Fe resident

Joseph Henry Sharp, *24*
Born 1859 Bridgeport, Ohio
1883 Santa Fe and Albuquerque visitor
1893 Taos visitor
1897 Summer in Santa Fe and Taos
1898, 1902–1911 Summers in Taos whenever possible
1912–1952 Taos resident
Died 1953 Pasadena, California

Eugenie Shonnard, *113*
Born 1886 Yonkers, New York
1927–1978 Santa Fe resident
Died 1978 Santa Fe, New Mexico

Will Shuster, *71*
Born 1893 Philadelphia, Pennsylvania
1920–1969 Santa Fe resident
Died 1969 Albuquerque, New Mexico

Aaron Siskind, *94*
Born 1903 New York, New York
Died 1991 Providence, Rhode Island

John Sloan, *37*
Born 1871 Lock Haven, Pennsylvania
1919 Santa Fe visitor
1920–1932, 1934–1950 Summers in Santa Fe
Died 1951 Hanover, New Hampshire

W. Eugene Smith, *83*
Born 1918 Wichita, Kansas
1947 Santa Fe and Taos visitor; *Life* (magazine) assignment
Died 1978 Tucson, Arizona

Frederick Sommer, *99*
Born 1905 Angri, Italy
Works primarily in Prescott, Arizona

Alfred Stieglitz, *50*
Born 1864 Hoboken, New Jersey
Worked primarily in New York
Died 1946 New York, New York

Paul Strand, *48*
Born 1890 New York, New York
1926 Taos visitor
1930–1932 Summers in Taos
After 1932 New Mexico occasional visitor
Died 1976 Orgeval, France

Earl Stroh, *80*
Born 1924 Buffalo, New York
1947 Summer in Taos
1947–1948 Albuquerque resident
1948 to present Taos resident

Roger Sweet, *145*
Born 1946 Huntington Park, California
1972–1974 Corrales resident
1975–1980 Albuquerque resident
1981 to present Jemez Springs resident

Andree Tracey, *139*
Born 1948 La Jolla, California
1987 to present Albuquerque and Santa Fe visitor

Alex Traube, *128*
Born 1946 New York, New York
1973 Abiquiu, Santa Fe, and Albuquerque visitor
1974 Tesuque resident
1974–1977 Española resident
1980–1981 Las Vegas resident
1981–1991 Santa Fe resident

Andy Tsinnajinne, *110*
Born 1918 Rough Rock, Arizona
1932–1936 Santa Fe resident
ca. 1945 to present New Mexico visitor

Willard Van Dyke, *59*
Born 1906 Denver, Colorado
1931, 1933, 1937 New Mexico visitor
1980–1986 Santa Fe resident
Died 1986 Jackson, Tennessee

Theodore Van Soelen, *76*
Born 1890 St. Paul, Minnesota
1916–1919 Albuquerque resident
1920–1922 San Ysidro resident
1923–1925 Santa Fe resident
1934–1942 Summers in Tesuque
1926–1933, 1943–1964 Tesuque resident
Died 1964 Santa Fe, New Mexico

Frederico Vigil, *115*
Born 1946 Santa Fe, New Mexico
1946–1972, 1976 to present Santa Fe resident

Todd Webb, *85*
Born 1905 Detroit, Michigan
1955–1957, 1959–1960 Abiquiu visitor
1961–1971 Santa Fe resident
1977, 1981 Abiquiu and Santa Fe visitor
1987 Santa Fe visitor
1988 Santa Fe visitor

Cady Wells, *86*
Born 1904 Southbridge, Massachusetts
1931 Taos visitor
1932–1933 Taos summer visitor
1940s–1950s Taos studio part-time
1933–1954 Jacona resident
Died 1954 Santa Fe, New Mexico

Jerry West, *130*
Born 1933 Glenford, Ohio
1934–1940, 1959–1969, 1976–1979 Santa Fe resident
1940–1941 Española resident
1956–1958 Albuquerque resident
1964–1969 Summers in Las Vegas
1969–1970 Las Vegas resident
1972–1973 Alamogordo resident
1987 to present Santa Fe resident

Edward Weston, *52*
Born 1885 Highland Park, Illinois
1933 Taos and Santa Fe visitor
1937–1938 Gallup, Moriarty, Tesuque, Taos, and Albuquerque; Guggenheim Fellowship
1941–1942 Las Cruces, White Sands, Santa Fe, Galisteo, San Cristobal, Cordova, Truchas, Taos, Albuquerque, Pojoaque, Chimayo, and Trampas visitor
Died 1953 Carmel, California

Emmi Whitehorse, *161*
Born 1957 Crown Point
1957–1974 Crown Point resident
1975–1982, 1987 Albuquerque resident
1987 to present Santa Fe resident

Joel-Peter Witkin, *143*
Born 1939 Brooklyn, New York
1975 to present Albuquerque resident

Adja Yunkers, *88*
Born 1900 Riga, Latvia
1947–1950 Summers in Albuquerque
1950–1952 Corrales resident
Died 1983 New York, New York

Biographical data have been verified by three bibliographical sources, personal interviews, and can be researched in the Artists Biographical Files, housed at the Museum of Fine Arts Library.